The Battle
of the
Washita

Stan Hoig

The Battle
of the
Washita

*The Sheridan-Custer
Indian Campaign
of 1867–69*

University of Nebraska Press
Lincoln and London

First Bison Book printing: 1979
Most recent printing indicated by first digit below:
5   6   7   8   9   10

Library of Congress Cataloging in Publication Data

Hoig, Stan.
  The Battle of the Washita.
  Reprint of the ed. published by Doubleday, Garden City, N.Y.
  Bibliography: p. 253
  Includes index.
    1. Indians of North America—Wars—1968–1869. 2. Cheyenne Indians—
Wars—1866–1895. 3. Custer, George Armstrong, 1839–1876. 4. Sheridan,
Philip Henry, 1831–1888. I. Title.
[E83.869.H64 1979]   973.8′1   79–14844
ISBN 0–8032–2307–2
ISBN 0–8032–7204–9 pbk.

Reprinted by arrangement with Doubleday & Company, Inc.
Manufactured in the United States of America

∞

TO MEL, LISA, AND BRENT

CONTENTS

LIST OF ILLUSTRATIONS

MAPS

INTRODUCTION

In the early morning of November 28, 1864, a Cheyenne Indian village under Chief Black Kettle was attacked and massacred by troops under the command of Colonel John M. Chivington at Sand Creek in Colorado Territory. Several chiefs, including White Antelope, Standing in the Water, and War Bonnet, and over one hundred Cheyenne men, women, and children were killed. The village was burned and several hundred horses captured.

Almost exactly four years later, at daybreak on November 27, 1868, the 7th Regiment of United States Cavalry, commanded by Lieutenant Colonel George Armstrong Custer, attacked and massacred this same village of Cheyenne Indians under Black Kettle on the Washita River in the Indian Territory. Black Kettle and Chief Little Rock were killed, along with more than a hundred other men, women, and children of the tribe. The village was burned, and nearly eight hundred horses were shot.

That both events were massacres—which utilized the element of complete surprise against a people who did not consider themselves to be at war and in which troops who had orders to kill anyone and everyone before them made no attempt to allow surrender—is hardly deniable by any accepted use of the word "massacre." Despite this, the latter incident has come to be known to history as "the Battle of the Washita," a title which this book has accepted in deference to long-standing use.

But what of the circumstances surrounding the two events? Was there justification for either? Who was in the right in these mortal conflicts between the white man and the red man? Army, Congressional, and historical investigations of the Sand Creek attack have clearly tagged it as an unwarranted breach of faith and an act of perfidy on the part of Chivington and others, despite stubborn attempts to establish Chivington as a military hero for his act.

And what of Custer? Was he hero or villain? Sherman, Sheridan, Custer, Hazen, and others have made vigorous defenses of the Washita attack, denying a comparison of it to Sand Creek. The points they made were essentially these:

(1) That the attacks made by a Cheyenne war party on the Saline and Solomon River settlements in August 1868 gave clear justification for open warfare against the entire Cheyenne nation.

(2) That where Black Kettle's band had been promised sanctuary at Fort Lyon prior to the Sand Creek attack, the band had been refused sanctuary by General Hazen at Fort Cobb just prior to the Washita fight and had been further warned that troops were in the field.

(3) That evidence reportedly found in Black Kettle's village after the attack proved that he and his people were engaged in depredations against the whites.

(4) That the Plains Indian was a barbaric savage whose habits and war culture could be changed only by the force of arms.

Those in opposition—principally Peace Commissioner Tappan and Agent Wynkoop, both of whom had also been the principal opponents of the Sand Creek Massacre—countered by arguing these points:

(1) That it was barbaric to punish an entire tribe for the acts of a few, particularly when those acts had been incited by the deeds of frontier whites and the government's lack of faith in fulfilling its treaty promises.

(2) That the Fort Cobb sanctuary, which Sherman had implied to the Indian Bureau would encompass all friendly Indians, had been a lure to Black Kettle, whether or not Hazen had offered them sanctuary.

(3) That there was question as to the legitimacy of the evidence offered by Custer and Sheridan of depredations by Black Kettle's band reportedly found in the destroyed village, evidence which, even so, could hardly have been known *prior* to the attack.

(4) That the claim by Custer that he followed the trail of a Cheyenne war party to the village, which he attacked without knowing even to which tribe it belonged, was invalid, as the Kiowas insisted that the trail had been made by a war party of theirs which was returning from a raid against the Utes of Colorado.

(5) That the Plains Indians, despite the acts of war by hot-blooded young warriors, were in reality a family-loving, peaceable race who had been forced into situations of war through deception, starvation, and attacks by whites.

To place the Battle of the Washita in historical perspective, it is necessary to consider the inability of the frontier army to catch and defeat the Plains warrior on the open prairie and the government's failure to reach an honest agreement with the Indians at Medicine Lodge regarding their hunting grounds in western Kansas. Obviously, the invasion of the Indian Territory, of which the Washita attack was the principal event, was a tactical maneuver aimed at accomplishing what the other tactics had failed to achieve: the removal of the Indians as a barrier to the railroads and the advancement of white settlements onto the central plains.

But the end results of the campaign had far wider significance than Sherman or Sheridan ever intended. The Sheridan-Custer campaign of 1868–69 destroyed, both in concept and in reality, the Indian Territory as the red man's last refuge from the onslaught of white civilization. The campaign was the vanguard invasion by the white man of lands that would ultimately form the territory and then the state of Oklahoma. There is more than a coincidental relationship to the fact that a member of the 19th Kansas Volunteer Cavalry that accompanied Sheridan and Custer, Captain David L. Payne, led the famous Boomer movement of the 1880s to open the Oklahoma lands to white settlement. There can be no question but that the reports of mineral and oil wealth and of fertile farming and grazing lands made by those in the campaign contributed greatly to white agitation that the lands be taken from the Indian and given to the whites.

The Battle of the Washita was probably the most significant Indian battle fought within the borders of present Oklahoma. Still, it has somehow evaded in-depth study by historians, who have largely contented themselves with surface information as reported by Custer and others. Left unresolved are a wide range of questions concerning the incident to which common curiosity begs answers. How many of Custer's soldiers were killed during the fight? Where were they buried? Were they all accounted for? Was the number of Indian dead listed by Custer an actual battlefield count, as he claimed? Who was the white woman Custer reported killed during the fight? Who were the two white children he claimed were rescued? Where were the bodies of Mrs. Blinn and her child really found? Was Mo-nah-se-tah Custer's mistress or is the charge merely historical gossip? Was Hamilton shot by his own men, as some historians have claimed?

This study attempts to search out the answers to these and other questions concerning the Washita engagement, though quite likely some of them will never be resolved with total certainty. Every effort has been made to separate the multitude of fiction from the facts of the event. It is intended that this work, to the extent possible, be neither pro- nor anti-Custer, pro- nor anti-Indian. It assumes the position that neither the whites nor the Indians were all good or all bad, leaving each reader to make his own judgment concerning who was the more right and who the more wrong.

The site of the Battle of the Washita has been named a National Historic Site, and Oklahoma has established the Black Kettle Museum in the nearby town of Cheyenne. It must be left to the conscience of each individual to decide which is commemorated by the marker erected there: a great victory for Custer or a tragedy for the Cheyennes.

Acknowledgment of very helpful research assistance must be paid to Mr. Robert Richmond and Mr. Joe Snell of the Kansas State Historical Society; Mr. Jack Haley and Mrs. Boyce Timmons of the University of Oklahoma Division of Manuscripts and Phillips Collection; Mrs. Alene Simpson and Mrs. Manon B. Atkins of the Oklahoma Historical Society; Ms. Elaine Everly of the National Archives; Mrs. Dorothea Ray and Mrs. Lois Filbeck of the Central Oklahoma State University library; and Mrs. Earl Armold of El Reno, Oklahoma, Carnegie Library. And once more I must recognize the invaluable help of my wife, Pat Corbell Hoig.

The Battle
of the
Washita

Chapter I
A CERTAIN IMPETUOSITY

When Brevet Major General George Armstrong Custer arrived at Fort Riley, Kansas, on October 16, 1866, he brought along four horses, a greyhound, a bulldog, and several staghounds. He fervently hoped there would be some good hunting in Kansas to break the monotony of postwar service on the barren desert-prairies of the West. He had little idea then that he would soon be hunting a far more wily and elusive foe than any he had yet encountered. Nor could he know that he was beginning a long, difficult trail to his one and only victory over the Indians, a victory shrouded with question and one for which, many believe, he and the 7th Cavalry would ultimately pay in blood on the Little Bighorn in 1876.

The youngest man—at the age of twenty-three—to rise to the rank of general during the war, Custer came to the Kansas plains with a brilliant military career behind him and a high reputation as a flamboyant and dashing soldier. Described by one newspaper writer in Kansas as the "beau ideal" of a cavalry officer, he was cited as an excellent horseman, a man who was fearlessly brave, a "capital shot," and one who did not drink, swear, or use tobacco. "There is no better man," the writer went on to say, "than the long-haired hero of Shenandoah."

Custer's reputation was no fluke. He had come by it legitimately, as proved by the fact that during the war he had had eleven or twelve horses shot from under him. An avid campaigner, Custer's forte was daring charges against the enemy and long, fast marches that allowed him to suddenly appear where he was not at all expected to be. He was by nature an irrepressible romantic who saw himself and the service in cavalier terms. He was constantly exhibiting a flare for the dramatic in his habits and dress, letting his hair grow long during the war on a wager that he would not cut it until the war was won. An officer from General Meade's staff saw Custer lead a charge at Culpeper Station and wrote home to describe the young general as looking like a "circus rider gone mad."

Custer emerged from the war as one of the most glamorous military figures in the nation, his 3rd Michigan having suffered the highest casualties of any federal cavalry unit during the war. Following the conflict, Custer saw service in Texas, where he was mustered out of the Army early in 1866. Receiving an interesting offer from Juárez, the President of Mexico, to command the Mexican cavalry against Maximilian, Custer was first required to secure the permission of President Andrew Johnson. Instead of giving his permission, Johnson assigned Custer as his own personal bodyguard during his travels around the country.

After failing to secure the newly created post of Inspector of Cavalry, Custer accepted an assignment in one of the new cavalry regiments authorized by Congress. He was first ordered to Fort Garland, Colorado, which he preferred because it offered good sport hunting. But his orders were changed to Fort Riley, where the situation of the Kansas Pacific Railroad was threatened by the hostile Plains tribes, particularly the Cheyenne, Arapaho, and Sioux.

American expansion westward across the central plains following the war had necessitated that Congress reorganize the old Union Army into an Indian-fighting force. The Division of the Missouri was established under Lieutenant General William Tecumseh Sherman with headquarters at St. Louis. The division encompassed all of the central plains from the border of Mexico to Canada and comprised four departments. One of these, the Department of the Missouri, covered the whole of the state of

Kansas. It was placed under the command of Major General Winfield Scott Hancock.

Hancock established his headquarters at Fort Leavenworth and assigned the newly designated 7th Cavalry Regiment to Fort Riley. Custer was appointed to fill the lieutenant-colonelcy, second in command of the unit, under Colonel (Brevet Major General) Andrew J. Smith, an over-fiftyish veteran of the Mexican War. Smith left it to Custer to organize the officer corps—a hodgepodge of ex-officers of high rank from various parts of the Union Army—which soon divided itself into pro- and anti-Custer alignments that would hover over the 7th Regiment all the way to the Bighorn.

Custer was also responsible for the training of a mostly green enlisted force. Though called away to Washington for over a month, from November 9 to December 16, he was directly involved in developing the regiment into a disciplined fighting unit. Cavalry drills and tactics were based upon Civil War experience; no one yet knew a thing about fighting Plains Indians. The first opportunity to learn came in the spring of 1867. In response to reported Indian depredations in western Kansas, Hancock recommended to the Army that a punitive expedition be conducted against the Indians there. The plan was approved, and preparations for an imposing show of military might were begun.

Hancock was a handsome, soldierly-looking man who had gained fame at Gettysburg. Following the war's end, he had been in charge of the military district around Washington, D.C., when Lincoln was assassinated, and it was under his command that the Booth conspirators had been tried and executed. Talkative and outgoing, Hancock was already being mentioned as a presidential candidate, which he would eventually become, in 1880.

In late March, the 7th Cavalry was alerted for its first field operations, marching to Fort Larned, where it was joined by six infantry companies, a battery of artillery, white and Indian scouts, a sizable wagon train, and General Hancock. All together, Hancock's army consisted of some fourteen hundred men, which

Custer thought would so impress the Indians that "they would accept terms and abandon the war-path." He was, in fact, more concerned about getting a chance to do some sport hunting on the trip, taking along three horses and five staghounds.

At Fort Larned, the expedition was joined by two newspaper correspondents. One was a reporter-artist for *Harper's New Monthly Magazine,* Theodore Davis. The other was a young roving correspondent who wrote for the *Missouri Democrat,* the New York *Tribune,* and other papers on a free-lance basis. His name was Henry M. Stanley, who was later destined to find lasting fame as the discoverer of the lost Livingstone and as an explorer of Africa. Stanley adeptly described Custer in one short sentence, observing, "A certain impetuosity and undoubted courage are his principal characteristics."

A late-spring blizzard struck the area, bringing severely cold weather and dumping a heavy snow on the ground. This delayed a council between Hancock and chiefs from a sizable Cheyenne and Sioux camp some forty miles up the Pawnee Fork from Larned. The meeting had been arranged by Lieutenant Colonel Edward W. Wynkoop, former commander of Fort Lyon, Colorado, good friend of Black Kettle, and now agent for the Cheyenne and Arapaho tribes. Finally the chiefs arrived, two hours after dark on April 12, and were fed. They then took seats on logs beside a roaring campfire in front of Hancock's tent. Hancock had his officers in full regimentals to impress the chiefs, but the Indians were equally impressive to Stanley. He described them, wrapped in their red blankets, some wearing blue army overcoats, their faces painted and ears bedecked with large brass earrings. Silver armlets on their upper arms, copper wrist bracelets, multicolored beads, peace medals bearing the likeness of President Andrew Johnson, and silver disks attached in long strings to their scalp locks all glistened in the light of the campfire.

After shaking hands all around, the chiefs went through their inevitable filling of pipes and smoking before the council could begin. An Arapaho boy who had been captured at Sand Creek and since exhibited in a circus was turned over to the chiefs. Hancock then rose to his feet and made a speech, which one of

his scouts, Cheyenne half-blood Ed Guerrier, interpreted sentence by sentence. Hancock said that he had heard that some of
the tribes had bad hearts and would go on the warpath and that
he was ready to fight those Indians. The bad Indians, he told
them, would not be allowed to kill white people and stop travel
on the overland routes. He said the Indians who were friendly to
the white man would be well taken care of.

Cheyenne chief Tall Bull answered that the Indians did not
like the idea of the railroads that were being built through their
country. Hancock, ignorant of the Indian protocol of letting
every man have his say in full, interrupted him to threaten, "If
you should ever stop one of our railroad trains, and kill the people on it, you would be exterminated." The general demanded to
know why there were not more chiefs there to talk with him.
When he was told that the Indians' horses were too poor to
travel, Hancock stated his intention of moving his command
closer to the Indian encampment so he could talk with more
chiefs. Tall Bull and the others were much alarmed at this, saying that the women and children still remembered all too well
the attack on Black Kettle's village at Sand Creek and would be
very frightened.

Though Wynkoop attempted to dissuade Hancock, on the following morning the frontier-inexperienced general began marching his troops up the Pawnee Fork. In order to keep the soldiers
from camping too close, the Indians burned off the grass around
the village. Hancock went into camp some twenty miles up the
river, and that evening he was visited by Sioux chief Pawnee
Killer and White Horse of the Cheyenne Dog Soldier military society. They assured Hancock that the chiefs of the village would
meet him in council the following morning. Bull Bear appeared
the next day, saying the chiefs would be there when the sun was
as high in the sky as he indicated by pointing—which was
judged to be around nine o'clock in the morning. When noon
came and the chiefs had not arrived, Hancock impatiently resumed his march toward the Indian village. A few miles from the
encampment, he came face to face with a large force of
Cheyennes and Sioux drawn up in battle line. Hancock ordered
his cavalry, infantry, and artillery into battle formation, and a

command of "Draw sabers!" brought the 7th's blades out flashing in the morning sun.

War chiefs rode along the Indian lines exhorting the braves to deeds of valor, and a fight appeared to be imminent. Stanley described the confrontation as involving some three hundred-plus chiefs and braves of the Cheyenne and Sioux nations, each warrior with bow drawn and arrows ready in hand. At their lead, Roman Nose carried a white flag of peace, but as the troops were brought into formation about a hundred yards distant, the Indians became increasingly excited and disturbed.

It was Wynkoop who broke the stalemate. He rode forward and talked with Roman Nose and the other chiefs, leading them back half way under a flag of truce to talk with Hancock's party of officers. Hancock demanded to know if the Indians wanted peace or war, to which Roman Nose replied that the Indians didn't want war. If they had, he said, they would not have come so close to the big guns of the soldiers. The Indians now retreated toward their village, Hancock's forces following and making camp some three hundred yards from them. At around five that afternoon, scouts were sent to the village. They returned to inform Hancock that only the chiefs and fighting men were in the village, the women and children, fearing another Sand Creek, having fled while the men were delaying the troops.

Feeling he had been tricked, Hancock was furious and sent for the chiefs, who came immediately: Tall Bull, Bull Bear, Roman Nose, Grey Beard, and the others. The officer demanded that the chiefs send for their people, and when they replied that their horses were too poor, Hancock furnished them fresh mounts for the assignment. Later that evening, scout Guerrier, who had accompanied the chiefs back to their camp, reported that the chiefs and the fighting men were preparing to leave also.

It was nearing midnight when Hancock had Custer awakened with orders to quietly turn his 7th Cavalry troops out of their blankets and surround the Indian village. Custer himself provided a ludicrous picture of how he and his troops crept up on the Indian village on their hands and knees during the night "like some huge anaconda about to envelop its victim." But he was too late. The Indians had already fled, leaving behind only an old Sioux man and a young girl of eight years. The girl had been brutally raped, and an unresolved controversy arose as to whether she was a white girl raped by the Indians or an Indian girl raped by soldiers. She and the old man were taken to Fort Dodge, where both soon died.

Hancock now ordered Custer in pursuit of the Indians with eight companies of the 7th, accompanied by Guerrier and a party of Delaware Indians as scouts and guides. As soon as it was light on the morning of April 15, with the Cheyennes and Sioux now having a twelve-hour start, a confident Custer took out on his first Indian hunt. By the time Walnut Creek was reached, the discovery of campfires still burning indicated they were close on the heels of the fleeing tribe. At one point, the Indians had even deserted some of their ponies, the pack of one containing an ornamental war bonnet that Guerrier said belonged to Roman Nose.

The abandonment of lodge poles and other equipage led Custer to leave his wagons behind and push on in anticipation of contacting the Indians before dark. But here Custer learned his first lesson about Indian fighting. The trail he followed began to fork off into a number of smaller trails, and these in turn split down to even more. Frustrated, he followed the middle trail each time, but finally the whole thing petered out to nothing. Distant moving bodies turned out to be either buffalo or wild horses. After marching some thirty-five miles, Custer went into camp with the Delawares unable to continue the trail, though smoke signals were to be seen on virtually all sides. The Indians had vanished, and, as Hancock later reported with some disgust, Custer had let "fifteen hundred Indians escape and not one is seen."

But Custer was not so concerned about the matter that, on the second day out, he would not take time out to enjoy his first buffalo hunt, despite Hancock's orders against straggling and his previous refusal to allow buffalo hunting on the expedition. Custer's action was certainly imprudent on his part and almost disastrous. As his column marched northward toward the Smoky Hill River, he rode on ahead with his dogs and his chief bugler. Spotting a large buffalo, he began a chase that separated him from the bugler. The buffalo turned when Custer caught up to him and charged Custer's horse, actually his wife's very favorite mount.

In controlling the reins with both hands, while one held his pistol, Custer accidentally shot the horse in the head, killing it. Just as suddenly, Custer found himself afoot facing the buffalo, which now rambled away, and completely lost in the vastness of the open prairie. Custer began walking in which he hoped was the direction of his command. Finally a line of dust proved to be that of his troops, and he was rescued from what had been a very foolish adventure for a commander of troops on an Indian hunt.

The 7th Regiment reached the Smoky Hill early on the morning of April 17, after a long night's march, and went into camp. Custer dispatched Captain Louis Hamilton, about the only officer who had been in that country before, to look for the stage road and a station. This turned out to be Downer's Station, and there Hamilton learned that Indians had been crossing the river headed north and that Lookout Station, east of there, had been attacked, with the three employees there killed and burned. Custer immediately dispatched couriers to Hancock, who had been vacillating over whether or not to burn the Indian village at Pawnee Fork.

By Civil War standards, it would look good to be able to report large amounts of enemy goods captured or destroyed. Hancock had suggested to Wynkoop on the night of the fifteenth that, because the Indians had acted so treacherously toward him by fleeing, they deserved to be punished and he would burn the village the next morning. Wynkoop reacted with an official letter of complaint, cautioning Hancock to ponder well the matter. Colonel Smith of the 7th was against burning the village, and on the seventeenth Hancock wrote Smith indicating that he would wait "until we hear if the Indians have committed hostilities anywhere; if they have, we will regret not having destroyed this camp."

Custer's messenger brought the news Hancock wanted, though Custer could not say which Indians had committed the crimes on the Smoky Hill. On the morning of April 19, Hancock ordered some 251 lodges destroyed—111 Cheyenne and 140 Sioux—saving forty others for the Indian scouts at Fort Dodge. All of the lodges and goods of the camp were thrown into huge piles and set on fire, including some 436 saddles, 942 buffalo robes, and other accouterments. Stanley estimated it would take three hundred buffalo to replace the destroyed Indian lodges.

On the same day, Major Wickliffe Cooper, commanding two companies of the 7th at the Cimarron Crossing, west of Fort Dodge, attacked six unmounted Cheyennes and killed at least two of them. Though Cooper reported all six Indians killed after they were caught skulking around the unit's horse herd, Wynkoop insisted the attack was unprovoked. The agent also reported to his superiors that he felt Hancock's entire operation was "disastrous . . . the result of which will be a general war."

Custer continued on down the Smoky Hill to Fort Hays. There he expected to find forage before continuing his chase of the Indians, whom he considered as unworthy foes because they ran instead of standing to fight. General Sherman, meanwhile, had devised a plan calling for the friendly Indians between the Smoky Hill and the Platte to come in to the forts along the Platte while Custer scoured the country for hostiles to punish. But Custer remained inactive, forced to sit and wait at Fort Hays through the last of April and all of May for supplies to reach the post. The horses were out of condition from feeding on dry prairie grass. His officers even had to share the hard bread, bacon, and beans of the troopers, and several cases of scurvy were reported. The weather turned cold and rainy, and through it all Custer yearned for the appointment to Fort Garland, where he could have his wife with him and the hunting was good.

Finally, on June 1, Custer led six troops of the 7th, or about three hundred and fifty men, and twenty wagons off northward in the direction of Fort McPherson, on the Platte trail. Guiding him was Will Comstock, a young frontiersman with a wealth of knowledge about Indians. An extremely superstitious man, having in Indian fashion a "medicine" for almost everything, Comstock quickly became a favorite of Custer, who relied upon him heavily during the summer's campaign. Ed Guerrier and a frontiersman called California Joe were also along, as was *Harper's* reporter Theodore Davis.

The march to McPherson was so uneventful as to allow Custer plenty of hunting excursions along the way. On the sixth day, a band of about a hundred Indians was seen, and one squadron was sent halfheartedly in pursuit. On June 8, while encamped near Medicine Lake Creek, a tragic occurrence took place. Captain Edward Myers came rushing into Custer's tent to announce that Major Cooper had just shot himself. Cooper was found slumped to the ground, pistol in hand and a pool of blood beneath him. He was dead. Though Cooper, whose wife was pregnant at the time of his suicide, was one of the anti-Custer officers of the unit, no reason for his death was ever given other than that he was drunk at the time. Custer ordered all the other officers to view Cooper's corpse to illustrate the danger of excessive drink, which was prevalent among the officer corps.

The 7th Regiment arrived at McPherson on June 10. While the unit was replenishing supplies of food rations and forage for the horses, Custer conducted a council near the fort with Pawnee Killer and other Sioux chiefs who had come in. Custer and the Sioux leader professed friendship, and the Indians were given presents of coffee, sugar, and other goods. It was later discovered that it had been Pawnee Killer who had killed the men at Lookout Station. General Sherman, who arrived at the post on the day following, was critical of Custer, feeling that he should have taken hostages. Sherman naïvely ordered Custer to go out and find Pawnee Killer's village and force him to move closer to the fort, where he could be watched.

While doing this, Custer was to scout out the country around the forks of the Republican, drive back northward to Fort Sedgwick, where he would replenish his supplies and perhaps receive new orders, and then march westward along the Republican to the South Platte. He also had the liberty to follow the Indians "to hell or Denver" if he found a hot trail.

Custer reached the forks of the Republican in four days, still without encountering the Sioux or other Indians. Going into camp there, he dispatched Major Joel Elliott with ten men and a guide northwestward to Fort Sedgwick, from where Sherman could be reached by telegraph for any new orders. It was a hazardous assignment at best, and Elliott left under cover of darkness on the twenty-third of June.

On the same day, Custer sent the wagon train off for supplies, not to Fort Sedgwick as directed by Sherman, but to Fort Wallace, under escort of one company under Lieutenant Samuel Robbins. Captain West was to accompany the train with another troop as far as Beaver Creek, there to halt and search for Indians while the train continued on. Lieutenant William Cook was in charge of the wagon train. Cook carried with him a letter from Custer to his wife, who he thought would be at Fort Hays, suggesting she meet him at Fort Wallace and join the expedition. Custer's anxious desire to have his wife with him indicates that he had gone against Sherman's instructions for personal reasons.

Custer still had found no Indians, but on the morning of the twenty-fourth they found him. At dawn a party of some fifty Indians attacked the camp, wounding the sentry. The attack was repulsed, and when Indians appeared on a nearby hill Guerrier was sent forward. The guide rode his horse in zigzag fashion to indicate "peace" and then in a circle to indicate a council was desired. Taking six officers and a bugler with him, Custer advanced to parley with chiefs of the attacking Indians, discovering, much to his surprise, that they were led by none other than Pawnee Killer himself.

The Sioux still professed friendship, but, as they talked, some of the warriors attempted to edge up. Custer noticed this and threatened to signal his bugler, who was posted at a distance behind. He also refused the Sioux's request for coffee, sugar, and ammunition. As soon as the meeting broke up, Custer ordered his troops in pursuit, only to learn another interesting fact about Indians. The Indian ponies were much speedier than the heavier army animals and had greater stamina. Furthermore, they could subsist well on the natural prairie grasses, while the army animals required grain forage to maintain their strength. The Sioux quickly outdistanced the troops and led them on a merry but futile chase.

Shortly afterward, a small party of Indians was sighted, and Captain Hamilton led two companies in chase. But he found that as he crested a hill where the Indians had been one moment before, they now would be on another hill, just beyond. In this fashion, the Sioux cleverly led the troops on, causing Hamilton to divide his command of fifty men into two groups, one under the command of First Lieutenant (Brevet Lieutenant Colonel) Tom Custer. Once the unit was separated, a much larger force of Indians suddenly appeared and attacked Hamilton's unit. Hamilton, however, coolly dismounted his men to a kneeling firing position and held off the whooping encirclement of warriors, finally driving them away.

Concern began to grow over the fate of Elliott, but on the twenty-seventh he arrived back in camp. Since the officer had encountered no Indians to the north, Custer feared that they were concentrated to the south and might well have seen the wagon train heading for Wallace. He was right about the Indians, for the Cheyennes had been hitting the Smoky Hill stage route daily, even attacking Fort Wallace, which was then commanded by Captain Miles W. Keogh of the 7th Regiment.

Custer ordered Captain Edward Myers to take a company of troops to Beaver Creek, there to join Captain Robert West, and the two companies to proceed toward the Smoky Hill to lend strength to the wagon train and its escort. They found the train on its way back but under heavy attack by a large force of Indians. The wagons had been formed into two parallel lines of march, the cavalry horses led between them, and the dismounted troopers surrounding the train. The entire unit continued to move forward, returning the fire of the Indians, who encircled the train in a galloping ring and fired from under the necks of their ponies.

From a high butte, where the prairie could be viewed for miles in any direction, an Indian lookout spotted the far-distant columns of Myers and West. The Indians, realizing their ponies would be too tired for another fight, ceased their attack on the train and left, with Will Comstock taunting them in their own tongue.

Elliott had brought no new orders, and Custer decided to carry out Sherman's instructions to march to the South Platte, despite the fact that Comstock had stated his belief the Indians could be found on the Beaver, to the south. The 7th marched westward up the North Fork of the Republican, staying with the river for about sixty miles before turning north toward the South Platte, some sixty-five miles distant. This part of the march was through country scorched dry by the blazing July sun, badly broken by ravines, and so thick with cactus that Custer's staghounds had to be put into wagons. It was a torturous march for both horses and men, whose only water supply came from digging in dry creek beds.

On the evening of July 4, Custer sighted the South Platte through his field glasses. With three others, he pushed on ahead of the command and reached the river just above Riverside Station, so weary that they collapsed on the riverbank and slept through a rainstorm without waking. The command arrived later that night. By wire from Riverside, Custer learned that Sherman had sent him later instructions ordering him to Fort Wallace. The orders had been dispatched by Second Lieutenant Lyman Kidder with ten men and guided by a Sioux chief named Red Bead.

Custer also discovered that he had marched himself into a serious predicament. Since its formation, the 7th Cavalry had had a very high rate of desertion. Many of the soldiers, often called "snow birds," enlisted merely for the winter months. Disliking the rugged, harsh life of soldiering on the frontier, the men were easily tempted by jobs on the railroads or by high wages offered by the Colorado mines. The South Platte road led directly to those mines.

Resting only one day from the grueling, exhaustive, and fruitless march, Custer ordered the command back over the line of march they had just endured. In the early morning of July 7, before the troops were to march, more than twenty men deserted, taking their horses and equipment with them. Others followed. Short on supplies and anxious to discover the whereabouts of the messenger Kidder, Custer could not afford to go after the deserters.

After marching fifteen miles back toward the Republican, the command halted for a noon break. As the march was about to be resumed, an officer reported to Custer that several more men,

seven on horseback and six on foot, were blatantly deserting
right then. Angrily Custer called for the officer of the day, Lieutenant Henry Jackson, to go after them. While Jackson was trying to round up his guard, many of whom had already taken up
the march, Custer shouted to the officers near him at the time to
go after the deserters themselves. Excitedly he yelled out orders
to "Shoot them. Bring none back alive." These officers—Elliott,
Cook, and Tom Custer—immediately jumped on their horses
and headed after the men, overtaking those on foot.

Three of the six on foot were shot: one in the right arm; another in the shoulder, ribs, and hand; and another in the left side
and in the temple, the ball coming out his jaw. This last man,
whose name was Johnson, later died at Fort Wallace. Elliott
claimed that the men were ordered to throw down their Spencer
rifles, and all but Johnson did so. When Johnson raised his rifle,
according to Elliott, the firing began. Other witnesses, however,
claimed that the soldiers were chased about by the officers on
their horses and that Johnson was on his knees begging for his
life when he was shot. One of the deserters later testified that it
was Lieutenant Cook, not Elliott, who actually shot Johnson.
Tom Custer stated that a scout named Atkins threatened to blow
Johnson's brains out if he touched his carbine.

The six deserters were placed in a regular army wagon and
brought back into camp, Custer refusing to allow Dr. I. T.
Coates, assistant surgeon, to treat the men for more than two
hours, and then only in secret so that the other men would not
know about it. Coates did not dress the wounds for two days, because the only water to be found was the dirty water in buffalo
wallows. The doctor gave his medical opinion that gunshot
wounds often did better when the blood was allowed to congeal
on them. He gave the wounded men opiates throughout the
rough, jolting ride in the wagon.

Custer prevented further dissension during the march by placing every officer on duty fully armed, walking the company
streets every night with orders to shoot any man appearing outside his tent. Under this tight security, the command reached
their old camp at the forks of the Republican, having found no
sign of Lieutenant Kidder's party. Reasoning that Kidder may

have mistakenly followed the larger wagon trail to Fort Wallace instead of his own trail to the northwest, and with the fort as his destination anyway, Custer headed in that direction.

Eventually, Comstock and the Delaware guides discovered Kidder's trail: the marks of twelve shod horses moving for a time at a walk. Then a dead white horse was found, and Elliott recalled having seen a "white horse" unit at Sedgwick. The tracks now were joined by the marks of smaller, unshod horses. Presently buzzards were spotted at a distance. Investigation soon revealed the bodies of Kidder and his party, all dead and badly mutilated. The Sioux guide, Red Bead, had been scalped, and the scalp lock had been tossed contemptuously beside his corpse, giving strong indication that it was his own tribe, possibly Pawnee Killer's band, who had caught up with the courier group. Kidder and his men were buried in a trench at the massacre site.

Arriving at Fort Wallace on the afternoon of July 13, the 7th set up camp near the post. From Captain Myles Keogh, whose Company I of the 7th was garrisoning the post, Custer learned that the Butterfield Overland stagecoach line had virtually shut down because of the incessant Indian raids on their posts and coaches. Captain Albert Barnitz, commanding Company G of the 7th, was also in the area, having gone to the relief of Pond Creek Station when it was attacked on June 26 by the Cheyennes. In a fight that lasted three hours, the Cheyennes under Roman Nose had lured the soldiers into a trap, killed six of them, and wounded eight more before Barnitz could get them out. Keogh and his troop had just returned from Denver with General Hancock, who had gone on east. Lieutenant Frederick Beecher, 3rd Infantry and post quartermaster, wrote: "We sit up nights and sleep by turns during the day."

Custer later claimed as justification of his ensuing actions that there were no rations or forage at Fort Wallace and that scurvy and cholera had broken out. While it is true there was no forage for the worn-out horses or horseshoes needed to refit the mounts and supplies were running dangerously low, the cholera had not yet reached Fort Wallace while Custer was there.

Still chafing to see his wife and extremely disappointed that he did not find a letter from her waiting for him at the post, Custer once again displayed his impatience and imprudence. From the six companies that had been with him on the march to the South Platte, Custer ordered his officers to select the men with the twelve best horses in each troop. His plan was to make another forced march eastward along the Smoky Hill trail to Fort Harker, which was then the railhead of the Kansas Pacific Railroad, purportedly to escort a supply train back to Fort Wallace. At dusk on July 15, with barely two days' rest for men and horses, Custer departed Wallace with seventy-two troops and three officers, these being Captain Hamilton, Lieutenant Tom Custer, and Lieutenant Cook. Reporter Theodore Davis, who had been with Custer all the way, accompanied the cortege on his way back to New York.

Traveling at night as fast as the badly jaded horses could go, the unit made the 150-mile march to Fort Hays in fifty-five hours, reaching there early on the morning of July 18. The trip was not without incident, and Custer was to be severely criticized for his rashness in making such a grueling march ostensibly to secure supplies but actually for the purpose of seeing his wife, whom he expected would be at Fort Harker.

Near Monument Station, Custer met a supply train under the escort of Captain (Brevet Lieutenant Colonel) Frederick Benteen and Company H of the 7th Cavalry. It was this train which carried the cholera germs that were to infect Fort Wallace. Forage was obtained from the train, and the expedition hurried on. At Castle Rock Station, on the second day, Custer stopped two mail coaches and went through their mailbags looking for letters or orders for himself, but none were found.

The men were beginning to drop out because of their weary animals or because they themselves went to sleep in the saddle. Custer assigned Sergeant James Connelly the chore of going back and picking up the stragglers and shooting the fagged-out horses rather than leaving them for the Indians. On the morning of the seventeenth, while the force was halted west of Downer's Station for coffee, Custer ordered Connelly to take six men and go back to pick up a soldier who was riding a mare belonging to Custer. While doing so, Connelly's party was attacked by Indians. The men made a dash for Downer's Station, leaving behind two soldiers, one of them wounded and one fairly certain to have been killed. The affair was reported to Custer while he was eating at the station. Infantry captain Arthur Carpenter, in charge of the station, described the incident in a letter to his parents: "While at dinner his rear guard was attacked about 3 miles west of here, and those who came in reported two killed. Custer remained unconcerned—finished his dinner, and moved on without saying a word to me about the bodies, or thinking of hunting the Indians." Carpenter went out and brought in the wounded man and the dead trooper. Custer's lack of concern caused angry threats of mutiny among the men with him.

At Big Creek, near Fort Hays, Custer left Captain Hamilton in charge of the troops, secured four government mules and an army ambulance, and proceeded without pause to Fort Harker. There he found that Mrs. Custer had gone back to Fort Riley. Undaunted by the fact that it was nearly two o'clock in the morning, Custer went to the quarters of Colonel Smith, who commanded the District of the Upper Arkansas as well as the 7th Cavalry, and awakened him. Reporting his activities to the groggy Smith, he then stated his intention of going on to Fort Riley by train. Smith woke Lieutenant Weir, his adjutant, to take Custer to the railway station. The next morning, when Smith had considered the matter afresh, he sent a telegram to Custer ordering him to report back to Harker immediately. Custer complied as soon as he could catch a train, whereupon Smith had him placed under arrest on the charge of deserting his post at Fort Wallace.

With Hancock pressing him hard to do so, Smith filed other charges against Custer. The counts alleged that Custer had absented himself from his command at Fort Wallace without proper authority and, in making a forced march, had overused the horses which were already unfit for service. Further, Custer was accused of procuring a vehicle and government mules for his own personal use, of not attempting to rescue his men at Downer's Station, and of not recovering their bodies when he learned that they had been slain.

To these, other charges were added. Captain West, who was very angry over the killing of his trooper Johnson, preferred charges relative to Custer's ordering the deserters to be shot and then refusing them proper medical attention. There was an additional, personal vengeance behind West's charges: while at Fort Wallace, Custer had had West placed under arrest for being drunk.

There is no question of the dissension with Custer among the officers of the 7th. A letter written by Lieutenant Charles Brewster to Custer on September 7, 1867, gives an interesting clue as to the feeling of the various officers relative to their commander. In it Brewster stated that Lieutenant Wallingford wished to be of help to Custer and that Hamilton was friendly to him also. But West was very bitter, Keogh unfriendly, and not another officer then at Wallace could be counted on, these including Elliott, Myers, Robbins, Barnitz, Commagere, Hale, Jackson, and Leavy.

On the morning of September 15, 1867—even as Jefferson Davis was being tried in Richmond and impeachment action was being recommended against President Andrew Johnson—Custer's court-martial board convened at Fort Leavenworth. The board of officers who tried Custer consisted of Colonel William Hoffman, 3rd Infantry; Colonel Benjamin Grierson, 10th Cavalry; Colonel Pitcairn Morrison, retired; Major M. R. Morgan, commissary of subsistence; Lieutenant Colonel Franklin Callendar, ordnance; Major Henry Asbury, 3rd Infantry; and Major Stephen Lyford, ordnance.

After lengthy testimony by men and officers of the 7th, Custer was found guilty on all counts. It was, of course, a mortifying experience for the youthful Custer, who felt he had been wrongly accused and plotted against. He pointed to the exceptional situation of deserters, which plagued the Indian campaign, citing a telegram he had received from General Hancock advising him to "capture or kill the deserters." And he complained bitterly that four of the members of the court were inferior to him in rank, that three of them were on Hancock's staff, that one member had once been censured by him for corruption in issuing rations to the soldiers, that three of them had never commanded in the field, and that one had openly expressed a strong bias against him. Nevertheless, the guilty verdict held.

On the evening of November 25, 1867, the 7th Regiment fell out in full-dress uniform on the Fort Leavenworth parade ground. The columns of blue-clad troopers, four abreast, wheeled their mounts into line to face the group of officers assembled there, colors to the center, while the troop commanders took positions beside their swallow-tailed guidons, their sabers slashing the air in brisk salutes. At the center of the reviewing party was Custer, sitting astride a magnificent black stallion.

Custer wore full regimentals, golden epaulets on the shoulders of an immaculate blue tunic, double row of buttons glistening in front, a twin slash of aiguillettes—gold-braided and tasseled—over the breast and more gold in broad stripes on the cuffs. His hands, overlapping the reins of his saddle pommel, were covered with white kid gloves. On his head Custer wore an ornate regimental helmet, the front of which carried a large emblem of an American eagle. On the top of the helmet was a pedestal-mounted plume of brilliant scarlet, while from under the back curled Custer's long, flaxen hair. The trousers of his uniform were gray with a broad yellow stripe down the side. His saber dangled in its metal scabbard to the left, reaching to the heels of his ebony cavalry boots.

Custer's campaign-reddened face was passive on the surface, but beneath the bushy eyebrows and the heavy mustache which overcurled his mouth he hid his anger and deep humiliation. He felt he was being victimized by those who were jealous of him and used as a scapegoat to blunt the rising criticism for the failure of Hancock's Indian campaign in western Kansas. Now he must endure with dignity the rank indignity of facing the regiment he had commanded in the field for the past six months while his enemies victoriously read the sentence of his court-martial.

Impatiently he listened to the droning voice repeating the charges, hearing himself pronounced guilty on all counts. A strangled silence followed as every soul on the parade ground waited in anticipation of the sentence. There had been much talk and even some betting around the post by officers and troopers alike as to what the military court would dare to do to the beau sabreur, the boy general of the U. S. Cavalry. Then the sentence was read. Custer was to be suspended from command, rank, and pay for one full year. A murmur of reaction swept through the ranks. Custer himself felt a sense both of anger and of relief. It could have been worse, considering the charges, however unjust they might have been. The bitterest part was losing field command of the 7th Regiment for a year, perhaps for good.

For now he could only bide his time and wait for another chance against the Indians. It was a mistake, he knew now, to try to catch the Indian warrior on the open plains. There was only one way: find his villages and attack them. But there would be another day. The famous "Custer's luck" would return and with it the enormous glory he had known during the war.

On January 4, 1868, Custer and Lieutenant Cook were brought to court in Leavenworth on the charge of murdering Private Johnson, the charge filed by Captain West. However, both were released when the judge ruled the charge was not sustained by evidence. Custer retaliated by charging West with being drunk on duty, for which he was found guilty and was suspended from rank and pay for two months.

The Hancock Indian campaign was over, a dismal military failure which had served only to make the Indian situation much worse. Hancock, now assigned to command the Fifth Military District at New Orleans, was being widely mentioned as the only Democrat who "could make a show against Grant" for the presidency. The Dog Soldiers and the Sioux were riding the prairies of western Kansas like angry hornets, and the ineptness of Custer in finding and striking them only increased the contempt of the Indians for the Army. Moreover, the Cheyennes took the burning of their village on the Pawnee Fork with a great deal more significance than Hancock might have suspected. To them it was a betrayal of the Treaty of the Little Arkansas of 1865 and another proof, if more than Sand Creek was needed, of the perfidy of the white man.

Custer, his glory now a bit tarnished, spent the fall and winter at Fort Leavenworth, enjoying the comforts of post life and talking of a possible trip to Europe. However, he returned instead to Monroe, Michigan, where he hunted, fished, and wrote self-praisingly of his adventures on the plains. But he was an unhappy and still impatient exile from his regiment, which during his court-martial in October had played escort to the peace commission at Medicine Lodge Creek under the command of Major Elliott. With the treaty signed under the false notion that the Cheyennes would still be free to roam and hunt over western Kansas, a new war on the plains was virtually assured. It would offer Custer new opportunity to rebuild his diminished reputation.

Chapter II
TREATY BY TRICKERY

A multitude of forces called for a solution to the Indian problem in Kansas in 1867. The wild tribes, especially the Cheyennes, were an interference with too many things. There was the immigration to the western states, mail and trade merchandise to be transported overland, railroads to be built across the plains, Texas beef to be driven across the Indian Territory and marketed at the Kansas railheads, land to be opened for homesteads, the expansion of new settlements onto the prairie, and other factors of national development to which the tribes were a barrier. The Indian problem had to be resolved; the nation debated the question of how to do it.

Both the Army and the frontier whites believed the only solution was to soundly punish the tribes and force them to remain on isolated reserves, if not to kill them off outright. Sherman expressed the opinion of many in July of 1867 when he wrote to Hancock: "We must not remain on the defensive, but must follow them on all possible occasions. We must clear out the Indians between the Platte and the Arkansas, and then move against the hostile tribes in force beyond those rivers."

The Indian Bureau and many citizens not living on the frontier sought a peaceful and humane solution, particularly in the wake of the Congressional reports concerning the Sand Creek attack. With the recent failure of Hancock and Custer to punish the Indians, it appeared to be time to give those whom Kansas editors had dubbed "the Olive Branchers" another chance. Accordingly, Congress approved a bill, which had been introduced by Senator John B. Henderson of Missouri, establishing a peace commission to work out new treaties with the various tribes of the central plains.

Henderson was named chairman of the commission, and appointed to serve with him were N. G. Taylor, Commissioner of Indian Affairs; Colonel Samuel Tappan, who had headed the army inquiry into the Sand Creek affair; Major General John B. Sanborn, who had commanded the Upper Arkansas District in 1865 and been a member of the peace commission at the Treaty of the Little Arkansas; Major General William S. Harney, known as an old Indian fighter from earlier conflicts with the Sioux and Cheyennes along the Platte, now retired; Major General Alfred H. Terry, commander of the Department of the Dakota; and General Sherman. Sherman, who made some ill-advised public remarks concerning the Indian problem which resulted in accusations by the press that he was not in agreement with the policy of making peace, was called to Washington from St. Louis by General Grant and replaced by Major General C. C. Augur, commanding the Department of the Platte.

In preparation for the peace council, excursions were made deep into the Indian country to find and "talk in" the various bands of the Cheyennes, Arapahoes, Comanches, Kiowas, and Plains Apaches. On September 10, Colonel Jesse Leavenworth, son of the namesake of Fort Leavenworth and now agent for the Kiowas and Comanches, took a party of men into Indian Territory and met with his charges on the Salt Fork of the Arkansas River. Through his interpreter, Philip McCusker, he induced Ten Bears and Iron Mountain of the Comanches, To-haw-son and Stumbling Bear of the Kiowas, and Iron Shirt of the Plains Apaches to attend the council.

Iron Shirt reported that he had only recently come from Wolf Creek, where Dutch Bill Griffenstein and his wife, Cheyenne Jenny, were operating out of Chisholm's old trading post fifteen miles from the Canadian. Iron Shirt complained that the Dog Soldiers had called the Apaches cowards because they wished to walk the road of peace.

Contacted by a courier from Leavenworth, Cheyennes Black Kettle and George Bent, who was married to Black Kettle's niece; Little Raven of the Arapahoes; and Poor Bear of the Apaches had gone to Fort Larned. There they talked with Superintendent Murphy and Agent Wynkoop on September 8. The chiefs insisted that the peace talks must be held on Medicine Lodge Creek, where there were good grass and water and where they would not be mistaken for hostiles by the soldiers. They also insisted that the tribes would need provisions to last them until the commissioners arrived.

On September 17, Murphy and Wynkoop, accompanied by forty Cheyenne, Arapaho, and Apache warriors, escorted a large train of provisions to Medicine Lodge Creek, some sixty miles south of Larned. There they found 171 lodges of Arapahoes, 150 of Kiowas, 85 of Apaches, 100 of Comanches, but only 25 of Cheyennes. Ed Guerrier was sent from there to guide trader Isaac Butterfield to find the Cheyennes. Butterfield was shot at by a band of hostile Dog Soldiers, who also took his horse, saddle, and pistol.

The Dog Soldiers were still highly incensed over Hancock's burning of their village on the Pawnee Fork. A party of ten Cheyennes led by Roman Nose visited Murphy's camp at Medicine Lodge and made a threatening move to get to Wynkoop with the evident intention of "lifting some hair." They were stopped by the Arapahoes, who grabbed their bridles, giving the surprised Wynkoop a chance to jump on his horse and flee the camp to the safety of Fort Larned. Murphy talked to the Cheyennes and persuaded them that Wynkoop was innocent; he also asked them to deliver his invitation for the Dog Soldiers, who were camped on the Cimarron, to attend the council.

In early October the peace commissioners gathered at Fort Leavenworth and moved by railway to Fort Harker. There they were joined by an escort of infantry, Battery B of the 4th Artillery with two Gatling guns, and 150 troops of the 7th Cavalry, all under the command of Major Elliott, who had been excused from Custer's court-martial proceedings at Leavenworth expressly for this duty. Governor Samuel J. Crawford and Kansas senator Edmund G. Ross (who in the following spring would be thrust into the fateful role of casting the deciding vote on the impeachment of President Andrew Johnson) also joined the commission train at Harker. On the morning of October 9, the caravan headed overland toward Larned.

With the commission train were a number of newspaper correspondents, more than had ever before covered an Indian peace council in the West. From these reporters would flow a barrage of colorful copy to American readers, providing extensive description of Indian culture, life on the frontier, events of the peace council, and opinions relative to the Indian problem. One of the most prolific, and most opinionated, was Henry M. Stanley, who fed a steady flow of copy to several newspapers. Another reporter was George C. Brown of the Cincinnati *Commercial,* who penned an excellent account of the expedition as it left Harker:

> First came the four scouts—hardy men of the Plains, with countenances bronzed with adventure, hats broad-brimmed, and eyes wild. Away ahead of the train they rode, generally together, and with eyes ever alert for objects suspicious. Danger none there really was, although some of the timid ones suggested some of the wild Kiowas and Comanches, who had not yet heard of the Commission, and were returning from their hunts, might be tempted to fire into our train, as other hostile bands have done, within the past fourteen days, to trains passing over the route we are now upon. Next came the one hundred and fifty mounted cavalrymen, on spirited steeds, each armed with revolvers, and carbines swung across their shoulders or dangling from their saddle pommels. By twos they marched, and, under command of Major Allen [Elliott] of the Seventh Cavalry, presented a fine appearance as ahead of the ambulances, in perfect order, they slowly wound up the crooked roads of the ravines, and anon dashed swiftly down steep descents, the heels of their steeds stirring up clouds of dust that, despite the rains of the day before, rolled away with a blinding effect. Close to the heels of the cavalrymen come the ambulances of the Commission—wide wagons on heavy wheels, covered with tight-fitting cloth canvass, impervious to both dust and rain, capable of seating comfortably four persons beside the driver and his companion, and each having wagon bottom enough for several valises and blankets. Stretching back, generally half a mile in the rear, are the baggage wagons, al-

ways behind hand, and driven by profane teamsters, who walk in
the dust, or, bestriding the "nigh wheeler," crack their long whips
and yell vociferously their slang and orders. At this rate we travel
about four miles an hour, and toward noon stop at Plum Creek, a
straggling stream where we tarried for lunch, General Harney
opening his capacious chest of superb French brandies and genuine
Bourbon whiskies, and General Sanborn uncorking several bottles
of genuine Heidseick [sic] Golden Wedding, all of which washed
down not unkindly the acceptable hard tack and cold ham. An
hour's halt in the hot sun, having made eighteen miles, and we are
off again.

The commissioners and their party arrived at Fort Larned on
the morning of October 11, and a number of them, along with
some of the correspondents, attended a gathering in a back room
of the sutler's store, where Agent Wynkoop treated them to some
of his private stock. Also present were the fat, good-natured
Arapaho chief Little Raven and the cunning, powerfully built
Kiowa Satanta, both of whom gave the white men prolonged
hugs of affection which left the victims covered with paint. Satanta, among others, drank his share before the meeting broke
up, though he was anxious to leave, as it "stink too much white
man here."

The commission went into camp on the bank of the Arkansas
River, where they rested for a day, until the morning of October
12. Then over two hundred wagons and other vehicles, thirty of
them loaded with gifts for the Indians, fell into line, crossed the
river, and headed for Medicine Lodge Creek, some sixty miles to
the south. Some wondered if they had enough protection, for
there was considerable uneasiness regarding the hostile Dog Soldiers.

Immense herds of buffalo were encountered on the march,
causing a great fever among the caravan for everyone "to immor-
talize himself by killing one of the monsters, and forthwith from
the train, everyone who could muster, beg, borrow or steal a
Rosinante, lame, blind, halt, windgalled or spavined, it mattered
not: the cry was, 'a horse, a kingdom for a horse!' Mounted, with
revolver, rifle and knife, off they started. Greenhorns, scouts,
teamsters, attaches, dogs and military, all intent on buffalo." Sa-

tanta, hung over and ill-tempered, was furious at the white men for killing the Indians' buffalo, many of which were left to rot on the plains. He complained strongly to General Harney, who issued orders that no more such sport hunting would be permitted.

Early on the morning of the fourteenth, the expedition arrived at the Medicine Lodge camping grounds, entering the Arapaho village "with a hundred dogs barking at our heels, boys and girls chasing behind us, whooping and yelling."

Black Kettle and some other Cheyenne chiefs came over from their camp and talked with the commissioners. Black Kettle's warning that the Dog Soldiers were still on the warpath and might attack the train if it were left unprotected caused "no inconsiderable panic among the commissioners." He told them, also, that the Cheyennes would need eight sleeps before the rest of the tribe could be brought in. The commissioners grudgingly accepted this. To encourage a friendly attitude among the Cheyennes, the commissioners issued them some military uniforms, which later caused Satanta and others to demand similar apparel.

That evening, a large party of heavily armed Cheyennes, led by Tall Bull and Grey Head, suddenly appeared at Commission Camp. Grey Head produced a safe-conduct note that General Harney had written for him nine years before, on July 17, 1858, on the North Platte. The chief and the old soldier slapped one another on the back happily, and Harney invited Grey Head to attend a hearing he was planning to hold regarding Hancock's operations against the Indians.

On the morning of the fifteenth, rations were issued to the tribes and a preliminary council was held. Black Kettle was the principal representative of the Cheyennes, along with Bull Bear, Tall Bull, Heap of Birds, Slim Face, Black White Man, and Grey Head. All together, they represented two hundred and fifty lodges of the Cheyenne Nation.

The chiefs came in full regalia, their faces dyed with red ocher and hieroglyphics drawn in various colors over their cheeks. All wore fully feathered headdresses except Black Kettle, who wore a tall dragoon's hat. Behind him trailed a long robe of the finest blue cloth. Some of them had colorful Mexican serapes, and others wore blue, red, black, and green blankets. All were adorned with breastplates with carved concave shells, huge silver crosses, and peace medals, plus the usual arm and finger ornaments. Their moccasins were beautifully beaded in designs of flowers, rings, stars, leaves, and other appropriate symbols.

Black Kettle listened to the speeches by Commissioner Taylor and chiefs of the other tribes but said little himself, merely stating that he was in agreement with what had been said and with the plan to meet again in four days. He explained that his people were involved in their annual rites of renewing the Sacred Medicine Arrows and that it would take several more days.

That afternoon Harney, who was outspoken in his criticism of Hancock's campaign, began taking testimony relative to the background of the Indian problem. Wynkoop talked at length about the burning of the Cheyenne village at Pawnee Fork and made charges of fraud in the handling of Cheyenne annuities. He testified that when the Cheyenne and other tribes received their annuities two years before, the blankets given them were badly rotted and virtually worthless. The Indians were charged eighteen dollars each for them. Barrels of sugar listed as full were more than half empty. Other goods, such as ladies' gaiters, bonnets, and other such gimcracks were entirely useless to the Indians, while, all together, less than a third of the annuity goods were even delivered.

Meanwhile the whites were investigating frontier life. Some of the correspondents visited the Arapaho village to trade, even entering some of the lodges, where they ". . . conversed with young women who were anxious that we should stay for improper purposes." Several of the reporters also attended an Arapaho dance, some even taking part in the affair. On one occasion, a party of horsemen with long hair were seen approaching the camp, and fear that the Dog Soldiers were attacking spread panic through the encampment until it was discovered the horsemen were Comanches. On the seventeenth, a knife fight broke out between a teamster and a correspondent who had gone into the Indian Territory with Leavenworth. The reporter, who signed his copy "Frontier," was stabbed twice in the ribs.

Tall Bull and Grey Head returned on the seventeenth and at-

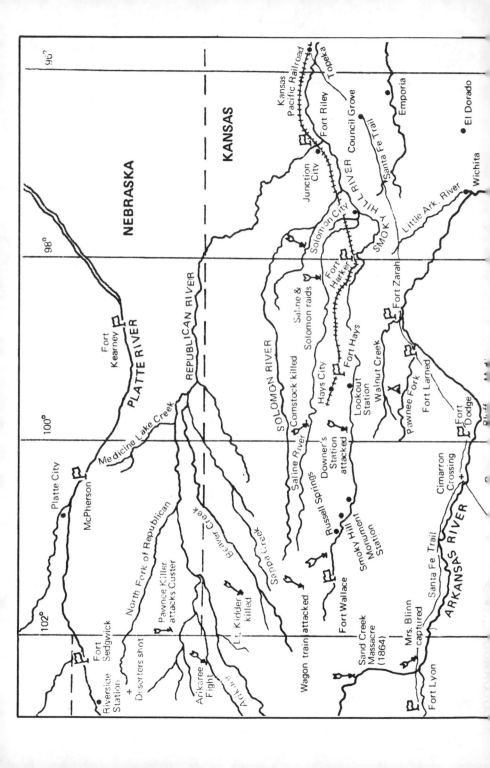

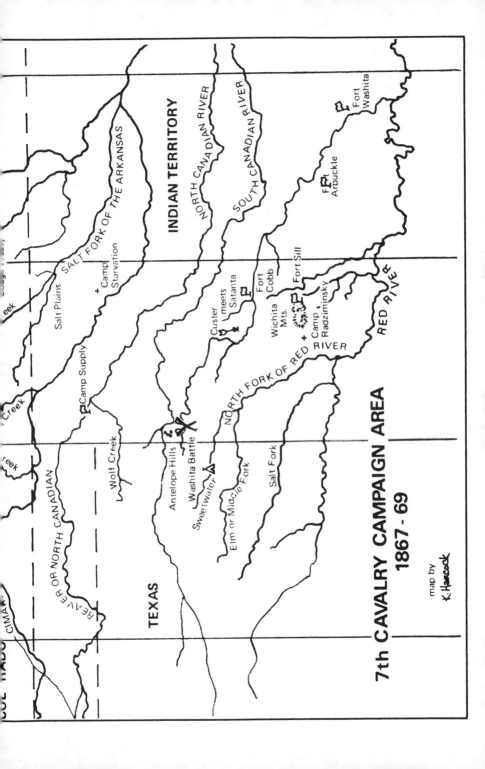

7th CAVALRY CAMPAIGN AREA
1867 - 69

map by
K. Hancock

tended the meeting with Harney. Grey Head claimed in his talk that the Sand Creek attack and the burning of their village on Pawnee Fork had made the Cheyennes very distrustful of white troops. After the council they shook hands with Wynkoop as evidence of their belief that he had not been responsible for the burning of the village. Later, they went to Black Kettle's camp and insisted that he come to the Cimarron and tell what he expected the Cheyennes to gain from making peace with the whites again. If he did not come, Tall Bull threatened, the Dog Soldiers would come and kill all his horses.

When the first general council was held, on the nineteenth, under a great arbor constructed of brush and limbs, the Dog Soldiers were still not there, though Black Kettle and Grey Head both returned. Grey Head spoke once during the meeting to say that the Cheyennes could make no commitment until the rest of the tribe, who were still conducting their medicine rites, had arrived. He indicated that Little Robe and some others would be in soon. Black Kettle remained silent throughout the meeting.

There were speeches by the chiefs of the other tribes, all of whom were very indignant that the council was being held up to accommodate the Cheyennes. Satanta, Ten Bears, Silver Broach (a Comanche), and Apache chief Poor Bear all spoke. Satanta and Ten Bears both said they did not want the houses that the government said it was going to build for them. Satanta made it clear he did not trust the commissioners: "I have not any little lies sticking about me. I lay aside my arrows and lance and come among you with nothing. I don't know how it is. The gentlemen of the commission may have something aside which I can't see."

At midafternoon the council was adjourned until the next morning. That night, a band of twenty Osages, war enemies of several of the council tribes, especially the Kiowas, suddenly appeared in camp asking to be fed. They were, and immediately afterward they left Commission Camp. The next day, some of the council Indians were drunk, and Harney was infuriated at the Osages, whom he blamed for selling them the whiskey.

At noon the next day, October 20, the council resumed. Elderly, spectacled Ten Bears and Satanta made statements of their tribal wishes, both again stressing that they did not want any of the white man's houses, barns, or schools. When Senator Henderson took the floor, he virtually ignored what the chiefs had said, blandly insisting that the government would build houses for the Indians. Satanta, gorgeously attired in a general's coat, bowed legs bare beneath, and a bugle hanging to his side, replied sardonically that the Indians would let them know when the buffalo were gone, and then they could build houses. Ten Bears and Satanta argued about Leavenworth as their agent; the Comanches liked him, the Kiowas did not.

The treaty, however, was duly signed by the Comanches and Kiowas on the following day, though many of the correspondents were convinced that they did not know what they were signing. Both Stanley and Major Elliott, who wrote an official report of the treaty, contended that the treaty was never read in full to the chiefs and that only a few pleasing extracts were read to the Indians by the interpreter.

By the treaty, the Comanches and Kiowas were forced to give up over sixty thousand square miles of territory which they considered their home, and accepted as a reserve a forty-eight-thousand-square-mile area in the southwestern corner of the Indian Territory. In return, the tribes would be provided with some thirty thousand dollars worth of houses, barns, and schools they did not want. There were many fallacies to the treaty, but possibly the most glaring was the misconception it promoted that the nomadic Indians would confine themselves to the reserve area except for occasional hunting parties.

Having taken care of the Comanches and Kiowas, the commissioners now turned their attention to the Cheyennes. The uneasiness concerning the absence of the Dog Soldiers continued to grow with each day. That same night of the twentieth, a severe rainstorm hit the camp, and out of it emerged a small party of Cheyenne chiefs that included Little Robe, Grey Head, and Min-im-mic. They appeared at Harney's tent, wrapped in soaking-wet blankets, explaining they had come to talk with Black Kettle, who was now with them. After some conversation in their own tongue, Black Kettle, who seemed visibly disturbed by the visit, explained that the Cheyennes were still conducting their

Medicine Arrows ceremonies and that it would take four more days to complete them.

This caused an argument among the commissioners. Henderson, who was very anxious to leave Medicine Lodge Creek, declared he would wait no longer for the Cheyennes. Angrily Harney threatened to place the senator under arrest if he tried to leave before the Cheyennes came in. Finally the commission agreed to allow the Cheyennes four more days, and Little Robe agreed that they would be in by then. With this the chiefs left the tent and rode off into the rainstorm, taking Black Kettle with them.

The Arapahoes and the Plains Apaches had not yet been attended to. Arapaho chief Little Raven requested that his tribe be dealt with separately from the Cheyennes, unlike in the treaties of 1851, 1861, and 1865. The Cheyennes misbehaved, Little Raven said, and were always getting the Arapahoes into trouble. He also informed the commissioners that some of his young men would be coming into camp with some whooping and firing of guns, but for the whites not to be alarmed. The Arapaho warriors had gone after some Kaw Indians who had stolen some of the Arapaho ponies. They had killed some of the thieves and were bringing back some scalps.

The commissioners virtually ignored Little Raven. The Apaches had asked that they be allowed to settle on the Kiowa-Comanche reserve, as they had been close to those tribes for years, and the commission found this an easy solution and incorporated them into the Comanche-Kiowa pact. The Arapaho question still remained open.

The camp now settled down to impatient and uneasy waiting for the Cheyennes. The Comanches and Kiowas, who had signed their treaties on the twentieth, were assembled on the twenty-second to receive their promised treaty presents. The wagons were unloaded, revealing the goods: "boxes of soap, beads, brass bells, long strings of tin cups, dozens of iron pans, bales of red, blue and black blankets, bolts of domestic and printed calico, a pile of revolvers, caps and ammunition, and dozens of butcher knives." This taken care of, the commissioners and correspondents now entertained themselves with visits to the Indian villages. On Friday, the twenty-fifth, the Apache treaty was signed by Poor Bear and others of his tribe.

Governor Crawford and Senator Ross had departed the council grounds on the twenty-second, Crawford having earlier reported to the commission his belief that the Plains tribes had united in an organized conspiracy to wage a general war against the whites. Crawford's charges of an Indian conspiracy, which sounded reminiscent of those made by Colorado Territorial Governor Evans prior to the Sand Creek Massacre, were strongly disputed by correspondent Milton Reynolds, who accused the governor of using the Indian problem for his own political advantage: "The politics of this state are terribly muddled and mixed and a systematic attempt has been made by Governor Crawford and his partisans to drag the Indian question into a dirty pool. Political aspirants induced the Government to proclaim the manifest falsehood that white settlers had a right to go on to Indian lands in spite of treaty stipulations."

Fear concerning the Cheyennes increased when Ed Guerrier, who had been sent to talk with the Dog Soldiers, returned on the twenty-fifth. He reported that he had great trouble getting to see the Cheyennes, whose camp was strongly fortified. They had told Guerrier that it would be three more days before they would be in. The commissioners sent word they would wait only as long as Monday, the twenty-eighth.

The persistent feeling of dread and suspense continued to grow in Commission Camp. Even the Arapahoes, who had long been traditional allies of the Cheyennes, did not know what to expect of the Dog Soldier warriors, and they were as concerned as the whites. Little Raven cautioned the commissioners against deception. On Saturday, Cheyenne chief Little Robe rode in to inform the camp that the Cheyenne warriors would be there soon and would probably fire their pistols in the air but that there would be no cause for alarm. The warning only added to the uneasiness of the whites.

It was especially quiet on Sunday morning. Some of the men were writing letters, some reading their Bibles, some sweeping the dirt floors of their tents and airing blankets and robes on the grass, others playing cards, and one group riding downstream to hunt for souvenirs in an abandoned sun-dance lodge. Shortly before noon, an Indian messenger arrived with the electrifying news: the Cheyennes were on their way!

A sense of near panic swelled through the camp. The Arapahoes scattered in fright, increasing the feeling of danger among the whites. A group of Kiowa and Comanche warriors quickly mounted their horses and, armed with lances, waited grim-faced to one side in a small knot. Major Elliott put his troops and Gatling-gun crews on alert, and everyone in the encampment checked the loads of his personal firearms. The commissioners, even now, argued. Harney wanted to put on a confident front by walking to the river's bank to meet the Cheyennes, insisting he had never known a Cheyenne to break his word. Others were not at all sure, but they hesitantly followed the old soldier's lead.

Then the cry went up: "Cheyennes, Cheyennes!" From the camp, a long, five-abreast column of riders could be seen through the trees as they crossed the sandy bluffs beyond. Now could be heard the warbling sound of war chants and the reports of pistols and rifles. Shortly the Cheyenne Dog Soldiers—described by one reporter present as "the bravest, ugliest, most vindictive and determined Indians of our day"—were crashing through the timber and tall weeds of the far bank to pull up there in a long, turbulent line of hooting, singing warriors and excited war ponies.

It was an impressive, blood-chilling sight for the white men: some four to five hundred well-armed and painted Cheyenne warriors, their silver crosses and medals glistening under the high noon sun, crimson blankets about their waists, eagle-feathered bonnets, white-red-and-blue-beaded moccasins, some wearing coats of the U. S. Cavalry that had possibly been taken from fallen troopers, their images and that of the tall, fluttering cottonwood trees behind them doubled by the mirroring waters of Medicine Lodge Creek. The braves hooted and chanted, still firing their guns and brandishing their rifles and lances above their heads, while through the din could be heard the tinkling of the little bells that adorned their ponies.

Behind them a bugle sounded, and the first line of warriors

kicked their ponies forward, splashing through the shallow
stream in a galloping charge upon the camp, the other lines of
mounted Indians following behind. The white-bearded Harney,
in full dress uniform and bemedaled, stood straight-backed and
unbudging in the face of the charge, the others frozen behind
him. Commission Camp was no place for the faint of heart that
day.

But the Cheyennes pulled their ponies to a dust-billowing halt
within a few feet of the commissioners and swung to the ground,
still firing and chanting until a group of chiefs led by Black Kettle broke through their line and walked up to the whites. The
Cheyenne chiefs shook hands all around, grunting "How" to
each. After agreeing on a meeting time for the next day, the
chiefs led the still-hooting Cheyenne warriors back to their own
camp.

At best it was a shaky experience for the white men, and all
were ready to leave Medicine Lodge Creek at the earliest possible date. The Cheyenne council was scheduled for the next
morning at nine o'clock. The Cheyennes came, ". . . armed to
the teeth with revolvers and bows . . . proud, haughty, defiant,
as should become those who are to grant favors, not beg
them. . . . They acted their character. They are the masters of
the Plains." Finally they were arranged in a huge semicircle in
front of the commissioners' tent, the Cheyennes to one side and
the Arapahoes to the other, the chiefs seated at the front and the
warriors behind. The front of the tent was opened to the view of
the commissioners, who sat behind a table, Harney to the center.

Senator Henderson opened the meeting with a speech apolo-
gizing for Hancock's burning of their village and then stating the
government's wish for them to stop raiding the railroads and
white settlements and to do their hunting south of the Arkansas
River. In exchange, the two tribes would be given livestock and
farming equipment, have a grist mill built for them, and be provided with a house on their reservation where annuity goods
would be sent to them.

The Cheyennes did not make their reply first, choosing to let
Little Raven of the Arapahoes speak. Little Raven asked that the
Arapahoes be provided a reservation near Fort Lyon similar to

the one that had been assigned by the Treaty of Fort Wise. He also asked for an "honest trader" among the Arapahoes. Addressing some of his remarks to the Cheyennes, Little Raven said the Arapahoes were willing to help them make war on the Utes, the Cheyennes' and Arapahoes' blood enemies of western Colorado, but not against the whites. Again the commissioners ignored Little Raven.

The Cheyennes remained silent in response to Little Raven's speech, offering none of the "Hows" usually given in approval. But now Buffalo Chief, who had been chosen to speak for the Cheyenne Nation, rose and took the floor. His speech was blunt and scolding in tone. He immediately made claim for the Cheyennes to the country north of the Arkansas, "where the bones of our fathers lie buried. . . . You think you are doing a great deal for us by giving these presents to us, but we prefer to live as formerly. If you gave us all the goods you could give, yet we would prefer our own life, to live as we have done. You give us presents and then take our land—that provokes war."

This was the key issue of the council and of the entire Indian problem: would the Cheyennes continue to roam and hunt the plains of western Kansas? That was what the peace commission had come there to change; that was what the Cheyennes insisted on the strongest, and they were at the council in a position of strength. Not only were the commissioners weary and anxious to be gone, but they were also fearful of what the Dog Soldiers might do if things did not go their way. One reporter summed up the Cheyenne attitude during the council. They had come to make peace, which the white man had asked for, and he could have it on their terms. They did not care for the houses or schools promised them, and they would hunt on their own grounds whether the white man liked it or not. But, if it would please the whites, they would be happy to sign a peace treaty with them. Though unspoken, this was what their conduct clearly implied.

The commissioners were perplexed. The treaty for the Cheyennes and Arapahoes was already drawn up and awaiting signature, but it did not agree with what the Cheyennes were saying. It provided hunting rights to the Cheyennes only on lands south of the Arkansas River. Something had to be done, and Senator Henderson did it. Calling the chiefs to one side, along with John Smith and George Bent to interpret, Henderson talked with them at length. To the reporters there, the chiefs appeared to respond in agreement before returning to their seats.

It was learned later that Henderson had instructed the interpreters to tell the Cheyennes that they did not have to go to their reservation immediately and that they could continue to hunt north of the Arkansas so long as the buffalo remained and so long as they kept away from white settlements. Later, when the buffalo were all gone, the Cheyennes could then move to their reservation, where the White Father would care for them.

This satisfied the Cheyennes. They had no concern about the buffalo being gone for a long while yet, if ever, and to them it appeared the whites were agreeing to their keeping the lands of western Kansas. The talking over, the commissioners and the Arapahoes began signing the treaty papers—when it was discovered that there was not a single Cheyenne chief still present.

Someone in Commission Camp had prematurely begun to break open the boxes of treaty goods, which were stacked ready for distribution to the Cheyennes once the treaty had been signed. The Indians, anxious to get their presents, had hurried over to watch the proceedings, leaving the treaty papers lying untouched on the table and the commissioners in an impatient sweat. Old John S. Smith was sent with coattails flying to round up the absentee chiefs and bring them back to the treaty table.

There was still some difficulty in getting Tall Bull to sign the treaty. He had signed the Treaty of the Little Arkansas, and when Hancock had burned the Cheyenne village at Pawnee Fork he had been blind with rage. He refused in sullen defiance to participate now. In anger Harney bellowed, "Damn you, sign," but Tall Bull still refused. Henderson now moved in and, through Smith, told Tall Bull that the Great Father in Washington would not recognize the treaty if the "great Cheyenne brave" did not sign. The flattery was successful, and the Cheyenne made his mark on the paper. Noticeably absent from both the council and the treaty signing were Medicine Arrow and Roman Nose.

Correspondent Stanley, calling it a "mock treaty," would later recount bitterly:

> The Chiefs have signed it merely as a matter of form. Not one word of the treaty was read to them. How, therefore, can the treaty have been a success? Bull Bear and Buffalo Chief, even while they signed, said: "We will hold that country between the Arkansas and the Platte together. We will not give it up yet, as long as the buffalo and elk are roaming through the country." Do the above words seem anything like giving up all claims to that country? And yet, if a white man, acting under the knowledge that all that country belongs to the whites, will go and make a home for himself, it will soon be a burning brand—a signal for war. If war is once thus commenced who are to blame? The commissioners.

Major Joel Elliott, in his official report of the council, made the same charge—that the chiefs had no idea what they were signing. Only Augur, he insisted, had protested when the Cheyennes were given the right to hunt north of the Arkansas, but the other commissioners had ignored him.

Correspondent Hall also stated the Cheyennes did not know, nor care much, what they were signing. He had been strongly impressed by the Cheyenne chiefs, whom he described as "singularly fine looking men—splendidly framed, and with impressive, characteristic faces. They showed by every look and gesture their fitness for command. The more I see of these Cheyennes the higher opinion I have of them. They are better looking than the others; they are cleaner and more of the old Spartan fire burns in their veins. Sooner death than captivity is the motto of these warriors of the plains."

After the treaty papers had been signed, distribution of the treaty presents began. The Cheyennes and Arapahoes seated themselves in a huge semicircle, the bales and boxes of goods piled at the center. Indian officers were appointed to divide out the blankets, army coats, multicolored cloth, felt hats, fruit baskets filled with beads, knives, and many other items. The Indians loaded the goods aboard their ponies and trudged off, their women and children following along behind. A festive mood reigned throughout the encampment.

Among the presents were defective cast-iron pistols that would not even snap a percussion cap. The commission had originally purchased more than a hundred Colt revolvers, a few of which were given to the Kiowas, and fifty-four Henry repeating rifles. None of these were issued to the Cheyennes or Arapahoes, however, evidently as a result of some second thoughts about further arming the belligerent Dog Soldiers. Little Raven had asked in his speech to the commission that his tribe be furnished with guns and ammunition with which to hunt and secure food. But, just as there was an implied promise that the tribes would be fed through the winter, the Indians were definitely expecting a future issuance of guns and ammunition, even though not specified by the treaty papers.

These matters, along with the misleading promise that the tribes would be free to roam and hunt in western Kansas just as always, would seriously strain the peace in the days ahead. Ironically, however, the event that would ultimately bring war back to the plains was the seemingly insignificant raid by the Kaws on the horse herds of the Arapahoes and Cheyennes during the council.

Chapter III
IN SEARCH OF AN ENEMY

The Kaws, or Kansas, Indians held a reserve in eastern Kansas at Council Grove, while the large and powerful Osage tribe was situated to the south of them. Both had long been enemies of the Cheyennes and the Arapahoes. In November 1867, a short time after the Medicine Lodge council, reports reached Superintendent Murphy of an Arapaho attack on a band of Osages. A man and a woman had been killed and 140 Osage ponies stolen. Osage agent Snow confirmed this, but added that the Big Hill band of Osages had since met a party of Arapahoes, killed quite a number, and taken about fifty mules and a large number of army overcoats, which were evidently treaty issue. Kaw agent Stover, meanwhile, claimed that it had been the Osages, not the Kaws, who had stolen the horses during the Medicine Lodge meeting.

Agent Wynkoop was asked to talk with his Cheyenne and Arapaho charges about the matter. He did so and stated that they claimed the Kaws and Osages had been the original aggressors by stealing the stock at the council. They said that in a recent fight the Arapahoes had lost five men killed and the Cheyennes six, with many others wounded. Wynkoop had given permission to some one hundred thirty warriors of the two tribes to proceed to Fort Zarah and retrieve the bodies of their dead braves. The Indians had promised not to bother the white settlements, but he had sent a white interpreter along, just in case.

On December 28, 1867, the Junction City *Weekly Union* reported that the town was full of Kaw Indians, who were selling some twenty-five Cheyenne scalps at ten cents each.

Otherwise during the winter of 1867–68, the Indian situation in Kansas enjoyed a quiet, post-Medicine Lodge interlude. Squaw man John Smith, who had been assigned by the Indian Bureau to live with the Cheyennes south of the Arkansas, reported some disturbing signs, but none of the authorities were greatly concerned. In March, Smith warned that the whiskey peddlers from Dodge were plying their trade freely among the tribes, creating a dangerous situation. No one knew better than old John Smith, who had lived with the tribe for thirty years, that mixing whiskey with a Cheyenne buck was potential trouble.

Moreover, Smith said, the Cheyennes felt that they were being cheated because the government had not fulfilled any of its treaty promises. There had not been a single issuance of annuities during the winter months, when the tribes needed them the most. They were much concerned, too, over the presence of surveying parties, which were now appearing even south of the Arkansas. Surveyors, they had learned well, meant more railroads. More railroads meant more whites, and more whites meant more buffalo killed and fewer for the Indian. The chiefs said they were still holding on to the peace made at Medicine Lodge, but the young warriors exhibited the same angry contempt for the government and the white soldiers as before.

During the early spring of 1868 an important change of command had been made in the military Department of the Missouri. Major General Phil Sheridan, the stocky, rough-talking general under whom Custer had served through the Civil War at Winchester, Chickamauga, Chattanooga, Missionary Ridge, Yellow Tavern, and the final, victorious Shenandoah campaign, had been the military governor of Louisiana and Texas until September of 1867. President Johnson charged him with "absolute tyranny" as well as insubordination and, over the wishes of Grant, transferred him to an Indian frontier command. Actually Sheridan merely exchanged commands with General Hancock, but after journeying to Fort Leavenworth, Sheridan took a leave of absence and left the Department of the Missouri under the temporary command of Colonel A. J. Smith.

In March of 1868 Sheridan returned to take over his command and immediately made a tour of the military posts along the Arkansas River, visiting Forts Zarah, Larned, and Dodge. When he arrived at Larned he found most of the Kiowas, Comanches, Arapahoes, and Cheyennes encamped near there waiting for annuities that had been promised them. The Indians requested an interview with him, but Sheridan refused, saying he was merely inspecting the posts and was not authorized to discuss matters with them at that time. Sheridan moved on to Fort Dodge, but the disgruntled chiefs followed him there and again requested a council. This time, Sheridan gave in and heard their complaints of how the government was not living up to the promises it had made at Medicine Lodge. There had been no annuities issued, and the chiefs had no idea as to where they were supposed to live. Their women and children were starving, they said. But Sheridan's advisers denied the Indians were in such bad shape, insisting there was an abundance of buffalo available for them to hunt.

In order to keep himself informed on the Indian situation, Sheridan moved his headquarters from Leavenworth to Fort Hays. Also, he employed the services of three highly regarded frontiersmen: Will Comstock, who had guided Custer through western Kansas the summer before; Abner "Sharp" Grover, who had lived among the Sioux; and a scout named Dick Parr. These three scouts were to report to Lieutenant Frederick W. Beecher, a young officer in the 3rd Infantry in whom Sheridan had great confidence. Comstock and Grover were to cover the territory west of Fort Wallace and report on the Indian activity there, while Parr was assigned to the headwaters of the Solomon and Saline rivers.

During April, Beecher and his scouts reported large bands of Sioux and Cheyennes in the region northwest of Fort Wallace. Beecher judged that they were not hostile, but many whites, who knew nothing of Henderson's verbal agreement with the Cheyennes at Medicine Lodge, were concerned that the Indians continued to hunt the area even though the treaty stipulated the Cheyennes could not hunt north of the Arkansas.

It was late April before the first annuities were finally delivered to the bands along the Arkansas by Agent Wynkoop. Black Kettle, Little Robe, Medicine Arrow, and Big Jake of the Arapahoes were provided several wagonloads of beef, flour, bacon, coffee, sugar and salt for their bands. The chiefs were happy enough to receive the food, but still there were no guns or ammunition among the annuities, as had been promised by the commissioners at Medicine Lodge. Many of the Cheyenne warriors said they were being cheated.

In May the first incidents of trouble began to be reported to Sheridan. A trader's store at Fort Zarah was burned on the nineteenth, and it was thought the Cheyennes were to blame. On May 26 a wagon train on the Smoky Hill route near Coyote Station was attacked, and the Cheyennes were again charged. Shortly afterward, scout William F. Cody, later of Buffalo Bill fame, was chased back into a railroad camp by a small party of Sioux, and Lieutenant Fred Beecher reported a man killed and scalped near Fort Wallace by Indians.

By late May the grass was high on the prairie, and the Cheyenne ponies were sleek and strong. The Cheyenne horse herds, which blanketed the slopes of the Pawnee Fork above Fort Larned, could provide at least five sturdy ponies for every warrior in the tribe, not counting the large numbers of American horses and mules in the herds. The warriors were well armed with rifles, carbines, and revolvers purchased from white traders, and the young bucks were restless for action. The time had come to seek revenge against the Kaws for the horses they had stolen and the Cheyenne and Arapaho warriors they had killed. Thus, early in June 1868, a large force of Cheyennes, probably between two and three hundred strong, left the Fort Larned area and followed the Santa Fe Trail eastward for the purpose of doing battle with the Kaws.

On the morning of June 2, alarmed settlers reported that some five hundred wild Indians had passed Marion Center, Kansas, and rumors spread that the savages were killing stock and cleaning out every house. Twenty-five families fled to Cottonwood

Falls for protection. But the Indians made no move against the whites; instead they went into camp on Diamond Creek near Cottonwood Falls, announcing that they meant the whites no harm and that they had come "to clean out the Kaws." Specifically, they said, they wanted seven Kaw scalps.

Militiamen from Junction City hurried to the Kaw Agency, as did A. G. Boone, former agent of the Cheyennes and Arapahoes, and Kaw agent E. S. Stover from Council Grove. They found the Kaws greatly excited. As Boone and Stover were trying to quiet things down, a party of some eighty Cheyennes riding bareback and each with two revolvers charged past the Kaw camp, whooping fiercely but not firing a shot. The Kaws did begin shooting, but the distance was too great to effect any damage. The Cheyennes formed on a distant hilltop, war-bonneted and primed for battle, but shortly they sent the white interpreter who had come along under a flag of truce to the Kaw camp.

The Cheyennes had heard that Boone, whom they had known in Colorado and who had effected the Treaty of Fort Wise with them in 1861, was in the area, and they wished to talk with him. Taking some tobacco for presents, Boone and Stover rode out to the Cheyenne party, which was led by chiefs Tall Bull, Whirlwind, and Little Robe. The chiefs agreed that they would meet with the Kaws and talk peace. But even as Boone and the chiefs were discussing the matter, the Kaws opened fire on them, some of the bullets buzzing dangerously close to the white men. One of the Cheyenne chiefs grabbed Boone's bridle and led him to safety even as the Kaws charged.

The white men watched as the two Indian forces charged and countercharged one another on the open plains, circling, whooping, and firing wildly. After what one witness described as "three hours of harmless scrimmage," the only casualties were a Kaw with a scratched hand and a Cheyenne shot in the foot. Finally a Cheyenne chief signaled a bugler, who directed the Cheyennes from the field in perfect order.

During the fracas the Kaws had called upon the militiamen to help them, but the whites shook their heads and answered: "No, Ingin fight." As the Cheyennes retreated through Council Grove, they burned two stone buildings occupied by Kaw half-bloods, robbed the home of three settlers and shot some beef cattle and a large number of dogs. When the whites suggested that the Kaws join them in going after the Cheyennes, the Kaws replied: "No. White man's fight. If white man want to fight Cheyenne, let white man go and do it."

After the raid, Kansas Governor Crawford personally went to Council Grove to investigate, and he reported that there had been no real damage done. The Emporia *News* of June 12, 1868, hastened to reassure potential Kansas settlers: "We wish to say to immigrants that there is no more danger here from Indians than there is of being garroted or being run off a railroad track in the East, and hardly as much." But the Kansas populace was greatly alarmed over the idea of large bands of wild Indians roaming freely through the settlements. Complaints quickly reached Washington. Commissioner of Indian Affairs N. G. Taylor wrote Kansas Superintendent of Indian Affairs Thomas Murphy on June 25 that the "Secretary of the Interior directs that on account of their recent raid on the white settlements, no arms nor ammunition be given them [the Cheyennes and Arapahoes] at present. . . ."

Thus when some twelve to fifteen thousand Indians gathered at Fort Larned on July 20 to receive their annuities, Agent Wynkoop had the unpleasant task of telling them that they were not to receive the arms and ammunition they expected. Though Wynkoop described the reaction of the chiefs as "disappointed, but gave no evidence of being angry," General Alfred Sully, commanding the District of the Arkansas, said the Indians threatened war. Sully was so concerned that he brought in all the troops he could muster from nearby posts, including six companies of 7th Cavalry from near Hays and two more cavalry units from Harker. Sully put on a bold front, telling the Indians that though he preferred peace he was ready for war, and this, he told Sheridan, held the Indians in check.

The Cheyennes, in fact, were angry and sullen enough to refuse to accept their arms-less annuities, sending the loaded wagons back to Larned. Wynkoop reported that the Indians "thought that their white brothers were pulling away from them the hand they had given them at Medicine Lodge Creek, nonetheless they would try to hold on to it, and would wait with patience the Great Father to take pity upon them and let them have the arms and ammunition which had been promised them. . . ."

Wynkoop now urged in the strongest terms the issuance of the guns and ammunition as soon as possible in order to prevent an outbreak of hostilities. Superintendent Murphy was ordered to Larned to make an estimate of the situation, and if it appeared Wynkoop was correct to give him the authority to proceed with the issuance of the arms and ammunition. On August 1, Murphy reported from Larned that he had met with the Arapahoes and Apaches, explained to them that the guns and bullets had been withheld in order to avoid a fight with the whites, and called for an end to the warfare with the Kaws and Osages. Little Raven replied that though the Kaws and Osages had clearly started the war during the Medicine Lodge council, he and his people were headed for the Purgatoire River in Colorado and would be making no more trips to the white settlements. He promised that the arms would never be used against the whites.

Murphy was satisfied and gave Wynkoop the go-ahead to issue the arms: 160 pistols, 80 Lancaster rifles, 12 kegs of powder, 1½ kegs of lead, and 15,000 percussion caps to the Arapahoes; 40 pistols, 20 Lancaster rifles, 3 kegs of powder, ½ keg of lead, and 5,000 caps to the smaller Apache band. The Cheyennes were not present but were expected in shortly to receive their share. Murphy said that he expected "no trouble whatever with them; they will come here to get their annuities, and leave immediately to hunt buffalo; they are well and peaceably disposed towards the whites, and unless some unlooked-for event should transpire to change their present feelings they will keep their treaty pledges."

Wynkoop, too, felt very strongly that the right thing had been done, reporting to Murphy that on the day before, August 9, he had made a complete issue of annuity goods, arms, and ammunition to the Cheyennes. The Cheyennes, he said, were satisfied and contented and had left for their hunting grounds. Wynkoop felt confident that because of this issue to them, there would be no trouble with the Indians of his agency during that season.

But, ironically, at the very moment Wynkoop was at his desk penning this optimistic prediction on that morning of August 10, the precise reverse of his hopes for peace was being perpetrated some eighty miles to the north on the Saline River. There a predominantly Cheyenne war party had entered the house of a settler, beaten the man, and committed repeated acts of rape upon his wife and her sister. This was only the first of numerous depredations that the war party of over two hundred warriors would commit along the Saline and the Solomon rivers during three days of brutal strikes at the white settlements.

Though there is no doubt that the Cheyennes committed the attacks, which included murder, rape, and capturing of women and children, there are the inevitable discrepancies between white and Indian accounts of the affair. According to newspaper stories originating at Ellsworth, Solomon City, and Salina, this is essentially what happened.

Around ten o'clock on the morning of August 10, a Monday, the Indians appeared on Spellman's Creek about sixteen to eighteen miles above Ellsworth. They went first to the homestead of a man named Shaw, beat him badly, and drove him from the house. The Indians then raped Mrs. Shaw and her sister, and perhaps another woman, reportedly for some time, with thirty or more Indians taking part and eventually leaving the women unconscious. The Indians then attacked other homesteads, being driven off from some, but overrunning others and raping other women, though the news accounts were not specific.

On August 12 the war party struck on the Solomon River some fifty-five miles north of Solomon City, killing a number of people, plundering and destroying homesteads, and running off stock. In one case the Indians entered the home of a family named Bell, mortally wounding the father. As the man lay dying, four of the Indians raped Mrs. Bell. Reportedly, during this her infant was wailing on the floor, and one of the raiders speared it in the back of the neck and head. Mrs. Bell was placed on a horse to be taken with the party, but she jumped off and was shot through the shoulder and breast. While lying wounded, she was violated several more times, the newspaper account stated. The two young daughters of the Bells were tied onto ponies and taken off with the war party.

A call for help was sent out to Fort Zarah, and Captain Frederick Benteen and a troop of 7th Cavalry responded. Their pursuit of the war party some ten miles in the direction of the Saline River eventually forced the Indians, whose ponies were already fatigued, to untie the two girls and drop them on the prairie. When the troops had been evaded, the Indians came back to find the two girls but could not. The children wandered lost on the prairie without provisions for three days, spending one night in an old abandoned house, before a search party finally found them. It was thought for a time that Mrs. Bell would live, but she died in early September.

Sheridan reported that thirteen settlers had been killed by the Indians during the attacks, and another army report listed the number at fifteen. Sheridan contended that the affair began when the Indians were given something to drink in a tin cup by the settlers. The Indians were insulted over this and threw it in their faces. Hazen wrote from Fort Cobb giving the Indian version of what had happened on the Saline. A Cheyenne-Arapaho war party went to attack the Pawnees and was beaten. When returning, one brave rode to the house of a settler for something to eat. He was ordered away, but did not understand. He was then fired upon by the man at the house, and a fracas commenced. "It is evident then that it was not premeditated, as the Cheyennes were trading away their arms, just issued by their agent, in large numbers, up to the day of the outbreak."

Another Indian version of the affair was provided when, on August 19, Agent Wynkoop met with Cheyenne chief Little Rock, whom he had previously sent out to learn by whom the depredations had been committed. With John Smith, scout James Morrison, and Lieutenant Sam Robbins present, Wynkoop interviewed Little Rock at length. Though the chief's account varied in numerous details with that of the newspapers, the chief was obviously telling the story as it had been given to him by warriors involved in the sordid affair:

> Wynkoop: "Six nights ago I spoke to you in regard to depredations committed on the Saline. I told you to go and find out by whom these depredations were committed and to bring me straight news. What news do you bring?"

Little Rock: "I took your advice and went there. I am now here to tell you all I know. This war party of Cheyennes which left the camp of these tribes above the forks of Walnut Creek about the 2d or 3d of August, went out against the Pawnees, crossed the Smoky Hill about Fort Hays, and thence proceeded to the Saline, where there were ten lodges of Sioux in the Cheyenne camp when this war party left, and about twenty men of them and four Arapahoes accompanied the party. The Cheyennes numbered about two hundred; nearly all the young men in the village went; Little Raven's son was one of the four Arapahoes. When the party reached the Saline they turned down the stream, with the exception of twenty who being fearful of depredations being committed against the whites by the party going in the direction of the settlements, kept on north toward the Pawnees. The main party continued down the Saline until they came in sight of the settlement; they then camped there. A Cheyenne named Oh-e-ah-mo-he-a, a brother of White Antelope, who was killed at Sand Creek, and another named Red Nose, proceeded to the first house; they afterwards returned to the camp and with them a woman captive. The main party was surprised at this action, and forcibly took possession of her, and returned her to her house. The two Indians had outraged the woman before they brought her to the camp. After the outrage had been committed, the parties left the Saline and went north toward the settlement of the south fork of the Solomon, where they were kindly received and fed by the white people. They left the settlements on the south fork and proceeded toward the settlements on the north fork. When in sight of these settlements, they came upon a body of armed settlers, who fired upon them; they avoided the party, went around them, and approached a house some distance off. In the vicinity of the house they came upon a white man alone upon the prairie. Big Head's son rode at him and knocked him down with a club. The Indian who had committed the outrage upon the white woman, known as White Antelope's brother, then fired upon the white man without effect, while the third Indian rode up and killed him. Soon after they killed a white man, and, close by, a woman— all in the same settlement. At the time these people were killed, the party was divided in feeling, the majority being opposed to any outrages being committed; but finding it useless to contend against these outrages being committed without bringing on a strife among themselves, they gave way and all went in together. They then went to another house in the same settlement, and there killed two men and took two little girls prisoners; this on the same day. After committing this last outrage the party turned south toward the Saline, where they came upon a body of mounted troops; the troops immediately charged the Indians, and the pursuit was continued for a long time. The Indians having the two children, their horses becoming fatigued, dropped the children without hurting them. Soon after the children were dropped the pursuit ceased; but the Indians continued on up the Saline. A portion of the Indians afterward returned to look for the children, but they were unable to find them. After they had proceeded some distance up the Saline, the party divided, the majority going north toward the settlements on the Solomon, but thirty of them started toward their village, supposed to be some distance northwest of Fort Larned. Another small party returned to Black Kettle's village, from which party I got this information. I am fearful that before this time the party that started north had committed a great many depredations."

Wynkoop: "Do you know the names of the principal men of this party that committed the depredations, besides White Antelope's brother?"

Little Rock: "There were Medicine Arrow's oldest son, named Tall Wolf; Red Nose, who was one of the men who outraged the woman, Big Head's son named Porcupine Bear; and Sand Hill's brother, known as the Bear That Goes Ahead."

Wynkoop: "You told me your nation wants peace; will you, in accordance with your treaty stipulations, deliver up the men whom you have named as being the leaders of the party who committed the outrages named?"

Little Rock: "I think that the only men who ought to suffer and be responsible for these outrages are White Antelope's brother and Red Nose, the men who ravished the woman; and when I return to the Cheyenne camp and assemble the chiefs and head men, I think those two men will be delivered up to you."

Wynkoop: "I consider the whole party guilty; but it being impossible to punish all of them, I hold the principal men, whom you mentioned, responsible for all. They had no right to be led and governed by two men. If no depredations had been committed after the outrage on the woman, the two men who you have mentioned alone would have been guilty."

Little Rock: "After your explanation, I think your demand for the men is right. I am willing to deliver them up, and will go back

to the tribe and use my best endeavors to have them surrendered. I
am but one man, and cannot answer for the entire nation."

Wynkoop: "I want you to return to your tribes and tell the
chiefs and head men when assembled the demand I now speak—
tell them I think that complying with my demand is the only thing
that will save their entire nation from a long and destructive war. I
want you to return as soon as possible with their answer. I will see
that you are safe in going and coming, and your service in this respect will be well regarded. You will be looked upon by the whites
as a good man, and one who is a friend to them, as well as to his
own people, and as the result of your action in this matter you will
be considered by the Government as a 'Great Chief,' one in whom
in the future they can always put the utmost confidence."

Little Rock: "I am here in your service, at the same time I am a
Cheyenne and want to do all I can for the welfare of my nation. If
the chiefs and head men refuse to comply with your demands, I
want to know if I can come with my wife and children (whom I
love) and place myself and them under your protection, and at the
same time act as a runner between you and my people?"

Wynkoop: "Should my demands not be complied with, you can
bring your lodge and family here, and I will protect you."

There had been, however, another incident of serious consequence which placed the Cheyennes even farther outside the
law. Shortly after the Saline and Solomon depredations, Lieutenant Beecher dispatched his scouts Comstock and Grover from
Walnut Creek to Fort Hays for the purpose of learning more
about the trouble. The scouts arrived at Hays on the fourteenth
of August, a Friday, and on Saturday rode out to a Cheyenne
camp northwest of Fort Hays. A resident of Hays City named
Fisher claimed the camp was that of Black Kettle, who was
known to be in the vicinity; George Bent later said it was Bull
Bear's Dog Soldier camp, while Grover identified it as the camp
of Turkey Leg, a northern Cheyenne.

According to Bent, Bull Bear, as a chief, was obligated by
Cheyenne custom to extend his hospitality to the two white men
despite the hostility felt toward them by the Dog Soldiers. Bull
Bear took the two men into his lodge, fed them, and gave them
quarters for the night.

Late on the evening of the next day, Sunday, August 16, a

party of warriors returned to camp from the Saline-Solomon raids. Comstock and Grover, considered to be spies, were ordered out of camp immediately. They rode out at once, escorted by four warriors and three young boys. After they had ridden some distance from the camp, the warriors suddenly yelled at the two scouts and at the same time raised their rifles and began firing. Comstock was killed instantly, shot through the heart, while Grover was knocked to the ground seriously wounded. Using his partner's body as a shield, Grover held off the Indians until dark and then made his way on foot to Monument Station on the Kansas Pacific Railroad, which then terminated at Sheridan City. There he was picked up by a work train and taken back to Fort Hays, where he remained for a few days until recovering enough to report to Colonel Bankhead at Fort Wallace.

Meanwhile, Little Rock never returned to Larned, undoubtedly fleeing south into Indian Territory with Black Kettle's band in order to avoid the war that now appeared certain. Wynkoop knew well enough the impossibility of his demands. Admitting with great disappointment that his Cheyennes were guilty, he wrote to Murphy:

> Though many may be inclined to deliver up the guilty parties, I am afraid this cannot be accomplished, and therefore knowing that the majority of the Cheyennes feel as Little Rock does in the matter, that they deprecate war and would prevent their people from entering into hostilities by every means in their power, yet they will be powerless to restrain their young men when once they fairly enter into it.

He suggested taking those Cheyennes who would respond to his call and locating them away from the others, protecting them with troops and letting those who refused to respond to a call to come in be considered at war and be properly punished. "By this means, if war takes place, which I consider inevitable, we can be able to discriminate between those who deserve punishment and those who do not. . . ."

Murphy, who was forced to agree that the Indians were best

left "in the hands of the military" until they gave assurance of keeping their treaty pledges, instructed Wynkoop to advise the Apaches, Comanches, and Kiowas to go south and remain in the vicinity of Fort Cobb in the Indian Territory until their agent got there. This would safeguard them while the military made war on the Cheyennes.

General Sherman, then in Omaha, received Sheridan's reports on the Cheyenne depredations and responded with an immediate call to "compel their removal south of the Kansas line, and in pursuing to kill if necessary. This amounts to war; but I hope on a small scale, confined to that locality."

Although only four Arapahoes had been involved in the Saline-Solomon raids, one of them being Little Raven's son, the Arapahoes were now considered to be at war also. Murphy virtually gave Sheridan a blank check on this when he wrote: "The Cheyennes and Arapahoes being confederated, each should be held responsible for the acts of the other; and while I am satisfied the Arapahoes, as a tribe, discountenance the last outbreak, still many of their young warriors are on the war path with the Cheyennes."

The Kiowas, Comanches, and Apaches were not considered to be allied with the Cheyennes and Arapahoes and were thus to be treated as friendly Indians. Following the Medicine Lodge Treaty, these tribes had ceased their raiding into Texas, where they had previously committed excessive depredations, including the taking of numerous children prisoners. They had even been receptive to white traders such as a Towanda, Kansas, man who passed through Emporia in May of 1868 with five wagonloads of buffalo robes which he had purchased from the Comanches and other tribes at Fort Cobb, in the Indian Territory.

During July the Kiowas had given up two white captives—a four-year-old boy and a thirteen-year-old girl—to Fort Dodge trader John Tappan, cousin of Commissioner Tappan. Also, while in a Comanche camp, Agent Wynkoop spotted another captive white girl. He compelled the Indians to give her up without ransom and took the girl, Melinda Ann Candle of Texas, into his home, where she was cared for by his wife. Wynkoop, obviously disheartened at the actions of his Cheyennes, requested a leave of absence and left Fort Larned on September 17 for Philadelphia, believing that he would return to find his agency transferred to Fort Cobb.

Although it was now agreed by the Indian Bureau and the War Department that old Fort Cobb would be established as a new agency and refuge for those tribes wishing to remain friendly, there was one major point of disagreement. The Indian Bureau considered that the friendly Cheyennes and Arapahoes were to be offered sanctuary along with the Kiowas, Comanches, and Apaches. Sheridan, however, made no such concession. Besides the arguments of supportive guilt which were charged against the entire tribe, he saw this as a convenient dodge for the guilty warriors as well. And both Sheridan and Sherman, knowing the inadequacy of the Army to catch the Indian warrior on the plains, were convinced that the only way to effectively punish the warring tribes was to find their villages and hit them.

"I am of the belief," Sheridan wrote to Sherman, "that these Indians require to be soundly whipped, and the ringleaders in the present trouble hung, their ponies killed, and such destruction of their property as will make them very poor."

Chapter IV
THE SOLOMON AVENGERS

Sheridan now concluded that a major campaign against the war-ring tribes of western Kansas was warranted and necessary, and he made plans for simultaneous operations both north and south of the Arkansas in order to deprive the Indians of using either area for a sanctuary. At his request, a group of frontier scouts had been authorized by Congress, and Sheridan selected an old Civil War comrade to head the command. Brevet Colonel (USA) George A. Forsyth, a major in the 9th Cavalry on detached service with Sheridan's staff, had become bored with camp duty and requested the assignment. Known as "Sandy" to his fellow officers, Forsyth was an energetic Scotsman who had entered the regular service as a private in 1861 and risen to the rank of brevet brigadier general of volunteers. Like Custer, he had ridden with Sheridan in the Shenandoah Valley campaign, making the famous ride from Winchester to Cedar Creek in 1864. He felt that a group of frontier scouts, traveling unencumbered by a wagon train, might succeed in catching the Indians where the regular army troops had failed.

In looking about for an officer as his second in command, For-syth was impressed with recommendations of Lieutenant Beecher, who was gaining a high reputation as an officer and scout on the frontier. Nephew of the famous New York clergy-man Henry Ward Beecher, and his own father a minister as well,

Beecher had led numerous patrols and scouting missions around Fort Wallace and had impressed Sheridan and others.

Born in New Orleans on June 22, 1841, Beecher had studied at Andover and Bowdoin College, where he was a good scholar and an accomplished gymnast. After graduating in the spring of 1862, he enlisted in the Union Army, being pronounced by the examining surgeon as one of the finest specimens to come out of Maine. He first served with the 16th Maine Regiment and soon rose to second sergeant, then second lieutenant, and then first lieutenant, participating in most of the battles of the Army of the Potomac from the first engagement at Fredericksburg to the Battle of Gettysburg. At Gettysburg a shell fragment hit him in the knee, causing a severe wound, and Beecher lay in pain for several hours before being discovered. He was near death from the wound for some time, but through the care of his mother, who came to the army hospital to be his nurse, he survived. He was still recovering when he was accidentally thrown from a carriage, breaking his wounded leg. When well again he was commissioned a first lieutenant in the Veteran Reserve Corps and stationed at Raleigh as adjutant to General E. Whittlesey. Later he was commissioned a first lieutenant in the U. S. Army and assigned to the 3rd Infantry on frontier duty.

Forsyth, however, learned that Beecher had developed the not-unusual army liking for liquor. Greatly disappointed by this, Forsyth wrote Beecher a personal letter advising him of the situation. Beecher answered with a forthright letter, acknowledging his habit and indicating a determined vow to stop his drinking. Forsyth and Sheridan were both impressed with the letter, and the twenty-seven-year-old New Englander was taken on with the unit.

Also assigned to the group was Dr. John G. Mooers, an ex-army surgeon then at Hays City, and W. H. H. McCall, a former brevet brigadier general who had drifted west looking for opportunity after the war and was now quite happy to serve as first sergeant of the group. McCall had distinguished himself during the siege of Petersburg when the Confederates had captured Fort Stedman. McCall had immediately led his regiment back into the fort and after heavy hand-to-hand fighting had recaptured the post. The others were an assortment of war veterans now caught on the frontier working at whatever jobs were available. To most, the chance to serve as a scout at fifty dollars a month, seventy-five dollars if they furnished their own horse, was a good opportunity.

Martin Burke, an Irishman, had served in the British Army in India and with a New York unit during the Civil War. John Hurst had fought Indians in Arizona and New Mexico with the First California Infantry before coming to Kansas as a teamster. Louis Farley and his son Hudson were farmer-settlers from the Solomon Valley and two of the best shots in the troop. Chauncey Whitney, who would later serve as sheriff of Ellsworth County, Kansas, and be killed trying to settle a card-game argument, was a Civil War veteran. Sigmund Shlesinger, a young Jewish boy whose family had immigrated from Hungary, had come to Kansas to work as a clerk and peddle everything from pies to newspapers to the soldiers and railroad employees. He was encouraged to join the unit by a man at Fort Hays who saw the chance to rent him a horse for twenty-five dollars. A. J. Pliley would later serve as captain of Company A, 19th Kansas Volunteers, in Sheridan's Indian Territory campaign. Almost all the men were war veterans of either the Union or the Confederate Army. The group nicknamed itself the "Solomon Avengers," vowing revenge for the Cheyenne murders on the Solomon and the Saline.

The theory behind the small force of scouts was that such a group of experienced frontiersmen, moving unencumbered by supply wagons, could catch up with the fast-moving Indians and prove themselves equal fighters to a much larger force, as was the standard frontier claim. It was, at best, an experiment that rested upon the belief that white frontiersmen were better shots and better fighters than the average army soldier and that a small number of such men could overcome a much superior force of Indians. The experiment sought to overcome the basic inability displayed by Hancock and Custer in catching and defeating the Plains warriors.

The small command of fifty-three men was outfitted at Fort Hays with good horses, saddles and bridles, Spencer rifles, Colt revolvers, and other equipment, such as blankets, lariats, picket pins, canteens, haversacks, butcher knives, tin plates, tin cups, and seven days' rations. Each man was issued one hundred forty rounds of rifle ammunition and thirty rounds for his revolver, these to be carried personally. Another four thousand rounds of ammunition, plus camp kettles, picks, shovels, medical supplies, and extra rations of salt and coffee were loaded aboard a pack train of four mules.

On August 29, 1868, the Solomon Avengers left Fort Hays due northward to beat out the country between the Smoky Hill and the Republican rivers, then moved northwesterly to the Beaver. Lieutenant Beecher acted as lead scout and guide. Eight days later, the scouts rode into Fort Wallace without having seen anything more than abandoned sites of Indian camps, Indian trails, and lots of buffalo. One man, who had been hurt by a fall from his horse when the scouts mistakenly charged the camp of a haying crew, was left at Wallace. Two new men joined the unit there, one of them being Sharp Grover, who was now sufficiently recovered from his wounds to ride again. He was named head scout.

Forsyth refitted at Wallace and was about to move on orders to Bison Basin when word came that a small group of Indians had attacked a freighter's wagon train near Sheridan, thirteen miles east of Wallace, killing and scalping two Mexican teamsters and running off with some of the wagons and stock. On September 10 Forsyth hurried to the point of action, where he took up the trail of what appeared to be a war party of about twenty-five Indians. With Beecher and Grover riding in advance and reading the trail, the command followed it, finding the cattle and two wagons the Indians had taken.

Forsyth pushed on northward until dark, when camp was made. Taking to the trail again the next morning, the scouts found that the Indians were dropping off one by one at points where the ground made their trail hard to read. Finally the signs of the war party vanished altogether some thirty miles from Wallace on Thickwood Creek. At this point, with the direction of the Indians pointing toward the Republican River, Grover and McCall cautioned the frontier-inexperienced Forsyth against the danger of running into large masses of Indians. But Forsyth was determined not to return without action to report, and he pushed on northward on Custer's old trail of the year before.

On the fifth day out from Wallace they discovered an abandoned wickiup on the banks of the Republican. Crossing the river, the scouts picked up another Indian trail and began following it westward up the Arikaree Fork of the Republican, the trail growing steadily broader with clear marks of Indian travois and fresh horse manure as well as discarded lodge poles and other Indian paraphernalia. Now swallowed completely by the wild, unknown country, with supplies running dangerously low and signs of a large body of Indians ominously close, several of the party again approached Forsyth to suggest turning around. But the officer would not listen to them, stubbornly asking if they had not enlisted to fight Indians, and the march continued on the following day, the sixteenth.

At about four o'clock in the afternoon the party reached a wide, comfortable, well-grassed valley on what they thought to be Delaware Creek, but was really the Arikaree Fork of the Republican, and went into camp to rest their jaded horses. Here the south bank of the river was a long, gentle slope while the north was a level plain for nearly a mile before being broken by a line of sand hills. The soft-flowing stream split into two channels (one then dry) in the valley to form a large sand-bar island. At its center grew a clump of willow and alder, with sage grass at its head and a small cottonwood tree near its foot. Forsyth camped, just opposite the island, on the north bank. That night a signal fire was seen on a hill some three miles away.

The camp was just stirring to life at dawn the next day, the seventeenth of September, and the coffeepots were on the campfires when the sudden cry of "Indians! Indians!" went up. The sentry had spotted several warriors rushing the horse herd, yelling fiercely and waving blankets in an attempt to stampede the stock, seven of which were driven away. Forsyth immediately issued orders to saddle up, but this was no sooner accomplished than hundreds of Indians suddenly appeared. They came out of the high grass surrounding the camp, from ravines and thickets, from the bed of the stream, and on horseback from over the hills to the north, all whooping and firing on the scouts.

The position occupied by the command was entirely exposed and untenable, allowing Indian sharpshooters to get within easy range without being detected. In desperation the scouts looked about for a place to take up positions and quickly chose the island, which offered the most opportune refuge immediately available. Having the advantage of surrounding open space in all directions for a field of fire, it would also allow the scouts to tie up their horses and all be available to fight. The scouts retreated in haste toward the island with Beecher, McCall, and Grover hanging back as a rear guard and holding the Indians in temporary check with their rifle fire. But in their haste the scouts left behind the pack mules with the few rations that were left, including forty pounds of bacon and twenty pounds of salt, plus one pannier containing all the medical supplies. All would prove to be critical losses.

Upon reaching the island, the horses were tied to bushes outside the perimeter of the defensive circle taken by the men. The Indians now dismounted a number of warriors as sharpshooters along the banks of the river and poured a heavy fire into the island positions. If they were intent upon getting the officers first, they were successful, for Forsyth was the first hit. He was issuing orders to the men to dig in on the sandy island when a bullet struck him in the right thigh, ranging upward. A short time later another shot hit him in the left leg, shattering the bone just below the knee. Conscious but unable to move, Forsyth was dragged to the hole occupied by Dr. Mooers at the west end of the island. As the doctor attempted to minister to Forsyth's wounds, he himself was hit squarely in the forehead by an Indian bullet. Mooers lay mortally wounded for three days before he finally succumbed without ever regaining consciousness.

Forsyth continued to issue orders through Grover, who dug a hole big enough for both of them. The others were also digging in, using butcher knives, tin plates, spurs, or their bare hands to scoop up the sand and pile it in front of themselves for a fortification. The Indian sharpshooters, meanwhile, were pouring a steady barrage of fire into the island while others were massing for a mounted charge on the scouts.

Though the exact sequence of events as described by the various accounts of the battle will probably never be satisfactorily resolved, it appears that the first of several charges was made at around nine o'clock that morning. One excellent account, written from an interview with the scouts after they had returned to Fort Wallace, and another by a scout with the relief column, who penned his version on October 1, the day they returned to Fort Wallace, list three to five separate charges. One describes a "Cheyenne chief, dressed in full war paint and trappings," while the other tells of a chief "with claws of birds and animals, the coronet of feathers and the eagle beak upon his head and all the insignia of command." Either description might well have been of the Dog Soldier chief Roman Nose, whose famous war bonnet had a single buffalo horn.

Possibly the most impressive warrior on the plains, Roman Nose was a superb figure of manhood, towering well above most others of his tribe, who were taller than most Plains Indians. He was described as being six foot three, broad-chested, and possessing a grandly sculptured head marked by a large mouth, fierce black eyes, and a strong, high-arched nose. Theodore Davis, when he saw Roman Nose at the Pawnee Fork, wrote that he had never seen so fine a specimen of the Indian race, an almost identical remark to one made by an army officer in describing him on another occasion. The officer felt it would be difficult to exaggerate the physique of this solemn-faced, majestic war chief of the Cheyennes.

George Bent, who was not at the fight, later said that Roman Nose led one of the later charges. Bent also claimed that Roman Nose had hesitated to go into the battle because a Sioux woman fed him out of a metal spoon, ruining his battle medicine. But when Bull Bear and White Horse appealed to him to lead a charge, he gave in and agreed to do so.

Along the bank, out of rifle range, an old Sioux medicine man rode about, excitedly beating his drum and shouting incantations and exhortations to the young warriors with Roman Nose to great deeds of valor. Atop the hills to the north, Indian women and children clapped their hands, danced, and sang. They had come to see the Cheyenne and Sioux warriors defeat the white soldiers. In the sand pits the beleaguered white men checked the loads of their Spencer rifles, six shots in the magazine and one in the chamber, and made certain of their pistols. The order went out from their wounded commander to "Aim low. Don't throw away a shot."

Around the bend came Roman Nose, stripped to the waist, his war bonnet trailing down his back and alongside his pony, his face striped with war paint. He wore only leggings, breech clout, and moccasins. Across his shoulder were strapped quiver and bow, cartridge belt around his waist, buffalo-skin shield in one hand, rifle and reins in the other. Close behind were his warriors, many of them young bucks, their scalp locks tipped with feathers, faces daubed with paint, the tails of their multicolored ponies tied up for battle. They spread en masse across the sandy river bed like a moving wall of horseflesh and whooping braves.

For many it was their first great battle, and the braves were feverish with wild excitement. Then Roman Nose threw back his head and clasped the palm of his hand across his mouth, sounding his shrieking war whoop. From somewhere off, a bugle sounded. Roman Nose's charge against what has come to be called "Beecher's Island," one of the classic incidents of Plains Indian warfare, was under way.

But the Roman Nose assault on the island was no more successful than the others. The steady fire of the scouts blunted the charge and caused it to falter. Scout Louis McLoughlin, who put the Roman Nose charge at about noon, stated that the Indians got to the upper end of the island. It was there that Roman Nose was hit and wounded mortally. Bent claimed that the warrior leader was struck in the back by a bullet but managed to ride back to his camp before he died.

During the charges, a number of Indians were knocked from the backs of their ponies. Most were hauled off by their fellow warriors, but three dead braves remained on the tip of the west end of the island, too close under the guns of the scouts to be retrieved.

It was evidently during the first charge that Lieutenant Fred

Beecher was twice hit. One of the bullets struck him in the side and then traveled on to sever his backbone. Beecher was no stranger to injury and pain, but the wound he suffered now left him in helpless agony. According to Forsyth, Beecher rose from his rifle pit after the first charge and, using his rifle as a crutch, dragged himself to Forsyth's position and lay beside him in the sand, face downward on his arm. He said quietly and simply, "I have my death wound, General. I am shot in the side and dying." Forsyth replied that surely it couldn't be that bad, but Beecher said, "Yes. Goodnight." The young officer sank into half-consciousness and Forsyth heard him murmur, "My poor mother." Possibly he was thinking also of his two sisters who had drowned the previous summer in a pond near the Beecher home. Beecher remained alive throughout the day, often delirious, at times begging to be shot and put out of his pain. It was sundown when he died.

When the Indians saw they were not going to be successful in easily overrunning the island, they set to work picking off the horses, which they would otherwise have liked to capture. It was not particularly easy work, since the counterfire of the scouts kept them back. The horses reared and screamed at their ropes as the Indians' bullets struck them. It was around two o'clock before the last horse was knocked to the ground. Then one young Indian warrior jumped to his feet and shouted with satisfaction in perfect English, "There! Their last damned horse is gone."

A scout named William Wilson was killed early in the fight. During the lull after the initial charge, McCall and George W. Culver were digging in behind a dead horse on the outside perimeter of the defensive circle when one of the men inside shouted: "If you fellows on the outside don't get up and shoot, the Indians will be charging us." Both men responded to the criticism by raising their heads and immediately drawing Indian fire. Culver was hit in the head and killed instantly. Another bullet grazed McCall's neck. Shortly afterward, scout Harrington staggered up with an arrow barb sticking in his head so deep that the others could not pull it out.

Having given up the idea of overrunning the island, the Indians resorted to their familiar technique of circling the embattled whites with mounted warriors who fired from under their horses' necks while the sharpshooters maintained a steady fire. However, the scouts were well entrenched now, and they suffered no more deaths, though they had some seventeen wounded. One of these was the elder Farley, who, though shot in the thigh, held his position in some tall grass on the north side of the island and shot two Indians through the head. A chief was seen on a hilltop west of the island prior to one of the charges, exhorting the braves by saying:

"Young warriors, we are many and the whites are few. The white bullets are almost gone. All now that is needed is one more big run to bring the whites in."

Grover reportedly understood the chief and yelled to him, "Hello, old fellow, what do you think now? This is pretty tough, ain't it?" The chief, surprised by this, looked in the direction of the island and replied, "You speak right straight."

Those who were still capable spent the night improving their defenses and helping the wounded. Some crawled out to the dead horses and brought in the saddlebags with the ammunition in them. Few of them slept at all that night, most lying with their eyes scanning the darkness for signs of movement and listening to the distant mournful wailings of Indian women who had lost men in battle.

Another dash was made upon the island on the following morning, a Friday, but it was not a strong one and it was unsuccessful in completing what was its primary aim, recovery of the bodies of the three dead warriors. During the remainder of the day, the Indians kept up a constant sniper fire on the scouts, but no further casualties were suffered by Forsyth's command. Only a scant amount of food had been recovered from the saddlebags, and the men now cut strips of meat from the dead horses, then jerked the meat and hung it to dry in the bushes. Late in the afternoon a party of twenty-five Indians appeared in the distance with a white flag, claiming they wished to recover the bodies of the three warriors that still lay at the head of the island. But the whites refused to parley with them, one of the scouts yelling out that this was no "peace commission" and driving them away with rifle fire. That night, Forsyth wrote a dispatch to Colonel Bankhead at Fort Wallace, and two volunteers, young Jack Stillwell and Pierre Trudeau, slipped away from the island in the darkness with their feet wrapped in blankets to avoid leaving tracks for the Indians to find.

The Indians returned again on Saturday morning, making another weak attack. During the day, water was secured by digging two wells on the sand bar, and trenches were made connecting all the rifle pits. That night, two more men, Chauncey Whitney and A. J. Pliley, started out for Wallace, but they found the Indians too thick around the island to make it through and returned. A heavy and cold rain that night caused considerable suffering among the wounded scouts.

Sunday was a quiet day, the first without an attack by the Indians. Mooers died early that morning, bringing to four the number of dead among the scouting force. So far, the horse meat was holding out, but the situation was growing increasingly more serious because of the wounds and the lack of food. That night, Pliley and Jack Donovan successfully slipped away from the island to try to reach Fort Wallace, since everyone was fearful that the first scouts had not made it.

A large body of Indians was seen moving south, and it now appeared that the main force of the attackers had left. Some of the men ventured back to the original camp site and found some of the scattered coffee and a coffeepot. Taking this happy find back to the island, they built a fire out of the arrows that littered the sand bar and enjoyed both hot coffee and soup made from horse meat. This helped lift the spirits of the wounded men considerably.

Still, the situation was growing steadily worse. The wounded were beginning to suffer badly, their wounds becoming infected and infested with maggots. The stench of the dead men and dead animals was becoming intolerable, and the threat of starvation hung over the group. By Tuesday most of the horse-meat jerky was gone. The men scouted about and found some prickly pears, and a coyote, coming up to the island after the dead horses, was shot and devoured. By the twenty-third, Wednesday, the men were becoming desperate with nothing to eat but the corrupted meat of the horses. Some of them ate even this, using gunpowder in lieu of salt, ineffectually, and some making soup from it. There was some talk of the well men leaving to save themselves, but a talk with Forsyth convinced them to all hang together to the end, placing their hopes on being rescued.

Thursday was the eighth day on the island for the scouts, and the desperation felt by the men is reflected in the diary entry of Whitney for that day: "My God! Have you deserted us?" But on the morning of the ninth day, September 25, relief came. At about nine o'clock in the morning, under a bright sun, the scouts spotted a movement on the horizon and watched it prayerfully. It turned out to be Brevet Lieutenant Colonel L. H. Carpenter and a troop of 10th U. S. Cavalry whom Donovan and Pliley had stumbled onto in the field southwest of Fort Wallace. Stillwell and Trudeau had also made it through the Indian lines, reaching Fort Wallace in three days and alerting Brevet Colonel H. C. Bankhead. Bankhead had also pressed forward in relief as urgently as possible, with one hundred men, two howitzers, and an ambulance. He was joined on the march by Major James Brisbin and two companies of 2nd Cavalry, both units arriving a day after Carpenter.

The scouts' welcome to Carpenter's unit was, as Whitney put it, of "unspeakable joy! Shouts of joy and tears of gladness were freely commingled. Such shaking of hands is seldom witnessed." Tents were quickly erected for the wounded, and food rations broken out. Dr. D. A. Fitzgerald attended the wounded. The elder Farley was in such bad shape that it was necessary to amputate his leg at the thigh; he died shortly afterward. On the twenty-seventh the wounded were loaded into the ambulance, and the entire force moved back toward Fort Wallace.

On the first day out, several soldiers came suddenly face to face with a small party of Indians, one of whom they killed and scalped. On the way to the battle site, Carpenter's command had discovered the bodies of eight to ten Indians buried on scaffoldings, obviously recently killed, but they had pushed on in their hurry to reach Forsyth. With the bodies were all the trappings of an Indian warrior. On the way back, however, these were examined more closely. Two of them were found to be the bodies of a Cheyenne chief and of a Sioux medicine man. One of Forsyth's men, Sigmund Shlesinger, tells of rolling the Cheyenne chief from his wrappings. This Indian wore a headdress "composed of buckskin beautifully beaded and ornamented, with a polished buffalo horn on the frontal part and eagle feathers down the back." It seems entirely possible this could have been the body of Roman Nose. Colonel Carpenter took the medicine man's drum and shield.

Forsyth and the scouts were back at Wallace on September 30, and the news went out that a great victory had been won over the Indians. In truth it had been a dismal failure, the survivors more than fortunate that Forsyth's overzealousness had not brought disaster to the entire unit. Frontiersmen could still brag that a small band of scouts had held off a much superior force of Indians, but Sheridan and the Army had learned still another way *not* to fight Indians. Forsyth was brevetted as a brigadier general in the regular Army for his "gallant conduct" during the Arikaree fight, as was Colonel Bankhead for his energy in relieving Forsyth.

During late December 1868, Sharp Grover led an expedition of 5th Infantry from Fort Wallace back through the snow to the battle site for the purpose of recovering the remains of Beecher. They found Wilson and Culver where they had been buried in the same grave, Wilson above Culver. Wilson's body had been found by the Indians and a Spencer carbine taken, but Culver's body had gone undiscovered. Farley's grave was also missed by the grave marauders. Beecher's burial site was located, and his body identified by the wool blanket in which he had been wrapped for burial and by the handkerchief used to tie his hands over his chest.

Sharp Grover, the highly regarded chief of scouts who had barely missed being killed by the Cheyennes himself that previous fall, was to meet his death in February 1869. Drunk and insulting in a saloon at Pond Creek, Kansas, he was shot and killed by another scout named Mooney.

There were other engagements north of the Arkansas that fall. Major William B. Royall, with seven troops of 5th Cavalry, was on the Republican in early October. As with Custer and Forsyth, he did not find the Indians; they found him. Royall having divided his troops and sent some off on a scouting patrol, his camp was struck by Tall Bull with a large force of Dog Soldiers, who killed two soldiers and ran off twenty-six horses. And on October 17 two companies of 10th Cavalry under Colonel Carpenter, then escorting Major E. A. Carr to Fort Wallace, were attacked by some two hundred Cheyennes on Beaver Creek. The troops corralled their wagons and held off the Cheyennes for six hours. On October 25, Major Carr, with seven companies of 5th Cavalry and fifty frontier scouts, discovered the trail of an Indian village on the Solomon. The Indians attacked and harassed the force until the village escaped, firing the dry prairie grass behind them, and Carr was forced to settle for killing ten to twenty warriors and capturing one hundred thirty ponies, a large number of lodge skins and poles, and various other Indian equipment.

Concurrent with these encounters were a series of Indian attacks on frontier settlements and transportation along the wagon roads. Three of these particularly have further significance. In mid-August six Indians rode up to the White homestead on Granny Creek near Concordia, Kansas, while White and his three sons were away from the house stacking hay. Two of the Indians seized the Whites' eldest daughter, eighteen-year-old Sarah, and rode off with her. The others continued on to where White and the boys were. They killed the father, but the boys escaped.

Early in October three Indians appeared at the homestead of James Morgan on the Solomon River near Delphos, wounded Morgan, captured his bride of one month, and carried her off into captivity. These two women would ultimately meet in a Cheyenne camp.

On October 9 a large body of Indians attacked a civilian caravan of wagons returning to Kansas from Colorado along the Arkansas road ten miles east of the mouth of Sand Creek. After stampeding the oxen of the train, they held the caravan under siege for several days. During this time they captured Mrs. Clara Blinn and her young child, a boy of two years. Her husband was seriously wounded. She, too, was carried off into captivity by the attacking Indians, believed to be mostly Cheyennes though the wagon master claimed he recognized Kiowa chief Satanta among them.

So far, none of the military operations north of the Arkansas had been able to inflict any serious damage upon the Indians. Nor could Sheridan find much comfort in the operations south of the river, where Brigadier General Alfred Sully was conducting a strike into Indian Territory at the same time Forsyth was in the field to the north.

Chapter V
RETURN OF THE BEAU SABREUR

In planning his two-pronged strike against the Indians during the early fall of 1868, Sheridan wrote to Governor Crawford on September 10, stating that his objective was ". . . to make war on the families and stock of these Indians. . . . All the stock and families of the Cheyennes and Arapahoes are south of the Arkansas River, and General Sully's movement will bring back all the raiding parties of those bands north of the river, for the protection of their own families."

Sully, the son of famous portrait painter Thomas Sully, had served in the infantry during the Seminole and Mexican wars and had pulled garrison duty in the West prior to the Civil War. After a distinguished Civil War career, during which he was several times brevetted, Sully had commanded in the Dakotas, when he drove the Sioux of the Minnesota rebellion of 1863 into the Black Hills and gained a reputation as an Indian fighter. Later he was active in a campaign against the northern Cheyennes along the North Platte. Now Sheridan had assigned him the chore of punishing the Cheyennes and Arapahoes south of the Arkansas.

To accomplish this, Sully accumulated a force of nine companies of 7th Cavalry, still under the field command of Major Joel Elliot, and one company of 3rd Infantry at Fort Dodge, Kansas. Sully saw the command as a "Triumvirate of S's—Sherman, Division Commander; Sheridan, Department Commander; and Sully, District Commander."

At four o'clock on the afternoon of September 7—the same day that Forsyth was refitting at Fort Wallace prior to the events of the Arikaree battle—Sully led his expedition west out of Fort Dodge. His command was not only much larger than that of Forsyth, but it was encumbered with a large, slow-moving wagon train carrying forage, ammunition, and supplies. Two troops of the 7th led the way as advance guard, two more rode each flank, and two followed behind as rear guard.

It was dark by the time the Cimarron Crossing was reached, and Sully led his escort across to the south bank, waiting there until the wagon train and the rear guard had followed. When they were all on the south bank of the river, Sully turned to his staff officers and announced with some sense of destiny: "Now we have crossed the Rubicon."

In an effort to avoid detection by Indians, Sully issued orders that the troops would observe the strictest silence possible. No bugle calls were to be sounded. Smoking, even, was prohibited. The wagon train was formed two abreast, and the cavalry regulated its pace to that of the slower wagons. Sully, an infantry officer himself, shunned horseback and took his place at the head of the column in an army ambulance, much to the disgust of the officers of the 7th.

After a silent march of about two hours, Sully sent out orders for the advance squadron to halt and allow the train to catch up. Captain William Thompson, commanding Troop B of the 7th, which was then riding advance, was a man who prided himself on his lung power, having at one time been a member of the Iowa Territorial delegation to Congress and a colonel in the 2nd Iowa Cavalry during the Civil War. When Sully's orders to halt reached him, Thompson issued the command to his troops in turn with a booming stentorian bellow: "Battalion. Halt!" The order exploded through the stillness of the night, and after its reverberations had faded away there came from somewhere along the line of march the mocking bray of an army mule. A rumble of laughter rolled through the columns of troops.

Sully was furious. He had purposely waited until dark to move south of the Arkansas, he said, and observed strict silence in order to avoid detection by the Indians. Now, he complained, his scheme had been "thwarted by Balaam's ass!" From there on, as the expedition moved southward through the night, orders were given in softer tones.

Once the march was under way, the infantry soldiers quickly disappeared into the canvas-topped wagons, adding to their already excessive weight. As a result, the movement of the expedition was slow at best, particularly when it came to getting the wagons up and down the hundreds of steep dry gulches, river crossings, and sand hills that abounded in the country south of the Arkansas.

John Smith, Amos Chapman, and Ben Clark—all frontiersmen with Cheyenne wives—rode in advance as scouts and guides. They were followed by an advance guard of one cavalry troop. Another troop trailed the caravan as a rear guard, while other companies of the 7th rode alongside the wagon train as flankers.

With his wagon train delaying him, Sully decided to send Elliott ahead with four companies of troops in search of Indians. On the tenth, the expedition regrouped on the Cimarron and began moving eastward down its north bank, the three scouts riding at the lead. Suddenly a party of Indians appeared over a hill, charging and cutting off Smith and his two friends from the command. The three scouts exchanged rifle fire with the Indians and held them off until a troop of cavalry came galloping to their relief. Sully reported: ". . . as soon as the detachment was within a short distance, the savages commenced firing upon them, but without effect, as our men drove them in every direction, killing two Indians and one pony."

That night, as the expedition encamped at the confluence of the Cimarron and Crooked Creek, the Indians harassed the camp with rifle fire and arrows even after dark. The troops broke camp the next morning, not realizing that during the night a large party of Indians had moved in close to them. The long caravan of wagons and troops was pulling out, Sully and his staff already a mile or more from camp at the head of the formation, when the Indians struck. Two straggling F Troop soldiers, a mess cook and his "striker," were haltering four horses when suddenly

the warriors, shrieking their war whoops, galloped out of a draw
where they had been hiding and swooped down on the two hapless cavalrymen. The Indians dragged their victims across their
ponies, grabbed the horses, and dashed away.

The rear guard of the train, under the command of Captain
Hamilton, heard the war whoops of the Indians and the cries of
the troopers and immediately wheeled about and took after the
Indians in hot pursuit. Another company, under Lieutenant E. A.
Smith, followed close behind, both groups pouring revolver fire
after the fleeing braves. The army horses were closing in on the
double-loaded Indian ponies when one of the Indians shot his
prisoner and dumped him on the ground. The soldier was retrieved badly wounded, but the Indians made off with the other,
screaming trooper.

Sully, who was at the front of the column in his ambulance,
was angered by this breech of formation. He sent a staff officer
with orders for the pursuing troops to halt and pull back into
line, preventing the second trooper from being rescued. Sully
reprimanded the two officers, Hamilton and Smith, ordering
their arrest and taking their sabers, but he eventually relented
from this course of action, much to the happiness of the other
7th Cavalry officers.

The command continued its slow march along the Cimarron,
then turned southward into Indian Territory, harassed all the
way by Indian snipers whom the scouts identified as Cheyenne
Dog Soldiers plus some northern Arapahoes. One of the scouts, a
half-breed, recognized an Indian he knew and exchanged words
with him. The Indians at one point conducted a well-organized
attack upon the command, using an army bugle to blow signals.
Sully claimed to have killed or wounded twelve Indians during
the march along the river, but since it was a common practice
for the braves to throw themselves to the far side of their ponies
when under fire, they often gave the appearance of having been
shot off when they really hadn't. Thus it was very difficult for
troops in their fights with Indians to tell for sure that they had
hit their targets.

On the morning of the thirteenth, the expedition marched
from the Beaver to the Wolf, the rear guard still skirmishing

with the Indians, who made a vigorous and determined charge upon Sully's caravan. Crossing the Wolf not far from its mouth, Sully began to see clear signs of travois marks, leading him to believe that he was close on the heels of an Indian village. In anticipation, he pushed his command forward, only to suddenly find his train mired axle-deep amid a series of sand hills. Then it began to dawn on him that the Indians had cleverly led him into a trap, the braves having tied stone-weighted poles to their ponies and dragged them to leave marks like those of a travois.

While the heavy wagons struggled through the loose sand, the Indians sniped at them from the tops of distant sand dunes. In frustration, Sully ordered Captain George W. Yates forward with a troop of cavalry in an attempt to drive away the Dog Soldiers. But the Indians were persistent. No sooner would Yates chase them from one hill than others would appear elsewhere. The Cheyennes taunted them from hill to hill and to increasing despair. One trooper was killed during this action. Finally, low on supplies and admitting to the hopelessness of the situation, Sully gave the order to withdraw and, though some of the 7th's officers argued in disgust that once through the sand hills they would have found the Indian village, the command turned about and headed back from whence it had come. Custer would later describe Sully's movement: ". . . up the hill and then, like the forces of France, marched down again."

The Cheyennes rode the hills just out of rifle range, taunting the troops and making derisive signs by standing up on the backs of their ponies and thumbing their behinds at the soldiers. By September 16, the day before Forsyth was attacked on the Arikaree, the 7th was back in camp at Bluff Creek, and Sully was unhappily penning his report. He claimed that though "it is too much the custom to report a very large number of the enemy killed" he could safely say that twenty or thirty Indians were killed as he himself had seen that many fall from their horses. The expedition had had three men killed, one accidentally shot by a corporal of the guard during a camp and six wounded. A number of horses and mules were lost.

As it was with Forsyth, Sully's Indian-hunting expedition was a signal failure in its avowed purpose of punishing the

Cheyennes. If anything, it had served only to reassure the Dog Soldiers and others that they could defeat the soldiers in the field. Sheridan was angry and disgusted. Fully aware that new tactics would have to be used against the Indians, he took serious consideration of a winter's campaign. He discussed the idea with other officers and with scouts and frontiersmen at Fort Hays, asking if they thought an army could be sustained on the open plains in winter. Many thought so, but some did not. The famed frontiersman old Jim Bridger, who was called in all the way from St. Louis to advise Sheridan, said: "You can't hunt Indians on the plains in winter, for blizzards don't respect man or beast."

But Sheridan already had his mind made up. He was convinced that winter would handicap the Indian and benefit the trooper. Indian ponies would be weak and thin and much slower in winter, while the grain-fed army animals would be stronger. Also, he looked to the element of surprise, since the Indians would be around their lodge fires, not expecting the troops to be out. It was obvious that his troops could not catch and defeat the Indian warrior in the field. As he had admitted to Crawford, it would be necessary to hit their home villages, even as Chivington had done at Sand Creek. But the public outcry against the Sand Creek Massacre was still reverberating through Congress, and Sheridan had to avoid leaving the impression that he was planning a similar operation.

Sheridan made his proposal to Sherman and General of the Army Ulysses S. Grant, who was then campaigning for the presidency, and was given approval. He now set about making his plans and accumulating men and supplies for a three-pronged drive into Indian Territory. Stores were collected at forts Dodge in Kansas, Lyon in Colorado, Bascom in New Mexico, and Arbuckle in the Territory. Six troops of 3rd Cavalry and two companies of infantry under Colonel A. W. Evans would march eastward from Fort Bascom, establishing a supply depot on Monument Creek. Another force, of seven 5th Cavalry troops under Brevet Brigadier General Eugene A. Carr, would drive southeastward from Fort Lyon toward the Antelope Hills and the headwaters of the Red. It was hoped that these units would either destroy any straggler bands they met or drive them eastward toward a third force moving southward from Dodge.

This third force, comprising eleven companies of 7th Cavalry, a battalion of five companies of infantry, and twelve companies of 19th Kansas Volunteer Cavalry, would march due south into the Territory and, within a hundred miles of Fort Dodge, establish a supply base from which a strike against the Indians could be launched. The 7th would be made available by using the 10th Cavalry, composed of Negro troops, to patrol the Smoky Hill road and other areas of western Kansas.

Sheridan was in dire need of a field commander in whom he had confidence, and that could mean only Custer, long a favorite with him. Sully, who blamed his lack of success in part on the youth and inexperience of Elliott, was in agreement that Custer was needed. A request to Sherman was all that was required to get Custer's court-martial sentence remitted. Custer, restlessly hunting and fishing away his exile at Monroe, Michigan, was delighted when, on September 24, he received a telegram from Sheridan stating: "Generals Sherman, Sully, and myself, and nearly all of the officers of your regiment, have asked for you, and I hope the application will be successful." Custer did not even wait for official confirmation of Sheridan's request. On the following day he was aboard a train headed for Hays.

Upon its return from the Territory, the 7th Regiment had gone into camp on Bluff Creek thirty miles south of Fort Dodge. Custer joined his old unit there in early October, immediately dubbing the site Camp Sandy Forsyth. He found that the encampment was under siege from bands of Indians who made hit-and-run strikes on the troops, displaying the disdain they held for the soldiers. Custer himself took his rifle to the line for some target practice, but "it was like shooting swallows on the wing." It was virtually impossible for the troops to ride out and catch the small parties of Indians. In fact, it was dangerous to try, since the Indians were adept at drawing a troop off with a smaller party and laying a trap for it with a much larger force.

Custer undertook to do something about the situation at once. Mounting four companies of troops, each with about one hundred men, he waited until dark and sent them out in separate directions. But none of them were successful in engaging the wily Indians. Custer now decided upon a march to Medicine Lodge Creek, from which direction it was reported the Indians were coming. Taking three companies of cavalry and a complete supply train carrying forage, tents, rations, and extra ammunition, Custer marched to the creek. Fifty well-armed braves struck at his rear guard on the way, but these were repulsed and the rest of the journey was void of contact with the redskins. The only tangible result of the expedition was a visit to a deserted medicine lodge, which Custer claimed contained a large number of white scalps of all ages and sexes. Not even recent trails of war parties were found in the river valley.

Returning to Bluff Creek, Custer now began preparing for Sheridan's planned winter campaign. Both he and Sheridan were convinced that the only way to fight Indians successfully was to "do that which the enemy neither expects nor desires to be done." Fresh horses were recruited and drilled. Each was newly shod, and an extra fore and hind shoe was fitted for each mount and carried in the trooper's saddle pocket. Officers learned to converse by mirror signals, "nature having formed admirable signal stations over this part of the territory."

An intensive program of target practice was initiated, and a sharpshooter corps was organized. The promise of a separately marched unit that was not to be assigned guard or picket duty, plus the honor of being one of the best shots, made each man compete anxiously to be among the forty selected. Lieutenant W. W. Cook was named to head the unit, now nicknamed the "*corps d'élite.*"

Custer also made another innovation with the 7th Regiment, instituting a practice that was to last with the United Sates Cavalry for years to come: "coloring the horses." Prior to this, the mounts of the regiment had been distributed without any consideration as to organization of color. Every horse in the command was led out and placed in line, and troop commanders were allowed to pick the color they preferred by rank. The horses were divided into six colors for distribution: four troops of bays, three of sorrels, and one each of chestnuts and browns together,

Brevet Major General George Armstrong Custer in full regimentals in a photo taken sometime after Washita. *Courtesy of Kansas State Historical Society.*

Major General Philip H. Sheridan, frustrated by the inability of standard cavalry tactics against the Plains Indians, decided upon a winter campaign which would strike the Indian in his home camp. *Courtesy of National Archives.*

Lieutenant General William T. Sherman, commanding the Division of the Missouri, which covered Kansas and the Indian Territory, backed Sheridan's military offensive into the Indian Territory. *Courtesy of National Archives.*

Major General William B. Hazen, who had once placed Cadet Custer on report at West Point, refused to allow Black Kettle and his band sanctuary at Fort Cobb. *Courtesy of National Archives.*

Major General Winfield S. Hancock, whose attempt at chastisement of the Indians was a signal failure, sought to protect his presidential political ambitions with a court-martial of his field commander, Custer. *Courtesy of National Archives.*

Brevet Brigadier General Alfred Sully led an inept and futile expedition into Indian Territory, later losing out in a struggle over command at Camp Supply with Custer. *Courtesy of National Archives.*

Kansas Governor Samuel J. Crawford resigned his political post to become commanding colonel of the 19th Volunteer Cavalry, which became lost in a snowstorm and arrived too late to take part in the Washita fight. *Courtesy of Kansas State Historical Society.*

blacks, grays, and a last group of assorted colors—roans, pie-balds, etc.—designated as brindles. The band and the trumpeters were mounted on grays.

Once the color separation had been made, the horses were led away to the various company grounds, where the men were allowed to select them, again by rank. Naturally there were many who did not want to give up a horse they had ridden and become attached to, but improvement of the regiment's appearance was, to Custer at least, well worth it.

Custer had already organized the scouts into a separate detachment of their own, selecting California Joe, a large, unruly veteran of the West, as his chief of scouts. Joe, however, filled his canteen with booze on the Medicine Lodge trip and became so drunk that he got lost and thought he was being led into an Indian camp when his mule brought him back to the command. Custer dismissed him as chief of the scouts, but Joe would be with the boy general nevertheless for many years and remain a favorite with him.

In addition to the white scouts, Sheridan and Custer also recruited a dozen Osage trailers, there being no love lost between the Osages and most of the warring Plains tribes. Meanwhile, Sully was finding good mules scarce, so he instead requisitioned a number of yokes of oxen with the intention of using them to haul supplies to the new post, then to snake logs for stockades, and finally to be slaughtered for meat. Both the army quartermaster and commissary departments were horrified, but Sully got his "bulls."

On November 12, 1868, a huge train of some four hundred fifty wagons, eleven companies of 7th Cavalry, three companies of 3rd Infantry, one company of 5th Infantry, and one of 38th Infantry began its march for the Indian Territory. General Sully was in command of the train, and the expedition followed essentially the same course he had taken two months earlier. Now the wagons were organized four abreast so that they would be less exposed to attack. An advance guard of two companies of 7th Cavalry rode ahead and another two guarded the rear. The remainder of the cavalry was divided into six detachments, with three riding each flank of the train, thrown out some distance for

protection. The infantry was distributed accordingly at the start
of the march, and a herd of beef cattle was driven along between the flanking troops.

With the 7th Cavalry was a correspondent who described the
expedition as it broke camp on the Arkansas River below Fort
Dodge on the morning of November 12:

> The regiment moved off in column of divisions or platoons, in
> which the horses were arranged by colors, as chestnuts, blacks,
> bays, greys, sorrels, browns, etc., presenting a magnificent appear-
> ance in the bright sunlight of a clear, cool morning, with just
> enough breeze to display the flags and guidons to the best advan-
> tage, and to waft down the column the strains of music from the
> Seventh Cavalry band, which was mounted on fine greys in the ad-
> vance. The music mingled with the roar of an immense wagon-train
> which moved in a quadruplicated column in the same course, and
> recalled to mind the scenes of yore, " 'way down in old Virginia."
>
> The band took occasion to remind us of "the girl we left behind
> us"—a period now quite too remote and obscure in the past, to ex-
> cite any tearful regrets in this instance.
>
> Everybody marched off, seeming cheerful—the men in the ranks
> particularly so—giving vent to their exuberant spirits in different
> ways quietly. While riding near the column this morning, I heard a
> trooper humming a version of "Out of the Wilderness," which ran
> in this wise:

> If you want to smell hell,
> Just join the cavalry, join the cavalry;
> If you want to smell hell,
> Then join the cavalry,
>   We're *not* going home.

> The huge supply train of several hundred army wagons contains
> materials and implements for constructing a new fort near the
> mouth of the Middle Fork of the Canadian River, 104 miles S.S.E.
> from Fort Dodge, and is designed for a base of supplies during the
> campaign.
>
> Riding near General Sully are some Osage Indians from a peace-
> ful tribe who are employed to hunt up and trace the enemy's trails.
> They are well mounted, and are adorned with the usual amount of

paint, feathers, leggings, blankets, etc., and look as savage as the enemy we seek.

Our ponderous, imposing column ploughs its way across the Arkansas River, where we fill our canteens with water, and when fairly over, and under way with hills about to shut out the view, we turn to take a last look at its restless surface, wondering what scenes and incidents will come to us before we look at it again.

The march is varied by an occasional chase after buffalo, wolves and antelope, all of which are abundant hereabouts.

We have reveille and breakfast before daylight, and the column is in motion at the first peep of day. We go into camp early in the afternoon, and all the animals are then allowed to graze until retreat.

The command saw a good many buffalo on the rolling plains south of the Arkansas but, surprisingly, encountered no Indians. The crossing of rivers and draws with the heavy wagons was the greatest problem. The steep banks of dry gulches and rivulets resulted in the breaking of coupling poles, bringing a barrage of whooping and cursing as the wagon masters urged their mules and oxen forward. The command moved from river to river, measuring the distance with an odometer: eight miles from Dodge eastward down the Arkansas; five miles from the Arkansas to Mulberry Creek on the twelfth; twenty-one miles to Bluff Creek on the thirteenth; fourteen and one-half miles to Bear Creek on the fourteenth; ten and one-half miles to the Cimarron on the fifteenth.

On this day the first winter norther caught up with them, it lasting all day and the ensuing night. That afternoon, Elliott was sent with three companies of infantry, one company of cavalry, and the heaviest wagons, with instructions to make camp on the Beaver. By the time the rest of the expedition had caught up and joined the advance party, the weather had turned very cold. Now turning eastward along the Beaver, the invasion force moved another eighteen miles and made camp on the Beaver's south bank, still having encountered no Indians or Indian trails.

But on the eighteenth, as the command cut southeastward toward the Wolf, the two-day-old trail of a large war party was discovered—estimated to be seventy-five strong and heading north. Custer, who sent scouts to pursue the trail for a short distance, wanted to take the 7th Regiment and back-trail the war party, feeling certain that it would lead him to an Indian village, "the ultimate object of the movement we were thus engaged in."

Sully, however, disagreed. Mistakenly possessed with the idea that the Indians must surely know about such a large train being in their country, he felt it would be impossible to surprise them. Custer was very indignant and annoyed with Sully for not permitting him to pursue the trail.

The command reached Wolf Creek three miles above its juncture with the Beaver at noon on November 18 and went into camp. They had now marched a little over a hundred miles from Dodge, and a reconnaissance was made in all directions for a suitable place to construct a post. DeB. Randolph Keim, a newspaper correspondent who arrived later with Sheridan, gave credit to old John Smith for having selected the site just above the confluence of the two streams.

The spot was considered an ideal one for the new post, now named Camp Supply. There was excellent winter grazing for the horses, including a mesquite whose seed was considered excellent for fattening the animals; good water on two sides; ample timber along both streams, heavy enough for the building of a stockade-type fort; and a great abundance of game: wild turkey, deer, elk, and buffalo in addition to rabbits and game birds such as quail, dove, and prairie chicken. Immediately, the troops were put to work building a fort under the direction of First Lieutenant Joseph Hale of the 3rd Infantry, and the stillness of the wild country of Indian Territory was soon broken by the sound of axes, the shouts of teamsters, and the occasional crack of rifles as hunters bagged fresh game for meals. Trenches for the stockades and water wells were dug, meadows were mowed for hay, and mule-whackers hauled fallen logs to the cantonment, where they were sorted into piles for use as palisades, upright walls, rafters, etc.

The stockade, about 126 feet square, was quickly raised. At the northeast and southwest corners were lunettes, allowing guns to sweep all sides of the fort. At the northwest and southeast were small blockhouses with loopholes. The north and east sides of the fort were log-cabin structures, while the west and south sides were stockade fences about fifteen feet high. The troops were quartered in tents outside the fort, but the compound allowed for protection of both troops and stock in case of an attack.

There now developed a struggle of command authority between Sully and Custer, both lieutenant colonels in regular rank. The Rules and Articles of War provided that when troops of the regular Army and volunteers served together, the officer holding the highest brevet rank would command. Had Crawford, who had resigned as governor to become commanding colonel of the 19th Kansas Cavalry, been there, he would have been the senior in rank. Sully, a brevet brigadier general, taking the position that the rule did not apply between regular army units, issued an order assuming command by virtue of being district commander. Custer immediately responded by issuing his own orders, taking command by virtue of his higher, brevet-major general rank.

Sheridan, meanwhile, had grown more and more anxious about the success of his winter campaign and decided he wished to be on hand to make certain that things went the way he wanted them to go. Leaving Fort Hays on November 15, he was caught in a howling norther that blew away his tent and forced him to spend a wet, freezing night under an army wagon remembering the warnings of Jim Bridger about the plains in winter. Continuing on through the snow and sleet storm to Fort Dodge, he picked up an escort of a cavalry troop and a group of scouts under Lieutenant Lewis Pepoon plus ten Kaw Indian trailers. Proceeding to Bluff Creek, he was met by two advance companies of the 19th Kansas, his entourage now consisting of nearly three hundred men, exclusive of officers, teamsters, orderlies, Indians, and servants, with a train of about twenty wagons.

When Custer received the news that Sheridan was approaching Camp Supply, he immediately rode out to greet his old commander and, without much doubt, to let Sheridan know how Sully had refused to let him pursue the Indian trail and was trying to assume command of the post. That night, Custer dispatched the 7th Regiment band to serenade Sheridan by performing "several popular airs, in honor of the occasion." Sheridan did not take long resolving the matter of command. He ordered Sully back to his district headquarters at Fort Harker under escort of Major Keogh and a detachment of troops. At the same time, he directed Custer to call in the troopers who had been working on the wood-hauling details and begin preparing for an immediate campaign, hoping to still backtrack the Indian war party and find a village. Buffalo-lined overcoats, leggings that reached to the hips, fur-lined mittens, and fur caps were ordered issued to the troops by Sheridan.

Sheridan and his staff presented Custer with a pair of buffalo overshoes and a fur cap with ear lappets. Custer searched through the horse herds and selected a beautiful brown horse that showed excellent spirit. The horse, which he named "Dandy," would be a favorite with him up to the Little Bighorn battle. On the evening before the 7th's departure from Camp Supply, November 22, it began snowing, and, writing to his wife a few moments before midnight, Custer reported the snow still falling rapidly and already five to six inches deep.

Sheridan's orders to Custer were simple and direct: "To proceed south, in the direction of the Antelope Hills, thence towards the Washita River, the supposed winter seat of the hostile tribes; to destroy their village and ponies; to kill or hang all warriors, and bring back all women and children."

Chapter VI
FORBIDDEN SANCTUARY

Though the Cheyennes and Arapahoes had ranged into the Indian Territory for many years, it had never been their home. Thirty years earlier, in 1838, the two tribes had fought an important intertribal battle with the Comanches and Kiowas on the high country between the juncture of Beaver and Wolf creeks. The conflict had been brought on by a growing enmity between the two sets of confederated tribes. The Cheyennes and Arapahoes had been ranging farther and farther south from the Black Hills region of the Dakotas, drawn in part by the huge horse herds of the southern tribes. During a horse-stealing raid against a Kiowa village on the Washita, a party of Cheyenne Bow String warriors had been caught afoot, killed, and scalped to the last man by the Kiowas.

In retaliation, the Cheyennes and Arapahoes attacked a Kiowa-Comanche camp about twenty miles from the mouth of Wolf Creek. Black Kettle is said to have been with the scouting party that discovered the camp. A long battle ensued, with both sides losing important chiefs and warriors. The Cheyennes and Arapahoes eventually withdrew, but the fight led to a peace council between the four tribes at Bent's Fort, on the Arkansas, in 1840. Presents were exchanged, and by agreements made there the Cheyennes and Arapahoes were conceded the privilege of hunting south of the Arkansas.

The Jackson administration had exiled the unwanted tribes of the South—the Cherokees, Creeks, Choctaws, Chickasaws, and Seminoles—to the hilly, wooded eastern half of the Indian Territory, along with smaller tribes such as the Quapaws, Senecas, Shawnees, and Kickapoos. But the western half of the Indian Territory, still largely unknown to the white man, was an ideal range for the Plains tribes. Away from the main transportation and migratory routes westward, the area was abundant in buffalo and other game. Numerous clear-channeled streams, their courses marked with cottonwood and willow, snaked their way through the country, which was sometimes sand hills, sometimes short-grassed prairie, sometimes stretches of sagebrush or the knee-high blackjack oak known to early visitors as the "Cross Timbers."

To the north was the Cimarron, which cut down from southern Kansas to join the Arkansas to the east. South of the Cimarron was the Beaver, draining the broken lands of the panhandle's high Black Mesa country and joining Wolf Creek to form the North Canadian. Below the Wolf was the South Canadian, where the Antelope Hills, or Boundary Mounds, rose in high plateaus above the level prairie to mark the river's crossing of the one-hundredth meridian, separating the Territory from the Texas panhandle. Farther south were the winding, red-banked Washita, the three forks of the Red River, and the Red itself, which provided a southern boundary line for the Indian Territory.

The Washita River, which looped off the southwestern corner of the territory, defined the principal home range of the Comanches and the Kiowas. The area included the Wichita Mountains, which took their name from the Wichita Indians, whom Colonel Henry Dodge had first visited in 1834 at their village on Cache Creek. In those days the Wichitas raised corn and vegetables and manufactured bows and arrows from the *bois d'arc* (better known as the Osage orange, or hedge apple, tree), which they traded for horses, mules, and buffalo robes with the Kiowas and Comanches, whose war parties ranged far south into Texas and even Mexico.

In 1858 the Comanches conducted a horse-stealing raid

against a Chickasaw settlement near Fort Arbuckle, on the Washita River, in central Indian Territory. An army officer at Arbuckle prevailed upon the Wichitas to go out and arrange for the Comanches to attend a peace council at the Wichita village sixty miles west of Arbuckle. Comanche chief Buffalo Hump agreeably led his village of nearly six hundred strong to the council. But Major Earl Van Dorn, then commanding four companies of U.S. 2nd Cavalry at Camp Radziminski, west of the Wichita range, knowing nothing of the council, discovered the Comanche trail and assumed it to be that of a raiding party. Following the trail on a forced march, Van Dorn, later to be a Confederate general, attacked the tribe's encampment at dawn, killing fifty warriors and two women and capturing over three hundred horses. He later struck them again, almost annihilating the band. The Comanches felt they had been betrayed by the Wichitas and swore revenge, causing the latter to flee their home grounds and seek refuge at Fort Arbuckle.

Though the southwestern corner of Indian Territory legally belonged to the Chickasaw and Choctaw nations by treaty, the agreement had also arranged for the lease of that area for the purpose of relocating the Wichitas and several other tribes there. In 1853 two reservations had been established in northern Texas for some of the Comanches and the smaller bands of Caddoes, Anadarkoes, Wacoes, Tawakonies, and Tonkawas. Attacks upon these reservation Indians by Texas citizen bands, however, made it necessary to close down the two reserves and move the tribes into Indian Territory, relocating them at a newly established Wichita Agency in a district leased from the Chickasaw nation near the Wichita Mountains. There they were joined by straggler bands of Kickapoos, Shawnees, Delawares, Ionies, and Kichais, and a few Shawnees and Delawares who were intermarried.

The Confederacy signed friendship treaties with some of the tribes, but many of the Indians fled to Kansas during the Civil War, along with some of the civilized tribes from the eastern half of the Territory, living out the war years in extremely destitute and diseased conditions. After the war, the tribes were returned to the Indian Territory, establishing themselves in the Fort Cobb area, where the government made minimal efforts to feed and care for them. The Kiowas and Comanches continued to roam freely as far north as the Arkansas, at the same time conducting persistent warfare against the Texas frontier settlements. They found that captive white women and children were profitable trade items with the whites, and Satanta of the Kiowas was reputed to be especially active in this.

Under the provisions of the act establishing the peace commission of 1867, Congress had allocated General Sherman, whose brother John was a U.S. senator, some five hundred thousand dollars for subsisting the needy Indians under the area encompassed by his Department of the Missouri. On August 10, 1868—the same day that the Saline and Solomon depredations began—Sherman issued an order establishing two large military districts on the central plains. The Northern District, including the huge Sioux reservation areas of the Dakotas, was placed under the command of Brevet Major General W. S. Harney. The Southern Indian Military District, covering the entire Indian Territory, was assigned to Brevet Major General William B. Hazen, a colonel in the 38th Infantry, who was to supervise and control the issuance of goods and supplies to the wild tribes of western Indian Territory.

Hazen, an opinionated and outspoken New Englander and graduate of West Point, had once served on the frontier in Oregon Territory and at Fort Davis, Texas, where he had been seriously wounded by a Comanche arrow. With the outbreak of the Civil War, he had been appointed as an assistant professor of infantry at the West Point academy. While there, in June of 1861, then-Captain Hazen placed a young cadet on report for not stopping a fight between two other cadets. The reported cadet's name was George Armstrong Custer. Though helped by a favorable recommendation from Hazen, which got him off with only a reprimand, Custer never really forgave Hazen for reporting him. It could not be expected that the flamboyant recklessness of Custer and the outspoken, critical nature of Hazen would be compatible under the best of circumstances; and the two generals would later fight public battles in print on various national issues. Also achieving an outstanding record during the Civil

War, Hazen in later life would become a brigadier general and head of the U. S. Weather Bureau.

In his new command, Hazen was directly responsible to Sherman in all matters except the military troops in the district, and in this he was answerable to General Sheridan. The appointment of a military man to the charge of an Indian post was questioned by many.

Hazen's first assignment was to assist in sorting out the peaceful Indians from the hostiles, and on September 18 he joined Sheridan at Fort Larned, where the Kiowas, Comanches, and Plains Apaches were still encamped. On the following two days, Sheridan and Hazen conducted talks with these tribes, instructing them that they should return to their reservation area in the Fort Cobb vicinity in order to avoid the forthcoming hostilities. Though the Kiowas under Satanta and the Comanches under Ten Bears were reluctant to go, it was eventually agreed that they would accompany Hazen to Fort Cobb. But since it was necessary to wait a week until rations had been delivered to Larned, the Indians were permitted to leave the overgrazed Fort Larned area and do some buffalo hunting south of the Arkansas. By agreement, they were to return at the end of a week and accompany Hazen to Fort Cobb.

On September 19, Sheridan spelled out the conditions of an agreement with Hazen and the Indians in a letter to Hazen. He would furnish rations to the Kiowas and Comanches until October 31 if they would at once return to Fort Cobb. "Their presence here," he wrote, "is very embarrassing to me and a great drawback in the prosecution of hostilities against the known hostile bands . . ."

After that date Hazen would subsist the Indians out of the fifty thousand dollars, plus clothing and stores, that Sherman had allocated to him for the care of the tribes in his district. Sheridan, however, did not have to feed the Kiowas and Comanches, for when the week was up they had not returned, choosing to continue on southward and hunt buffalo rather than return to Larned for Sheridan's promised rations. This left Hazen in somewhat of a predicament, for he now faced the danger of trying to reach Fort Cobb alone, with the hostile Cheyennes and Arapahoes between him and his destination and with no military escort available. Because of this, he was forced to reroute his journey roundabout to Fort Gibson, in northeastern Indian Territory, and thereby delay his arrival at Cobb.

When it became apparent that he was going to be too late to meet the Indians at Fort Cobb as scheduled, Hazen arranged for an officer from Fort Arbuckle, Captain Henry Alvord, to proceed to Cobb and take charge of the Indians until he arrived. Alvord, a West Pointer who in more civilized days would return as president of Oklahoma State University, reached Fort Cobb in mid-October with two companies of 10th Cavalry.

Chiefs of the Kiowas and Comanches had already visited Cobb and found no one to meet them. They immediately returned to the Antelope Hills and continued their buffalo hunting. They were cautious of Fort Cobb anyway, for Cheyenne squaw man John S. Smith, who, like Wynkoop, was suspicious of Sheridan's intentions and feared another Sand Creek, had told them at Larned that "General [Hazen] would not come as he had promised, through fear of an attack from the Cheyennes; that . . . they had better move south and west rapidly not going to either Larned or Cobb, for the military had set traps for them at both places."

Upon arriving at Fort Cobb, Alvord dispatched a courier to bring in some of the Kiowa and Comanche chiefs. Old Ten Bears sent back word that the Comanches would be in shortly. He said also that Black Kettle and his Cheyennes were just north of the Antelope Hills and planned to visit Cobb soon "to arrange for moving a large portion of the Cheyennes south for lasting peace."

On November 1, the main camp of the Cheyennes was reported to be on the South Canadian at the one-hundredth meridian, with the Arapahoes and a large party of Sioux nearby. There the Indians were conducting trading operations with a number of Mexican traders, swapping captured stock and robes for provisions and ammunition.

Hazen, who finally arrived on November 7 with a company of cavalry and one of infantry, faced a difficult situation at Cobb. There he discovered some seven hundred Comanches and over a thousand Indians from smaller tribes—Caddoes, Anadarkoes, Wichitas, Wacoes, Kichais, and Tawakonies—all looking to him for subsistence and guidance. None of the agents for the various tribes were there. S. T. Walkley, acting agent who replaced Comanche-Kiowa agent Leavenworth, had already left because of poor pay by the time Hazen reached Fort Cobb. Henry Shanklin, agent for the Wichitas and affiliated tribes, had taken a sudden leave of absence because of a "severe affliction of rheumatism" and later resigned without returning. Wynkoop was still on leave in the East, and it wasn't until December that A. G. Boone arrived to take up duties as Kiowa-Comanche agent.

The fifty thousand dollars, which Sherman had thought was a generous amount, proved to be grossly insufficient for Hazen's task. He estimated that he would need $115,220 just to feed the Indians at Fort Cobb, plus money to hire two clerks, a storekeeper, an interpreter, four scouts, one butcher, and a teamster, and to put a roof on an old storehouse. Neither the Army nor the Indian Bureau nor Congress would provide additional funds. Alvord had already reported the situation to be precarious at best. With only a half barrel of coffee and one hundred and seventy barrels of flour to be distributed among some seventeen hundred Indians, there seemed little chance to keep the tribes at Cobb. The Comanches had already threatened to head back for the buffalo ranges.

At mid-November the Kiowas and Apaches arrived at the post, and Hazen issued them rations for ten days. At about the same time, a small party led by Black Kettle and Little Robe of the Cheyennes and Big Mouth and Spotted Wolf of the Arapahoes arrived at Fort Cobb to visit Dutch Bill Griffenstein. The trader's wife, Cheyenne Jenny, had died in October, and Griffenstein had called in the Cheyenne chiefs to pick up her effects. The trader encouraged Black Kettle to talk with Hazen about making peace, and the Cheyenne principal chief agreed. On November 20 the four chiefs met with Hazen, Captain Alvord certifying a true record of the conversations. Black Kettle spoke first:

> I always feel well while I am among these Indians, the Caddoes, Wichitas, Wacoes, Keechies [Kichais], etc., as I know they are all

my friends, and I do not feel afraid to go among the white men, because I feel them to be my friends also. The Cheyennes, when south
of the Arkansas, did not want to return to the north side, because
they feared trouble there, but were continually told they had better
go there, as they would be rewarded for so doing. The Cheyennes
do not fight at all this side of the Arkansas,—they do not trouble
Texas, but north of the Arkansas, some young warriors were fired
upon, and then the fight began. I have always done my best to keep
my young men quiet, but some will not listen and since the fighting
began, I have not been able to keep them all at home. But we want
peace, and I would be glad to move all my people down this way. I
could then keep them all quietly near camp. My camp is now on the
Washita, forty miles east of Antelope Hills, and I have there about
one hundred and eighty lodges. I speak only for my own people. I
cannot speak for nor control the Cheyennes north of the Arkansas.

Big Mouth also made a short speech:

I have come down here, a long distance, to this country in which
I was born, to these prairies between the Wichita mountains and
the mountains on the Arkansas, over which I roamed when a boy,
to see all these Indians, my friends, and the white men, who are my
brothers, and to have a talk. I look upon you [General Hazen] as
the representative of the Great Father at Washington, and I came
to you because I wish to do right; had I wished to do any wrong I
never would have come near you. I never would have gone north of
the Arkansas again, but my father there [the agent] sent for me
time after time, saying it was the place for my people, and finally I
went. No sooner had we got there than there was trouble. I do not
want war, and my people do not, but although we have come back
south of the Arkansas, the soldiers follow us and continue fighting,
and we want you to send out and stop these soldiers from coming
against us. I want you to send a letter to the Great Father at Washington at once, to tell him to have this fighting stopped; that we
want no more of it. Although a chief, a kinsman of mine, has been
killed, with others, we will forget it, for we wish for peace.

The Cheyennes and Arapahoes represented by these two
chiefs posed a special problem for Hazen. His orders from Sherman, dated October 13, had read:

General . . . I want you to go to Fort Cobb, and to make provision for all the Indians who come there to keep out of war, and I prefer that no warlike proceedings be made from that quarter. The object is for the War and Interior Departments, to afford the peaceful Indians every possible protection, support, and encouragement, whilst the troops proceed against all outside of the Reservations, as hostile; and it may be that General Sheridan will be forced to invade the Reservation in pursuit of hostile Indians; if so, I will instruct him to do all he can to spare the well-disposed; but their safety now is in rendezvousing at Fort Cobb. . . .

Sherman had given further definition to whom he considered to be peaceful Indians when he sent a telegram to General Schofield, on October 20, stating that he wanted both agents Wynkoop and A. G. Boone sent to Fort Cobb with clothing for the Indians that had already been purchased and stored at Lawrence, and with as much money as the Secretary of the Interior could spare "to be used in taking care of all Indians who take refuge there in good faith to avoid the war."

Perhaps, as the critics implied, this would have been definite enough to a non-military man. But Hazen, though impressed by the sincerity of Black Kettle and Big Mouth, knew that Phil Sheridan had declared the Cheyennes and Arapahoes to be hostile. He reasoned that it might well be inviting another "Chivington" affair if he accepted the tribes at Cobb and then Sheridan found it necessary to invade the Fort Cobb reservation area, as Sherman had suggested to be both appropriate and possible. Accordingly, Hazen responded to the two chiefs negatively:

The "Great Father" in Washington sent for me when I was away out in New Mexico, because I had been much with the Indians and like them, to come here and take care of all the Cheyennes, Arapahoes, Apaches, Comanches, and Kiowas, to look after them and their agents and their traders, to get them on to the Reservations agreed upon a year ago at Medicine Lodge, and see they were treated right. Before I could come from New Mexico, the Arapahoes and Cheyennes had gone to war, so that I could not see them; but I saw the Kiowas, Apaches, and Tapparico [Yamparika] Comanches, at Fort Larned, and I have come here as I promised them. I am sent here as a peace Chief. All here is to be peace, but north of the Arkansas is General Sheridan, the great war chief, and I do not control him, and he has all the soldiers who are fighting the Arapahoes and Cheyennes. Therefore you must go back to your country, and if the soldiers come to fight you must remember they are not from me, but from that great war chief, and with him you must make peace. I am glad to see you, and glad to hear that you want peace and not war. I cannot stop the war, but will send your "talk" to the "Great Father," and if he gives me orders to treat you like the friendly Indians I will send out to you to come in; but you must not come in again unless I send for you, and you must keep well out beyond the friendly Kiowas and Comanches. I am satisfied that you want peace, that it has not been you but your bad men who have made the war, and I will do all I can for you to bring peace: *then* I will go with you and your Agent on to your reservation, and care for you there. I hope you understand how and why it is that I cannot make peace with you.

The chiefs replied that they understood. Hazen said he could offer them no subsistence, but Griffenstein gave them food and other goods. In his report to Sherman on November 22, Hazen defended his decision on the grounds that "To have made peace with them would have brought to my camp most of those now on the war path south of the Arkansas; and as General Sheridan is to punish those at war and might follow them in afterwards, a second Chivington affair might occur, which I could not prevent." He said that he did not understand that he was to treat for peace, and asked for more definite instructions. "To make peace with these people would probably close the war, but perhaps not permanently. I would prefer that General Sheridan should make peace with these parties."

Hazen also reported that while the Cheyenne chiefs seemed to be sincere in their desire for peace, the Kiowas and Comanches claimed that the young Cheyenne warriors were ready for more war because they could then get more mules. They said the Cheyennes bragged that in the spring the Sioux and the Dog Soldiers would come down and help them clean out the country. Hazen was concerned enough to request from the commander of Fort Arbuckle, Indian Territory, two more companies of 10th

Cavalry and two howitzers "remaining a week or two, during which time General Sheridan's movements from above will probably develop . . ."

In a letter to James A. Garfield, Hazen later made the interesting suggestion that he had offered Black Kettle a chance for personal sanctuary: "I again asked him whom he represented, hoping to give him personally, with his families, the protection of the Government, but [he] replied that he spoke for all the Cheyennes. . . ."

Black Kettle and the others returned to their camps up the Washita. A Cheyenne woman, Moving Behind, remembered that as a girl she was in Black Kettle's camp when the chiefs returned. She said Black Kettle's wife, Medicine Woman Later, was very angry and stood for a long while outside her lodge because the camp was not moved right away, saying, "I don't like this delay, we could have moved long ago. The Agent sent word for us to leave at once. It seems we are crazy and deaf, and cannot hear."

Chief Black Eagle of the Kiowas told interpreter Philip McCusker of another reason for concern among the Cheyenne villagers:

> On the night of the 26th November, a party of Kiowa Indians returning from an expedition against the Utes, saw on nearing the Antelope Hills on the Canadian river, a large trail going south towards the Washita. On the arrival of the Kiowas at the Cheyenne camp, they told the Cheyennes about the trail they had seen, but the Cheyennes laughed at them. One of the Kiowas concluded to stay at the Cheyenne camp that night, and the rest of them went on to their own camp, which was but a short distance off.

Black Kettle's village of Cheyennes, consisting of some fifty lodges plus one of Arapaho and two of Sioux, was encamped the farthest west of a series of encampments—Cheyennes, Arapahoes, Kiowas, Comanches, and Apaches—which were spread some ten to fifteen miles along the Washita River of the Indian Territory. Some six thousand Indians were in winter camp there along the river valley where nature had formed a wide basin bordered by sandy, red bluffs and dotted with unique, rounded knolls. In the bottom of this basin, the Washita wound back and forth in hairpin fashion before looping northward to form a large horseshoe bend. Spread along the top of the bend were the Arapahoes under Little Raven; below them, at the bottom of the loop, a larger Cheyenne camp under Medicine Arrow; another Cheyenne camp; then Kicking Bird's Kiowas; and on farther the Comanches and Apaches. It was an excellent winter camping ground, protected by the bluffs to the north and offering an abundance of water, grazing, and wood from the timber that fringed the river.

On the evening of November 26, 1868, Black Kettle invited the principal men of his village to meet with him in his lodge. He had recently ridden over a hundred miles through the snow in returning from Fort Cobb, where he had talked with General Hazen. Now he was calling a council to discuss the situation. The elders came and seated themselves cross-legged on robes spread around the lodge fire, drinking the hot, sugared coffee that Black Kettle's wife poured from a large pot, passing the pipe, and talking. Black Kettle told them what General Hazen had said: that he could not allow them to come in to Fort Cobb and that there presently were troops in the field under the command of General Sheridan. Hazen had advised the Indians to hold in their war parties and keep a sharp eye out for soldiers.

One of the Cheyenne men mentioned that a Kiowa war party had only that day reported a big trail north of the Canadian, but others scoffed at the idea that the bluecoats would be out in such cold weather. Most of them felt that surely they were far enough south of the Arkansas to be safe, especially with the heavy snow, which would keep the soldiers in their camps. Two boys were watching the pony herd to the northwest side of the village, but, just to be extra cautious, it was decided that on the next day the camp would move farther down the river, among the other tribes. Runners would be sent out to talk with any troops that might be headed their way to clear up any misunderstandings. Black Kettle wanted Sheridan to know that the Cheyennes south of the Arkansas did not want war.

When all had been agreed upon, the elders filed out one by

one and tramped the snowy paths back to their own lodges. The cold of the winter night closed about the silent village on the Washita as the last ribbons of smoke trailed off above the cone-shaped lodges. Outside the camp, the two young herders huddled close to their campfire until long after dark, before finally heading back in to the warmth of their lodges and bed robes. They had been but small children when, four years before, lacking only one day, their village had been attacked on Sand Creek by the Coloradans under Chivington. The Kiowa war party had passed by earlier, and there was no reason for the two boys to suspect that upriver the long columns of the 7th Cavalry were pushing through the night toward their village.

At about the same time that Black Kettle and the others returned to the bend of the Washita, Satanta, Satank, and Lone Wolf of the Kiowas, taking advantage of their accepted position as non-hostiles, had moved their villages to Fort Cobb, leaving only Kicking Bird's band of Kiowas on the river. Hazen welcomed the three Kiowa chiefs, issued them rations, and offered them shelter. Earlier, in a report to Sherman, Hazen had made the curious statement that ". . . all the Kiowas and Comanches are at peace, excepting their old habits of thieving and murdering in Texas."

Even as these events were taking place, another human drama was being acted out, one in which fate played a tragic role. Before Hazen had arrived at Fort Cobb, Agent Walkley had reported the release of five Texas children who had been held captive by the Kiowas and Comanches. Rescue of the children had been accomplished through the aid of an Indian woman, Cheyenne Jennie. In his report on the matter, Walkley wrote:

> Too much cannot be said in praise of "Cheyenne Jennie", (wife of Wm. Griffenstein,) for the interest she took and exertion she made in recovering the captive children from the Comanches, visiting their camps, invalid as she was, riding in her ambulance when she was not able to sit up, giving up her own horses for the McElroy children that they might go home with their Father. She also had great influence with all the wild Indians which she used in trying to have them keep on the straight road. "Her work is done; she has gone to her happy hunting grounds."

Cheyenne Jennie had also tried to rescue a white woman and her child from the Cheyennes. The woman was Mrs. Clara Blinn, who had been captured near Fort Lyon on October 9. Jennie had sent a man (Sheridan identified him as "Cheyenne Jack") to the Cheyenne camps to see what could be done about securing the woman's release. While there, the messenger gave Mrs. Blinn a piece of paper so that she could write a letter. Mrs. Blinn's letter, a pathetic transcript of frontier life, was released by the military command to the press, and it appeared in many Kansas and eastern newspapers:

Saturday, November 7, 1868

KIND FRIEND—Whoever you may be, I thank you for your kindness to me and my child. You want me to let you know my wishes. If you could only buy us of the Indians with ponies or anything, and let me come stay with you until I could get word to my friends, they would pay you, and I would work and do all I could for you. If it is not too far to their camp, and you are not afraid to come, I pray you will try. They tell me, as near as I can understand, they expect traders to come and they will sell us to them. If it is Mexicans, I am afraid they would sell us into slavery in Mexico. If you can do nothing for me write to W. T. Harrington, Ottawa, Franklin County, Kansas—my father. Tell him we are with the Cheyennes and they say when the white men make peace we can go home. Tell him to write to the Governor of Kansas about it and for them to make peace. Send this to him. We were taken on the 9th of October on the Arkansas, below Fort Lyon. Cannot tell whether they killed my husband or not. My name is Mrs. Clara Blinn. My little boy, Willie Blinn, is two years old. Do all you can for me; write to the Peace Commissioners to make peace this fall. For our sakes do all you can, and God will bless you. If you can let me hear from you again let me know what you think about it. Write my father; send him this. Goodby.

Mrs. R. F. Blinn

I am as well as can be expected, but my baby is very weak.

But, tragically, Cheyenne Jennie herself died even as Mrs. Blinn was being contacted. When the latter arrived at Fort

Cobb, Hazen forwarded it to military headquarters in Missouri, stating that he had given the trader Griffenstein "full care of this case with permission to trade with the friendly Indians nearest the Cheyennes, with directions to spare no expense in his efforts to reclaim these parties."

That was on November 25. On that same day, Custer's 7th Cavalry was crossing the snow-covered dividing ridge between Wolf Creek and the South Canadian; and Governor Samuel Crawford's force of 19th Kansas Volunteers, marching from Topeka to join Sheridan's expedition at Camp Supply, was floundering, badly lost and facing starvation, in the broken country of the Cimarron.

Chapter VII
MARCH OF THE 19TH KANSAS

It was not the most momentous military operation in history; in fact, it was one of the most disastrous. But there were few military marches in western history that were more difficult and trying than the one made by the 19th Kansas Volunteer Cavalry from Topeka to Camp Supply in November of 1868. It was commonly agreed by the men of the regiment who had served with the Union and Confederate armies that they had experienced nothing like it during the recent war.

Feeling against the Indians was fever-high in Kansas during the fall of 1868. An attempt to provide protection to the frontier settlements and lines of transportation had been made with the formation, in July 1867, of the 18th Regiment of Kansas Volunteer Cavalry, commanded by Major Horace L. Moore. Consisting of only four troops, and hard hit at the offset by cholera, the 18th was as ineffective as the 7th Cavalry had been in catching the fleeting Indians on the vast ranges of western Kansas.

Following the raids along the Solomon and Saline rivers in August of 1868, Governor Samuel J. Crawford had wired Sheridan offering to raise a battalion of picked men if the Army would furnish five hundred Spencer carbines with accouterments and ammunition. Sheridan immediately accepted the proposition, and on September 14 Crawford issued a proclamation calling for troops to be organized into a militia for service on the frontier.

Enlistment would be for a period of three months, each man to furnish his own horse. These five companies of state militia, known as the Frontier Battalion, were commanded by Major George B. Jenness.

Following the failures of Forsyth and Sully to punish the Indians, Sheridan secured authority to extend the enlistment of the new unit, now designated as the 19th Kansas Volunteer Cavalry, to six months. The Army would furnish the horses and clothing as well as equipment, arms, and subsistence. Sheridan wired approval of this to Crawford on October 9, and, on the day following, the fiery Kansas governor issued another proclamation call to arms.

Crawford, an adamant Indian hater, had led an eventful career as an officer during the Civil War, for some time commanding the 83rd United States Colored Infantry and eventually attaining the brevet rank of brigadier general of volunteers, at the end of the war. A Hoosier who had come to Kansas in 1859 to practice law, Crawford had received a commission as a captain of volunteers when the war began. He took part in the battles of Wilson's Creek and Shelbina under General Lyon during the early fighting, then returned to Kansas, where he helped to recruit the 2nd Kansas Cavalry. After serving in New Mexico, Missouri, and Arkansas, he was tendered the colonelcy of the black 83rd at Fort Smith, Arkansas. Crawford commanded this regiment in numerous clashes with the Confederates, and in leading his troops in a bayonet charge during the battle of Jenkin's Ferry, he had his horse shot from under him. When the Rebels announced they would take no prisoners from units that fought under the "black flag," Crawford responded by vowing to take no Rebel prisoners in kind.

In 1864 he was nominated by the Republicans in Kansas as their candidate for governor. But Crawford had to put politics to one side for a time, as Confederate General "Pap" Price invaded Missouri from Arkansas and threatened Kansas. As a member of General Curtis' staff, he took part in the battle of Westport, leading a cavalry charge against the Confederates and routing them. Two days later, on October 25, 1864, he led another saber charge at the battle of the Little Osage. There he was joined by a young colonel, "full of fire," named Frederick Benteen, whose "most gallant and desperate cavalry charge" helped to defeat the Rebels under Marmaduke and Cabell.

Two weeks later, on November 8, Crawford won the election for governor of Kansas, and he was installed the following January. When the war ended, he faced the Indian situation of western Kansas as his most severe problem. Quickly establishing himself as an exponent of the punitive policy in dealing with the Indians, Crawford led the cause in promoting strong military action against the "wild beasts and savage barbarians" of the plains. When twelve wagons loaded with presents for the Indians who were to attend the Medicine Lodge council arrived at Lawrence, Crawford had threatened to burn the whole outfit if Sherman did not prevent the train from reaching the Indians. Sherman was forced to place the train under the guard of a 7th Cavalry troop from Fort Riley, which escorted it to Fort Larned. There it was held until the treaty council.

Crawford's proclamation of October 10, 1868, was an impassioned plea for the settlers' cause in Kansas:

Executive Office, October 10, 1868

With scarcely an exception all the tribes of Indians on the plains of Kansas or contiguous thereto, have taken up arms against the Government, and are now engaged in acts of hostility. The peace of the exposed border is thereby disturbed, quiet and unoffending citizens driven from their homes, or ruthlessly murdered, and their property destroyed or carried away. In fact children have been carried into captivity and in many instances barbarously murdered; while many women have been repeatedly violated in the presence of their husbands and families.

Besides these instances of individual suffering, great public interests are being crippled and destroyed by this savage hostility. The commerce of the plains is entirely suspended. The mail routes, and the great lines of travel to the territory and states beyond us, are constantly being blockaded, and are sometimes completely closed for the space of several days.

Longer to forbear with these bloody fiends would be a crime against civilization, and against the peace, security, and lives of all the people on the frontier. The time has come when they must be

Major George A. Forsyth won a brevet lieutenant-generalcy for his brave but foolhardy invasion of the Cheyenne Dog Soldier and Sioux hunting grounds with a fifty-man force of frontier scouts. *Courtesy of Kansas State Historical Society.*

Colonel Samuel F. Tappan, whose sympathy for the Indian was well known throughout Kansas and Colorado, denounced Custer's victory at the Washita. *Courtesy of State Historical Society of Colorado.*

This photo of Major Edward W. Wynkoop was taken during his
military days as a member of the Colorado First Cavalry. *Courtesy of
State Historical Society of Colorado.*

Lieutenant Fred Beecher, who was killed during the fight on the Arikaree along with the famed Cheyenne war leader Roman Nose, was a nephew of Henry Ward Beecher. *Courtesy of Kansas State Historical Society.*

Major Joel Elliott, who had won a high rank in the 7th Cavalry through examination, was a zealous officer whose eagerness carried him to his death at the Washita. *Courtesy of Kansas State Historical Society.*

Captain David L. Payne, member of the 19th Kansas, which helped establish Fort Sill, later became famous as the leading boomer for the opening of unassigned lands within the Indian Territory. *Courtesy of Kansas State Historical Society.*

Ben Clark, who was married to a Cheyenne woman, served as a guide for Sully and with Custer at the Washita. His accounts of the Washita fight, given later in life, were often inaccurate. *Courtesy of Western History Collections, University of Oklahoma.*

met by an adequate force, not only to prevent the repetition of these outrages, but to penetrate their haunts, break up their organizations, and either exterminate the tribes or confine them upon reservations set apart for their occupancy. To this end the Major-General commanding this department has called upon the Executive for a regiment of cavalry from this State.

During October, Topeka began to fill with recruits from the towns, frontier settlements, and farms of Kansas—homesteaders, teamsters, ex-soldiers of the war, frontiersmen, raw youths, soldiers of fortune, men down on their luck and needing employment, professional men who thought that a bit of soldiering would be fun—all united in their conviction that the Indian must be killed or driven from Kansas. Most were under forty, a large number between eighteen and twenty-one. Two legislative halls of the statehouse were used to quarter the new arrivals until Camp Crawford was established on two farms which were rented near town. Trainload after trainload of clothing, arms, food, and other supplies began arriving from Fort Leavenworth. Hundreds of horses, accumulated from over Kansas, Iowa, and Missouri, were shipped or driven in. Each was inspected, branded, and shod before being placed in a newly fenced pasture on the edge of Topeka. One night the horses, many of them not yet halterbroken, broke loose and stampeded through the city, the ring of their shoes on the hard streets being heard for some distance.

Major Moore of the 18th was appointed as lieutenant colonel of the new unit. An unsmiling but good-natured man who had during the war served as a troop commander under Crawford and later commanded the 4th Arkansas Cavalry, he was well-liked by the men. There was a temporary rebellion among the men of the 18th, who refused to muster in when they learned that Captain Henry C. Lindsey of their Troop A was not to receive the major's post in the 19th. But Lindsey persuaded them to go ahead, and 108 of them were enlisted in the new regiment on October 20. George Jenness took command of Troop F, while another former 18th officer, David L. Payne, was made captain of Troop H. Payne would later gain fame as the leader of the

Boomer movement, which pushed for the opening of the Oklahoma lands to settlement.

A. J. Pliley, the highly regarded scout who had been with Forsyth at Beecher's Island, was given the command of Company A. Though only twenty-four years of age at the time, Pliley was referred to as "an old soldier and scout" by Kansas newspapers. C. P. Twiss of Allen County arrived in Topeka with one hundred eleven men he had recruited, and they were mustered in, with Twiss as captain of Troop C. All together, twelve companies of mounted troops were quickly recruited, enlisted, uniformed, and drilled into shape. The regiment was divided into three battalions.

On November 4, with orders from Sheridan to march immediately for the Indian Territory, Crawford resigned his governor's office to become commanding colonel of the new regiment. Troops D and G of the 19th were ordered to embark by rail with all their horses and equipment for Fort Hays. There they would serve as an escort for Sheridan and a wagon train of supplies headed for the Territory.

On the morning of the fifth, the handsomely uniformed 19th Kansas—their shiny new Spencer carbines slung across the backs of their blue tunics, a thousand strong led by twenty-one buglers and each platoon riding full abreast to fill the broad Kansas Avenue from curb to curb—rode proudly and confidently southwestward out of Topeka while throngs of citizens waved farewell from sidewalks, doors, and housetops. The regiment was followed by fifteen 6-mule wagons, which carried only five days' rations for men and animals. Sheridan had anticipated only a five or six days' march, but it had been planned that new supplies and forage for the horses would be available at the Little Arkansas River, some one hundred fifty miles distant.

The first camp was made that afternoon on the Wakarusa, with plenty of wood, a clear sky, and a happy feeling for this business of soldiering. However, the supply train did not reach camp in time for the evening meal, and the soldiers ate their food without salt, pepper, or bread—a mild initiation to much greater hardships to follow.

The last signs of civilization, except for an occasional homestead, quickly disappeared as the Kansas volunteers rode mile after mile over the rolling hills, eventually striking the rutted Santa Fe Trail, which led them to Burlingame and on to the Neosho River, where camp was made. It had rained most of the day, soaking the blankets in the wagons as well as the men, so much so that even fires would not dry out the bedding. That night, the wind blew fiercely, and the rain changed to a melting snow that soaked through the canvas pup tents where rain would not. Many of the men developed colds and sore throats.

Now came the nemesis of armies throughout history—mud! It was "long, ropey, stringy, sticky, Kansas mud" which clung like black mortar to the men and stock alike as they marched across the plains. It virtually pulled the shoes from the horses as they passed through it. Nor was there any relief when the unit reached Emporia, which "looked so discouraged and homesick that the soldiers floundering through the miry streets felt sorry for it." On the evening of November 7, camp was made near Cottonwood Falls, and on the ninth the regiment passed a man who was at work building a cabin. The man told the troops that he was starting a town, which he planned to name El Dorado. Later they encamped near a homestead settlement to the west which was called Towanda. There the troops saw the last lumber house they would see until returning home the following April.

The small settlement of Wichita, with some two hundred inhabitants and as many buffalo wallows, stood at the juncture of the Little Arkansas with the Arkansas. Some two miles distant was Camp Beecher, which consisted of a rudely constructed log building for army supplies, another, smaller one for the post sutler, one or two adobes, and four or five bark-and-grass wickiups belonging to some Kaw Indians. The 19th went into camp below the post, between the two rivers. Crawford had anticipated finding ten days' rations waiting for him at the camp, but he discovered that most of the supplies had already been consumed by the few regular troops stationed there, while only a portion of the forage for the horses and mules had arrived from Fort Riley. Nor were there extra wagons for transportation as had been expected.

Crawford faced a difficult decision. From here on, the country was virtually unknown, most white men having been kept out of the Indian Territory by the government, and the maps were extremely vague. To proceed into uncharted territory with grossly inadequate supplies, unseasoned horses, and only partially disciplined troops, during winter, was a hazardous undertaking. On the other hand, Sheridan had given orders and was waiting. According to the Camp Beecher troops, there were plenty of buffalo ahead. Sheridan had sent the 19th two scouts to serve as guides to the confluence of the Beaver and the Wolf; one was Jack Stillwell, who had been with Forsyth, and the other was a man called Apache Bill Seaman. Apache Bill declared himself familiar with the wild, unbroken region ahead, known only as "Dutch Henry's Trail." Among the men of the 19th, it was reputed to be a country from which few white men returned. In the words of one trooper: "Here I wrote a letter to my mother . . . as we were told it would probably be the last chance, as that was the end of civilization and few were known to come out alive that went South of the Arkansas River."

After a couple of days' rest, during which the horses were reshod and the command tightened up where it had shaken loose on the first half of the march, the 19th began crossing the Arkansas to the south bank on the morning of November 14. The cavalry crossed first, then double rows of horsemen snaked the wagons across with rope cables. A strange foreboding seemed to affect the men and horses alike in "this land of silence and desolation." The horses "were uneasy, and there seemed a smoldering excitement among them. John Linton, Captain Pliley's farrier, a fine horseman, said the night of the thirteenth: 'If I was superstitious I would look for something terrible to happen, them horses act so queer. I believe there is something on this side of the river that makes them homesick.'" He was correct: something soon did happen to the horses.

On the evening of the sixteenth, the regiment reached the Chikaskia, and there the last of the corn was fed to the horses, making it necessary for the animals to forage off the land from there on. Medicine Lodge Creek was reached on the eighteenth, and it was there that a near disaster struck the regiment. Having had only the dry prairie grass to eat, a source of little nutriment, the horses and mules were hungry and nervous. When the regiment went into camp that night, the troops formed by battalion a three-sided box inside of which the supply train was to be driven when it arrived. Most of the troops had dismounted, unsaddled, and hitched their mounts to the picket line when a soldier arrived late and unsaddled his horse. Anxious to grab a piece of firewood he had spotted, he tied his horse's halter rope to his saddle on the ground. When the horse moved and jerked the saddle, it frightened the animal, causing it to bolt, kicking and bucking with the saddle bouncing behind. The horse's panic quickly spread to the other animals of B, I, and K troops, the horses and mules rearing at the picket lines, jerking out the stakes, and erupting into a wild, screaming stampede. Joseph Phelps Rodgers, a member of Troop F, described the event:

> Now 100 horses tied to one line came through the camp, tearing down the tents, overturning the wagons. There was much confusion, the men trying to get out of the way. I think there were about 600 horses in the stampede. I happened to be on rear guard that day and just got off my horse and was going to unsaddle when here they came, our own Company horses, tore loose the line and before I had time was caught in the center of the line, my horse on the dead run, the cable around my back. I had the presence of mind to keep the spurs in my horse and as soon as I could get my knife out I cut the cable and was free, but kept right on with the stampede. Now and then a horse would fall when his halter strap would break. The next morning I found myself several miles from camp, rounding up what horses I could find. I soon had plenty of help, as about 100 had not broken loose.

About eighty horses were lost, and several men were injured. One man was caught in the picket rope and dragged nearly a mile, almost being killed. Captains Pliley and Finch trailed some of the horses nearly fifty miles, but the animals were headed home and were impossible to catch. The men without horses were put in the rear of the columns, ahead of the wagons, and the mounted men of their companies would trade off with them a few miles at a time.

The regiment moved out on the nineteenth completely without

forage for the stock and with few supplies for themselves. Evening mess in Troop F was two small hams, two pounds of flour, a few cans of tomatoes and sardines, all dumped into a camp kettle with some water. It was their only meal of the day and their last for forty hours. Hardtack had become "legal tender." It was expected that a wagon train would meet them, and when smoke was seen in the distance the men thought it was the relief train. But after marching some sixteen miles, the regiment arrived at a creek, and scouts searched more than ten miles up the stream without discovering even a trail. The men, who had marched all day on empty bellies sustaining themselves with visions of a feast that evening, were much disappointed, and considerable grumbling was heard.

It had begun to rain again, and by nightfall the men were soaked to the skin as a fierce north wind drove temperatures down close to zero. With the wagon train far in the rear, fires impossible to keep alive in the wind, the horses still starving and frightened, and the sky moonless and dark, the troops shivered through a long and painful night. Many of them remained at their horses' heads to quiet the nervous animals.

On the following day, when sent to search out a suitable place to cross the river, soldier James A. Hadley had an even more painful experience when he stepped off into deep water:

> Just as this happened the cloak of my overcoat was wrapped around my head by the wind. The sudden cold and surprise caused the horse to plunge and struggle, while I, disconcerted by the ducking and blindness, was not for the moment sitting firmly in the saddle, so was easily thrown off into deep water. Wearing very high boots, my overcoat buttoned and belted outside with two pistols, I came very near sinking. Being only twenty years old, and knowing that I was being introduced to death, I was full of panic, but had sense enough not to try to reach shore or struggle in any way. I finally got my face clear, the alarm was given, a rope was thrown to me, which I caught at last and was pulled out. When I reached the fire I was sheathed in ice. This was soon melted off, and I kept my place in the column all day without ill effects either from the ducking or the bitter experience of the night before. My clothes dried during the day in spite of the cold.

Since leaving the Arkansas River, the troops had been supplementing their meager rations with fresh buffalo meat killed for them by hunting parties. The men ate their slices of buffalo without salt, roasted over the coals of their campfires—"buffalo straight," it was called. On the twenty-second, just north of the Cimarron, the hunters were unsuccessful in finding any game. With the meat of the kill of two days before gone, the only food in camp that night was six barrels of sugar cubes for coffee in the officers' stores—"not a mouthful of rations in the entire command." On top of this, there was a tobacco famine among the men, and tempers were raw. Crawford ordered the sugar cubes counted out three to the man. Two men in Company L, both powerfully built, got into an argument over their rations of the sugar, and one of the hardest fights seen by the regiment occurred, the two "smashing each other beautifully 'till the guard interfered."

It had begun to snow that afternoon, the twenty-first, and by dark there was over five inches of snow on the ground, eighteen by morning. With the animals unable to graze in the snow, the troops cut down cottonwood limbs for them to eat. But this was far from satisfactory, and the hungry horses neighed and the mules brayed to set up a crescendo of complaint all the morning. "But those poor horses and mules," a trooper wrote; "it made one sick to see them begging."

Many of the animals died on the picket line, and almost all of them became too weak and exhausted to travel. The men, too, were in bad shape. Orders were given not to ride the horses without permission, though the men with frozen feet had to do so anyway. Some of them wept in regret that they had ever come on this expedition; some cursed the government roundly; and others muttered threats of desertion. When several men had deserted earlier, no one went after them, as hardly anyone could bring himself to really blame them.

It was a march impossible to adequately describe; horses stumbling and shrinking from the knife-like gale, men with heads down and covered with their overcoat capes, staggering after their file leaders, chilled to the bone and slapping, stamping, and pounding themselves in desperate endeavor to keep up a circulation of the blood.

It now became clear that Apache Bill had never been in this country before, and there was much talk among the men of hanging him for claiming to know the way when he didn't. The scout stayed close to Crawford during the remainder of the march.

Crawford decided to send a force on ahead to contact Sheridan, if possible, and have supplies sent back. Pliley was selected for the task, and with fifty of the best mounted men in troops A and C he rode off into the snowstorm on the evening of the twenty-second, the same storm in which Custer and the 7th Cavalry would march toward the Washita on the following morning. The rest of Crawford's command lay in camp on the twenty-third, the snow still falling so heavily that it was impossible to move. Private Spotts wrote in his diary on that date:

> Our hunters are out today but the snow is so blinding and the wind so cold that they return in a few hours with no success. We have no food so we just spread our ponchos on the snow and make our beds on them a little distance from the fire. We have a great pile of dry wood and we sit or stand around the fire and listen to the boys tell what they will do when they get to Camp Supply. When some one begins to curse the Government or some one for our condition, everyone jumps on him, calls him a growler or tells him he will know how to appreciate a "square meal" when we get to camp. The idea is to be cheerful under any circumstances and if we don't feel that way it is wise to keep still.

Finally the morning of November 24 broke clear, and the command moved out with the men leading their starving and exhausted horses. It was feared that if game was not found soon, the men would have to eat their horses, thereby nullifying any hope of being of assistance to Sheridan. All day the 19th tromped through knee-high snow, the various companies taking turns at the weary task of breaking a trail through the drifts and finding a course around the snow-covered canyons. At mid-morning a buffalo bull was killed, and each man got a few bites, or "1-1000th part of a buffalo." Later, shortly before sundown, a herd of bulls was discovered, themselves mired in the deep snow. The entire herd was killed, and that night the troops feasted on buffalo meat. Even without salt it tasted delicious to the hungry men, though it gave them severe diarrhea. Some boiled the meat in the briny water of the area, giving it a salty taste, while even the bones were roasted and broken open for the marrow.

Camp was made that night near some high hills that were covered with hackberry trees. The trees were loaded with berries, which were almost all seed and very little meat. But to the famished troops the berries tasted sweet, and the men climbed through the trees devouring the hackberries by handfuls, seeds and all, while others made tea from the berries. Later, when the seeds would not digest, many of the men became dangerously constipated, taking freely of castor oil and salts. One man almost died from eating hackberries and buffalo hoofs, which clogged his rectum. Though the name of this camp was officially designated as "Camp Hackberry Point," it became famous to the men of the 19th as "Camp Starvation." Again the wagon train was far in the rear when camp was reached, and the men slept the night of November 24 in the snow without blankets.

Another decision was now made. On the theory that it would be best to divide the command, leaving the sick, partially frozen, and dismounted men to subsist on the buffalo in the Cimarron Hills, Crawford and Moore would take the strongest and hardiest men and horses of the command and push on to join Sheridan, without food, bedding, or tents. Close to five hundred men were selected to go, while some six hundred were left behind under the command of Major R. W. Jenkins. The latter group was to remain at Camp Starvation until they could be rescued.

It was the afternoon of the twenty-fifth when Crawford led his segment of the 19th out of camp with the sun shining and the snow glistening brightly. Taking the course of a deep canyon that led to the Cimarron Valley, he blindly followed its tortuous course most of the day.

The snow thawed considerably as Crawford led his men, often dismounted, in single file winding around the cliffs and banks of the rugged Cimarron country. They were badly lost: "We were not certain where we were, nor where we were to go, nor where we were to get our future rations. We had been living on buffalo meat, without bread, salt, or pepper, from the 20th, . . ." wrote Assistant Surgeon Ezra P. Russell in a letter from Camp Supply later.

We marched southwest from the Cimarron, across the roughest country I ever saw. Bonaparte crossing the Alps was no comparison to our trip. It was the grandest sight I ever saw. The gulches were so deep, narrow and steep, that only one man could pass at a time, and lead his horse. The command numbered five hundred men, and you, with your fertile imagination, can imagine how they looked marching through these hills. We were three days making forty-five miles.

Finally a point was found where the steep-banked river could be crossed, and under a full moon camp was made on the high ground beyond. Snow was scraped away to allow the horses to graze on the frozen grass, and a killed deer provided a treat for the men.

On November 26, Thanksgiving Day, the Kansans were blessed with a buffalo to eat. At noon on the following day, as they struggled through deep, ice-crusted snow, the scouts discovered the trail of Pliley and his men. Following it, the command that night reached a wide-bedded river, which was judged to be the North Canadian. From among the oak and walnut trees along the stream, the men secured an ample supply of wild turkey as well as more venison. The spirits of the volunteers now began to lift and, during the march of the following day, those spirits soared:

About mid-afternoon a roar broke out in the column and followed back to the guard. When it faded a little, it broke out again, clearer and louder every time. It was good, hearty, old-fashioned cheering too. The occasion for the men having a conniption fit just there was, first, a stump whence the tree had recently been cut by the white man's ax; second, a wagon track since the snowstorm; third, some fresh chips on the snow! The fourth and last cheering was due to a messenger from the advance who informed Colonel Moore that Supply was in sight not five miles away.

Soon the men reached a high bluff from where they could see the white tents of the cantonment less than a mile away, and there was "the most beautiful of all inanimate objects, the flag, silently floating in dignified power over the garrison. Even as we looked a puff of white smoke appeared, the flag came fluttering down like a wounded bird, and in a moment or so the boom of the evening salute filled the whole valley."

Sheridan had a much appreciated camping spot readied for them. Snow had been scraped off, and tents pitched, with hay in every tent for bedding. No one could have enjoyed the luxury of sleeping under canvas and in the warm comfort of dry hay more than did the men of the 19th. Pliley and his fifty men had reached Supply on the twenty-fifth, and supplies had already been dispatched back to Camp Starvation. Jenkins and the remainder of the regiment reached Camp Supply later, the men badly constipated and in severe pain. When the wagon train had reached them, they had been allowed to eat only a little at a time, three hours apart. Some had not slept, fearing they would miss their share.

Sheridan had been very distraught over the failure of the 19th to arrive on time. As one of the officers of the Kansas regiment put it: instead of a "full regiment of gallant Kansas volunteers, finely mounted and equipped," Sheridan got a "disorganized band of half-starved men, a regiment of worn out and emaciated horses, so reduced that there was hardly a serviceable horse in the command."

Many of the horses would remain in such poor condition throughout the rest of the winter that the effectiveness of the 19th as a fighting unit would be seriously impaired. Sheridan angrily blamed Crawford for not relying on his guides. Still the march had been made without the loss of a man, and most considered this an accomplishment of merit in view of the circumstances of the unpredictable plains weather, the faulty supply efforts of the Army, and lack of capable guides to direct their course. Even so, this was only the first leg of a long journey for the men of the 19th Kansas.

Chapter VIII
CUSTER'S LUCK

The day before their departure from Camp Supply—November 22, Sunday—the men of the 7th Cavalry had been busy preparing for the march. "Everybody was in prime condition as regards health and spirits, and the whole outfit was in for it, whether it turned out to be a fight, a fluke or a frolic." Troops were released from fort-building details. Supplies for thirty days were drawn and loaded as compactly as possible into the wagons, three wagons to each troop, including one for troop mess, one for officers' mess and extra ammunition, and one for forage. Each man was equipped with a magazine-carbine Spencer and a Colt revolver with paper cartridges and caps. Horses were allowed to graze and were fed extra grain. Both officers and men discarded surplus clothing and personal items from their rolls and reduced their wardrobes to what they could carry conveniently with them on their horses. The camp bustled with activity as Custer's army of eight hundred effectives prepared for the first winter's expedition against the Plains tribes into a country barely known to the white man. As one officer described it: "Our exact destination was problematical, the location of the hostile villages was purely a matter of conjecture, and while we all knew we were operating on a 'war path' basis, our movements seemed to be enveloped in an impenetrable cloud of mystery."

That evening, it began to snow and the men retired to their

tents to pen a final letter to family or friends or to make the day's entry in a diary. It snowed all night, and when reveille pulled the troopers from their shelters at four o'clock the next morning, they found over a foot of snow on the ground, with still more being whipped down by a stinging north wind. The shivering horses received little grooming from the equally cold troopers, who quickly headed for the campfires, where, with the collars of their greatcoats turned up to their caps, they grabbed quick bites of breakfast and hot cups of coffee, standing in snow almost to their boot tops.

It was still dark when the general call sounded, ordering a dismantling of tents and final packing of wagons in readiness for the march. Mule skinners maneuvered their teams into position and harnessed them to the wagons with almost frozen hands, while each soldier caught and bridled his horse and led it into company formation. Then the bugler sounded "Boots and Saddles," and each man began saddling his mount and adjusting his gear. Soon the various commanders reported that their companies were ready to march. Custer, followed by his orderly, galloped to where Sheridan's tent stood in the snow, sentry in front.

Sheridan had been awake listening to the activity in the darkness outside, still with some doubts about sending troops out in such inclement weather. Custer, however, was ready and eager to march. The snow was just what he wanted, he told Sheridan. He could move; the Indians could not. Sheridan acceded to this, admonished his field commander to take good care of the troops, and returned to the warmth of his blankets.

Custer now ordered the call "To Horse" sounded, and each trooper took his place at his animal's head. Shortly, there followed the commands "Prepare to Mount" and "Mount," and officers and men wheeled their horses into line. Then the bugle notes sounded "Advance," and by "foursright" the line swung into four columns, forming a long line of dark shapes moving out to become swallowed from the view of those behind by the snowy darkness. At the head of the columns was the band, playing a marching tune, "The Girl I Left Behind Me," as it rode.

Originally, Custer had intended to go back up the Beaver and follow the Indian trail they had seen there on the way to Supply, but now it would be covered by the snow. Instead he headed up Wolf Creek with the intention of driving to the South Canadian, on down to the Washita and Fort Cobb, and then southwest to the Wichita Mountains.

The expedition moved southwestward along the northwest bank of Wolf Creek, scouts in advance, followed by Custer and his staff officers, the eleven companies of the 7th and Cook's sharpshooters, and, stretching a long distance behind, the lumbering wagon train. It was so dark and gloomy that even the Osage guides were unsure of their course, and Custer himself took the lead and guided the command with his compass. At around two o'clock in the afternoon, fifteen miles south of Camp Supply, the expedition forded the frozen Wolf Creek at what would become known as "Custer's Crossing." With his wagon train far behind and the horses of the regiment wearying quickly, Custer selected a wooded clump in the Wolf Creek Valley and made an early camp.

Soon the cooks had the coffeepots on, while officers and men, all wet to the skin from the snow, busied themselves in clearing places for their tents. The valley was alive with rabbits, and rabbit stew was the fare for most company messes that day. Many of the cavalrymen later suffered sore backs from the warping of their saddle trees which was caused by the wet snow soaking through the saddle leather. Private Winfield Harvey of Troop K penned in his diary: "At night we had to lay in snow eighteen inches deep with our clothes all wet and freezing, although we had plenty of wood and good fires to keep us warm."

Reveille was sounded at four the next morning, and the troops arose to find that the storm had abated during the night, leaving the countryside a vast expanse of snowy whiteness. California Joe pronounced that the clear sky meant "the travellin' was good overhead." But when time came to move out, several wagons were still unhitched; in fact, some of the teamsters' tents were still pitched. Custer was furious. He ordered the guilty teamsters and their wagon masters arrested by the officer of the day. As punishment he forced them to march on foot through the deep snow for several hours until they humbly promised to be ready whenever the military units were prepared to move in the future.

Wolf Creek had bent sharply to the west at about the point of crossing, and now Custer's army headed along the south bank, away from the bright morning sun, which glistened brilliantly upon the snow and caused many cases of eye discomfort and some snow blindness. Buffalo which had bunched in groves of trees for protection against the storm were seen in number, as well as an occasional deer. The Indian guides and white scouts kept the command in good supply of fresh meat, particularly of buffalo meat, since the hapless animals could barely move in the deep snow. Custer, ever ready to enjoy some sport, took time out himself to try his luck, as he describes in *My Life on the Plains.*

Seeing a fine herd of young buffaloes a short distance in the advance, I determined to test the courage of my stag-hounds "Blucher" and "Maida." Approaching as near the herd as possible before giving them the alarm, I managed to single out and cut off from the main herd a fine yearling bull. My horse, a trained hunter, was soon alongside, but I was unable to use my pistol to bring the young buffalo down, as both dogs were running close to either side and by resolutely attacking him endeavoring to pull him down. It was a new experience to them; a stag they could easily have mastered, but a lusty young buffalo bull was an antagonist of different caliber. So determined had the dogs become, their determination strengthened no doubt by the vigorous blows received from the ready hoofs of the buffalo, that I could not call them off; neither could I render them assistance from my pistol, for fear of injuring them. There was nothing left for me to do but to become a silent although far from disinterested participant in the chase. The immense drifts of snow through which we were struggling at our best pace would soon vanquish one or the other of the party; it became a question of endurance simply, and the buffalo was the first to come to grief. Finding escape by running impossible, he boldly came to bay and faced his pursuers; in a moment both dogs had grappled with him as if he had been a deer. Blucher seized him by the throat, Maida endeavored to secure a firm hold on the shoulders. The result was that Blucher found himself well trampled in the snow, and but for the latter would have been crushed to death. Fearing for the safety of my dogs, I leaped from my horse, who I knew would not leave me, and ran to the assistance of the stag-hounds. Drawing my hunting-knife and watching a favorable op-portunity, I succeeded in cutting the hamstrings of the buffalo, which had the effect to tumble him over in the snow, when I was enabled to despatch him with my pistol.

Crossing several small tributaries of Wolf Creek, including the Little Wolf, the Indian-hunting expedition continued another eighteen miles westward up the river before making camp on the second afternoon. Resuming the march again on the morning of the twenty-fifth, still having encountered no sign of an Indian war party having crossed Wolf Creek, Custer ordered a change of direction to due south, toward the Antelope Hills. The march between rivers was difficult and slow. Cresting the dividing ridge between the Wolf and the South Canadian, the command reached the Canadian Valley after dark. They went into camp a mile from the river on a fresh-water tributary, likely Commission Creek.

Though he quite probably did not know it, Custer was only a short distance from Little Robe Creek, where on May 12, 1858, Captain John "Old Rip" Ford and a force of Texas Rangers and friendly Anadarkoes had attacked a Comanche village. Ford claimed to have killed seventy-six Comanches, undoubtedly many of them being women and children but one of them being the chief Pohebits Quasho, or Iron Jacket. It was reported that when the rangers peeled back Iron Jacket's robes they found that underneath he wore a suit of Spanish armor.

That evening, Custer held a council with his staff, scouts, and Indian guides. It was the general opinion that the snowstorm would be driving back homeward any war parties that were out and that they would likely cross the South Canadian somewhere in the vicinity of the Antelope Hills, which now loomed against the sky just ahead. Since the direction of his march was to the southeast, toward Fort Cobb, Custer decided to send a scouting party up the river westward to look for Indian signs while the rest of the command would cross the icy, swollen South Cana-dian and march downstream some five or six miles to camp.

Major Elliott, second in command, was dispatched early the

next morning with three full troops—G under Captain Albert Barnitz, H under Captain Frederick Benteen, and M under First Lieutenant Owen Hale—to scout along the river some fifteen miles. If he should discover the trail of a war party, he was to take up pursuit and send back a courier to apprise Custer of the action. A few Osage and white scouts were assigned to Elliott, some of them to serve as messengers. The reconnoitering force rode off at daybreak, and Custer turned his attention to getting the wagon train to the south bank of the river. California Joe was assigned to locating a crossing. There was a great deal of quicksand in the river, but a comparatively safe fording place was found and the 7th Regiment led the way across, followed by the wagons.

Custer, accompanied by several officers and his chief bugler, galloped up the snow-covered bed of the South Canadian, from where the 7th Cavalry was making its crossing near the mouth of Commission Creek. South of the river loomed three giant plateaus, which with two other giant mounds, standing off to the southeast, constituted the Antelope Hills, sometimes called the Boundary Mounds. The center of the three closest to the river presented a steep but sloping side which allowed Custer and his party to reach its summit on horseback.

Rising two to three hundred feet above the prairie floor, the plateau provided a panoramic view in all directions, displaying an "immense circle of snowy whiteness," broken only by the lines of winter-black treetops and the jagged marks of snow-filled ravines. From the west, where the Texas panhandle lay not fifteen miles away, snaked the rusty-red river's channel, cutting around the north of the mounds in a huge oxbow and winding on eastward until it vanished from sight. Custer swept the snow-shrouded land with his field glasses, finding it frozen and silent.

He could see that the main column of the regiment, some six miles away and ant size at that distance, had already made its crossing of the icy channel at the top of the bend. As the troops regrouped on the high ground, the wagon train followed in line across the river and up the long incline of the south bank. Custer noted that the rear guard was closing up in good fashion behind the train and turned his glasses westward, up the river, in the direction he had sent Elliott. Custer was rewarded when in the far distance he spotted the dark figure of a horse and rider struggling through the snow field toward him.

Custer waited anxiously, wondering what news the courier could be bringing. Had Elliott not been able to find a crossing and sent for new orders? Had there been trouble of some sort? He had heard no firing. Or could it be that an Indian trail had been discovered, as had been hoped? Eventually the scout, Jack Corbin, pulled his winded mount up to the side of Custer to make a hurried report. After moving up the north bank of the river for some twelve miles, Elliott's command had found the trail of a large war party, estimated to be from one hundred to one hundred and fifty strong and to have passed there not more than a day earlier, since the tracks were only partially drifted with snow. Elliott had already crossed the South Canadian and was headed south by east in hot pursuit.

It was exciting news! This was the very thing Custer had hoped for the most, a trail that would lead them directly to an Indian village. Below him, his army was well armed, strongly mounted, and never more ready for a fight. Ahead was the great victory he sought and a return to the glory of past days. There could be no doubt: the famous "Custer's luck," on which many a cavalryman would have bet his wages until the Kansas affair, had returned, appropriately on this twenty-sixth day of November, Thanksgiving Day.

Custer was elated at Elliott's discovery. Ordering a fresh mount for the scout, he sent him hurrying back to catch up with Elliott, carrying orders for the unit to stay on the trail and to keep Custer advised if the Indians changed direction. The remainder of the regiment would drive directly south to join them before eight o'clock, if possible. If not, Elliott was to halt his command and wait for Custer.

Riding back to the regiment, Custer ordered the bugler to sound the call for all officers to join him. They did so, excited and anxious to know what Corbin had reported. Custer quickly explained the situation, that Elliott had no doubt found a "hot trail," and outlined his plans. The main command would move forward in just twenty minutes without the baggage train proper.

One wagon would be assigned to each squadron (two troops), one to Troop G and the teamsters, and one to headquarters— seven in all—and one ambulance, all under the command of quartermaster Lieutenant James M. Bell.

Each trooper would take only what supplies he could carry on his person or strap to his saddle. This would include a hundred rounds of ammunition, a small supply of coffee and hard bread, and an equally small amount of forage for his horse. There would be no extra blankets or tents. Eighty men, detailed from the various troops, would be left behind to guard the baggage train under the command of one officer. It was standard procedure that a different officer be detailed each day to command the train guard. It so happened that, on this particular day, that officer was Captain Louis Hamilton.

Captain Louis McLane Hamilton of Poughkeepsie, New York, was a grandson of Alexander Hamilton. He was also a grandson of Louis McLane, Secretary of State under President Jackson. When the War of the Rebellion had broken out, Hamilton had shunned any special privilege and enlisted in the 22nd Militia, serving at Harper's Ferry. Later he enlisted a company for the 159th New York Volunteers and could have received a commission then. Instead he joined the 3rd Infantry as a private and, with that unit, performed gallantly in combat, winning a field commission of second lieutenant. Later, when the regular brigade from the Army of the Potomac arrived in New York to control public rioting, Hamilton was placed on the staff of General Ayres. At the close of the war he preferred to continue his successful military career, and in the reorganization of the service was placed in the 7th Regiment as a ranking captain.

By all accounts, Hamilton was well liked by both men and officers. In part this was because of his zealous devotion to his role as a soldier and because he, more than any other officer in the 7th, represented the genteel tradition of the "gentleman officer," yet at the same time sought no special reward because of his family background.

Along with the other officers, Hamilton had watched the courier ride up and confer with Custer, then mount a fresh horse and gallop away to the south. When the officers were told that they were to advance quickly upon the enemy's trail, his excitement was unbounded. But then came the chilling realization that it was he who was the officer of the day on this moment in which history was about to be made, and it would be his responsibility to stay behind and command the train guard. Surely this could not happen. Surely, Custer would understand and make it possible for him to accompany the regiment.

Spurring his horse to Custer's side, Hamilton pleaded that he should be allowed to go along. Custer was in sympathy with him but said that he did not feel it would be just to another officer to make him replace Hamilton on duty with the train. Officer friends of Hamilton put in a word for him. One argued: "General, we ought to have Hamilton with us"; another: "It will kill Hamilton if he has to remain behind and his men are led into battle by another."

Finally Custer agreed that if Hamilton could find another officer who would willingly substitute for him, then an order for the change would be issued. The New Yorker spurred back down the line and soon returned to announce that he had found a junior officer, Second Lieutenant E. G. Mathey, who was probably persuaded that he suffered snow blindness and who disqualified himself from joining in the pursuit of the Indians. Custer then obliged Hamilton by allowing the officer to rejoin Troop A, which he normally commanded.

Meanwhile, the troops had been making ready for an accelerated march. Ammunition boxes were jerked from the wagons, their lids quickly pried open, and troopers grabbed handfuls of cartridges for their saddle pouches. Since they would likely be sleeping without tents, many of the men donned extra clothing. The best horses of the command were selected, and inferior ones were assigned to the wagon train. An air of hurried excitement prevailed as officers barked commands and troopers wheeled their horses into formation. Custer had said twenty minutes; in that time the command was ready.

It was midmorning of the twenty-sixth when Custer moved the regiment ahead at as fast a pace as the drifted snow would allow. The lead horses soon became badly fatigued by the work of plowing a trail through the drifts, and frequent changing of positions among the troops was necessary. All that day, the 7th Regiment moved forward in anticipation of catching up with Elliott's force, not pausing even for the slightest rest or food. Midafternoon came, and still there was no sign of the others. Custer grew more and more concerned that perhaps the Indians had changed course and Elliott's courier had not been able to find him. Flankers were kept out wide to scout for the trail, but evening came and there was still no word of Elliott's trail having been seen. Finally, as the sun was falling with winter quickness toward the western horizon, a scout yelled out his discovery of a trail in the snow. The shod-hoof marks indicated it was Elliott's force.

Now following the already broken path, Custer pushed ahead more rapidly. Even so, the flat country allowed visibility for miles, and no indication of life was to be seen through Custer's field glasses. A special detail of troopers and scouts was sent ahead at a gallop to overtake the unceasing Elliott and tell him to halt and await the main command. Once rejoined, they would rest the horses and troops for one hour before taking up the pursuit again.

The melting snow of the day concerned Custer, who feared that another day of sun might permit the Indians to escape. Neither men nor horses had rested or eaten since four o'clock that morning, and all were showing signs of fatigue. Still Custer pushed forward, and another three hours passed before finally, at nine o'clock, they came upon Elliott and his troops camped near a small stream, a tributary of the nearby Washita. With great relief, the men of the 7th swung from their saddles, stretched, rubbed their rumps, and stomped circulation into their feet. Horses were unsaddled, unbitted, and watered, and feed bags with oats were slipped over their noses. Custer allowed small fires for coffee to be built under the shelter of the riverbanks.

One hour, no more. A bright moon had now risen, with only thin clouds interfering. By ten o'clock the horses were resaddled and the unit re-formed without the use of bugle calls. Now that Elliott was overtaken, attention was focused on the main objective: catching the Indian war party they trailed. Custer moved slowly and carefully now, following eastward along the north bank of the Washita. Two Osage scouts led the way on foot several hundred yards in advance of the remainder of the scouts. Custer rode with the advance guard, while the 7th followed four abreast, "our long, dark column winding through the valley like a huge, black monster." The combined sounds of the horses' hoofs on the snow could be heard for some distance through the thin, cold air of the night. No one spoke above a whisper. Occasional howls of wolves floated to the ears of the troops, who felt a strange and undefinable sensation as they moved stealthily through this unknown, wild land of the Indian.

Again the march continued unceasingly, mile after mile. The men were drowsy in their saddles. The steady march was first broken when Custer was informed that the two lead scouts wanted to see him. Sending orders back along the line to halt, he rode forward, where one of the Osage scouts sniffed the air and declared, "Me smell fire." But when neither Custer nor any of the officers or white scouts could detect any unusual odor, it was decided that the Indian was imagining the smell. The march was continued cautiously, but within half a mile the scout again halted the column and this time pointed to where, some seventy-five yards off the trail, were the dying embers of a campfire.

The discovery caused considerable excitement and speculation as to the potential of Indians in the vicinity. Custer dispatched the Osage guides under Little Beaver and Hard Rope to advance with rifles ready to check on the fire. As the guides disappeared into a dark grove of trees leading toward the fire, Custer's command was forced to wait anxiously on their horses in the clear moonlight, extremely vulnerable to attack. Fortunately, however, the Osages soon returned to report that the campfire was abandoned. From the tracks that surrounded it, the Osages judged it to be the fire of Indian boys who were tending a pony herd. The news gave Custer and his officers reason to sigh in relief, and the march was taken up again with even greater caution.

Custer now rode with the two scouts at his horse's head. As each hill was approached, one of them would go forward in Indian fashion and take a cautious look beyond. It was after one such careful peek over a ridge that the Osage guide returned to report: "Heaps Injuns" ahead. This was the long awaited news indicating the possibility of an Indian village. Custer hurriedly dismounted and crept to the crest of the hill with the guide. In the moonlight he could see shapes that appeared to be a herd of buffalo nearly half a mile away. The guide said this was an Indian pony herd and meant that a camp was nearby.

"Me hear dog bark," the Osage added. The party listened intently, and soon the statement was confirmed by the sound of a dog barking and then reaffirmed by the tinkle of a bell. Custer nodded, conceding that buffalo were not in the habit of wearing bells but that Indian ponies sometimes did. Then came a final confirmation: the sound of an infant child's wail drifted to them from the river valley below.

Leaving the two Osages as lookouts, Custer returned to the regiment and brought his officers forward, ordering them to first remove their sabers. They then accompanied Custer to the hilltop, where they could take a look at the situation. As they viewed the valley beyond, Custer pointed out the horse herd and where, inside a loop of the Washita's south bank among some trees, he suspected there to be an Indian encampment. Returning to the command, Custer ordered the troops countermarched quietly to a distance where their chances of discovery were lessened. The wagons under First Lieutenant Bell and Troops H and M under Captain Benteen had been halted two or three miles back on the trail.

Scouts Ben Clark, Joe and Jack Corbin, and Romero, a Mexican who had been raised among the Cheyennes, were sent to reconnoiter closer to the river and determine the exact location and size of the suspected village. Carefully, so as not to alarm the Indian horse herd grazing between the command and the river, the three scouts crept to the north bank. Ben Clark later described the lay of the village:

> We drew close enough to see the smoke curling from the tops of the lodges and found that the village was on the south side of the river. It was an admirable camping place, in a big bend of the river on a level stretch of ground. Beyond the village and parallel to the swinging shore line of the river was an embankment, probably fifty feet high, with an almost perpendicular face. This embankment was

the abrupt termination of an undulating prairie which stretched away still further to the south. The lowland close to the river continued for several miles down the stream and merged gradually with the lessening height of the embankment into comparatively level ground. About a mile above the village was a trail which crossed the Washita. On the north side of the river were low spurs of hills, which increased in height northward until they reached much higher hills, to which they were almost at right angles. An Indian trail, followed by the war party, led down the river on the north side.

Heavy timber surrounded the camp site, but the scouts were able to count about fifty lodges. When they had reported back, Custer held a council with his officers, outlining his plan to divide the 7th into four units, which at a prearranged signal would strike the village simultaneously. Major Elliott would take companies G, H, and M and swing in a wide loop around the hills to the north of the village and attack from the timber to the northeast side below. With Elliott would go troop commanders Barnitz, Benteen, and Hale, plus second lieutenants T. J. Marsh and H. W. Smith.

Captain William Thompson would lead troops B and F to the crest of a hill south of the village and connect, if possible, with Elliott's battalion. With Thompson would be Captain George Yates, commanding F, and lieutenants D. M. Wallingford and F. M. Gibson.

Captain Edward Myers would lead companies E and I to the right down the Washita and attack from the timber above, taking up positions in the woods along the river valley about three quarters of a mile to the right of Custer's center column. With this contingent would be First Lieutenant Charles Brewster, commanding Troop I, and First Lieutenant J. M. Johnson.

Custer's command consisted of troops A, C, D, and K, along with the sharpshooter company under Lieutenant Cook and the scouts. Troop commanders were Captain Hamilton, A; First Lieutenant Matthew Berry, C; Captain T. B. Weir, D; and Captain Robert West, K. Other officers with this attack unit were first lieutenants Tom Custer, Edward Godfrey, Myles Moylan and Samuel Robbins, and second lieutenants A. E. Smith and

Edward Law. This force would attack from a position overlooking the village from the west. There would be two columns, one led by Hamilton and the other by West. All together there would be approximately seven hundred troops surrounding the fifty-one Indian lodges.

The signal to attack would be made at dawn by Custer. This would give some four hours for the troops to get into their assigned positions. Custer sent Lieutenant Godfrey back to instruct Benteen to come forward and leave Bell with the camp guard to hold the wagons until the attack. Bell was to move up and retrieve the overcoats and haversacks the troops would leave behind. Elliott waited for Benteen to join him, then moved out first, followed by Thompson and Myers (see Appendix A).

Now the troops faced the task of waiting out the bone-chilling cold without fires and in strict silence. The men were instructed not to stamp their feet or even walk around in the snow to keep warm, lest too much noise be made. Troopers buttoned their coats tightly around themselves, collecting in small groups to talk about the coming fight. Some stayed close to their animals for warmth while others lay back in the snow and found such comfort as to bring sleep. Custer himself later claimed to have slept for over an hour.

Off to one side, the Osage guides clustered to themselves, wrapped in their blankets in a tight circle. There had grown among them the ever-present suspicion that they might not fare well if things went badly for the soldiers. The Osages saw the possibility that they might even be sacrificed if the whites did not win. Also, once the battle began it was likely that an Indian would be an Indian to the troops. The guides decided that the safest place for them would be directly behind the flag-bearer to avoid being mistaken for enemy Indians.

The men of the 7th Cavalry waited. Soon there would be battle.

Chapter IX
THIS BLOODY GROUND

Elliott and Thompson having moved out with their detachments, the remainder of the 7th Regiment huddled through the cold night behind the ridge. Custer watched the sky for signs of dawn, and when the first faint light was visible he called his officers together for a final council. During the early morning hours, a fog had settled over the river valley, and it caused a prominent morning star to glitter brilliantly as it rose above the village. It was so bright that Custer at first thought it to be some sort of warning signal sent up by the Indians.

The growing lightness of the sky told Custer it was time to move his troops forward to their points of attack, where they would await the signal for battle. Now the men were ordered to remove their overcoats and haversacks containing their rations, leaving one man from each troop to guard them. Myers' detachment moved off to cross the river above the village, where, with half of his troops dismounted, he would take up positions in the timber along the south bank. Custer himself led the remainder down the long slope toward the grove of trees that lined the north bank of the Washita where it bent around the village, almost due west of the encampment.

The slope seemed unexpectedly long and the sound of the horses' hoofs crunching through the snow's crust extra-loud as the troops advanced upon the village. Indian ponies were encountered along the way, and they shied from the soldiers like a flock of blackbirds across the snow. Through the trees, the Indian village could now be seen—a picture of frozen silence, the dark, conical lodges with their crisscrossed poles at the top looming against the sky.

The village was so still that Custer was concerned, wondering if perhaps the Indians might have slipped away from him again just as they had that night on the Pawnee Fork. Nor was he at all certain that Elliott and Thompson had been able to reach their assigned points of attack. He checked the positioning of his own command. To the right was Major West's detachment, Troops C and K, mounted in line among the trees, the officers with their bridles is one hand, pistols in the other. The troops sat with carbine butts at rest on their thighs, their horses chafing for action. As an afterthought to the instructions already issued, Custer sent his courier with a new order to West. Lieutenant Godfrey and Troop K were to drive on through the village without stopping and round up any pony herds to be found on the other side.

To the left, Hamilton's squadron, Troops A and D, were likewise mounted and poised. The major rode along his line, reminding his men in soft tones to keep cool, fire low, and not to hurry their shots. In advance of his line and spreading along the bank northwest of the encampment, Cook's forty sharpshooters had been dismounted for better firing accuracy and positioned among the trees close to the edge of the river. Custer was at the center, and directly in back of him, mounted on grays, was the regimental band, the leader with his cornet ready. At Custer's side was the color guard, the regimental standard with its huge golden eagle hanging stiffly above. Behind the guard, clustered in a small knot, were the Osage scouts. Nearby, the white scouts held their mounts in check, California Joe being perched atop his mule, looking uniquely unmilitary but just as tense and apprehensive as the rest. In the village, several dogs commenced barking.

The swelling light over the horizon meant that daybreak was imminent. The time had come. But even as Custer turned in his saddle to give the signal to his bugler and the band, the sound of a rifle shot rang out from the northeast side of the Indian camp.

Later it was learned that an Indian buck had heard the dog barking and had come out to investigate. As he was looking about, a trooper in Elliott's command, which had moved in close to the edge of the north bank of the Washita just across from the camp, stuck his head up for a look. The movement was spotted by the Indian, who immediately fired the shot of warning to his village.

Quickly Custer completed his signal. The brisk notes of the bugle blared forth against the surrounding bluffs and resounded across the Washita Valley. Simultaneously, the rollicking, airish tune of "Garryowen" began, only to break off raggedly after one strain because the breath moisture in the musical instruments had frozen. Troopers jabbed spurs to their horses and reinforced their battle courage with whoops and cries of "Huzzah!" as they swept forward toward the Indian encampment with the rattle and crack of gunfire peppering the air about them.

Custer, riding a black stallion and accompanied by his scouts and staff, led the charge down the steep bank of the Washita, clearing the trail crossing of the Washita at a single jump. Inside the village area he encountered a Cheyenne warrior, who jerked up his rifle to draw a bead on the cavalryman. But, according to his own claim, Custer quickly proved the value of past battle experience and his accuracy with a pistol. He shot the Indian through the head before he could get off a shot. Custer's horse knocked another Indian to the ground as he headed directly for a small knoll to the south of the area, from which he watched the battle and issued orders as it progressed.

Elliott's command also launched its attack from across the river, to the northeast of the village. The young officer's three troops had circled widely to the north around a chain of ragged hills and bluffs, finally locating a place of descent into the river valley. A thick stand of trees and underbrush lined the north bank, and Elliott's troops fanned along the riverbank as it curved tightly around the village and meandered on eastward.

Myers' detachment, troops E and I, moved on the village from the southeast, half of the unit making the traditional cavalry charge and the other half advancing on foot as skirmishers to catch Indians trying to escape in that direction. Myers, himself suffering a severe case of snow blindness, had relinquished command of Troop E to Lieutenant Johnson.

Thompson's force, troops B and F, had been compelled to take a circuitous route around the south of the village to reach its assigned position. In doing so, it lost its bearings somewhat. Further, the long, treeless slopes of the land to the south of the Indian encampment did not afford the convenient cover available to the others, and Thompson was forced to remain behind a ridge farther from the camp than were the rest. As a result, his right flank failed to make a juncture with Elliott's left flank, leaving an open avenue between them to the southeast. It also caused Thompson's unit to be the last to reach the village during the charge.

Both Custer and Elliott had had to cross the river before reaching the Indian camp. The north banks, on the outside of the river's arc, were high enough to stymie a full charge. The troops had to guide their horses down the incline, and this brief delay gave the Indian camp a few precious seconds to come alive. Instantly, the lodges produced the darting shapes of Indians, some war-whooping their wild defiance, some stringing their bows with arrows, some with guns in hand. But even as they emerged, the troops were upon them, the cavalry horses thundering through the lodge aisles, the blue-shirted troopers firing and slashing at anyone not mounted. There was no quarter given.

The village area had become a melee. The air resounded with whooping and war cries, the curses of soldiers, and the screams of the wounded—all mingled with the blasts of pistol fire. Every man found his own private engagement or victim. Those Indians who chose to stand their ground or who could not find an avenue of escape were shot point-blank or whacked down. The braves, and many of the women and young boys, fought as best they could, but the odds were too much against them. It was impossible to hold back the overwhelming avalanche of mounted troops. Within ten minutes, the Cheyenne village was under the control of the 7th Cavalry.

But the fighting was not over. The Indians took up positions behind trees and in ravines and began firing at the troops, many of whom now dismounted to fight on foot. Units of the 7th charged the Indians' positions, eventually wiping out most of them. But the stubbornest resistance came from a group of war-riors—Custer said seventeen of them—who had established themselves in a gulley. Charging them proved unsuccessful, and it became necessary for the sharpshooters to find vantage points from which they could pick off the Indians man by man as they raised their heads to fire.

Many of the Indians retreated to the river, which offered the most available protection and chance for escape, the refugees plunging half-clad into the icy water. These Indians became prime targets for Cook's sharpshooters. Some managed to escape the fusillade of bullets by hanging close to the bank and working their way downstream. Those who went in other directions were mostly unfortunate, running head on into the charging troops or dismounted skirmishers.

As was customary for chiefs, Black Kettle had his horse tethered near his lodge, and with his wife mounted in front of him he headed for the river crossing of a trail that led from the village down-river along the north bank to other Indian camps. He managed to get almost across the river before a bullet struck him in the back, knocking him from the pony. He hit face down in the stream, his long role as a peacemaker ended. His wife was also struck by a bullet and fell dead in the stream, and there the two were later found by friends, after the soldiers had left.

The Cheyenne woman Moving Behind, who was fourteen at the time, later told of the fight, and her role in it:

> Many Indians were killed during the fight. The air was full of smoke from gunfire, and it was almost impossible to flee, because bullets were flying everywhere. However, somehow we ran and kept running to find a hiding place. As we ran, we could see the red fire of the shots. We got near a hill, and there we saw a steep path, where an old road used to be. There was red grass along the path, and although the ponies had eaten some of it, it was still high enough for us to hide.
>
> In this grass we lay flat, our hearts beating fast; and we were afraid to move. It was now broad daylight. It frightened us to listen to the noise and the cries of the wounded. When the noise seemed to quiet down, and we believed the battle was about to end, we

raised our heads high enough to see what was going on. We saw a dark figure lying near a hill, and later we learned it was the body of a woman with child. The woman's body had been cut open by the soldiers.

The wounded ponies passed near our hiding place, and would moan loudly, just like human beings. We looked again, and could see the soldiers forcing a group of Indian women to accompany them, making some of the women get into wagons and others on horses.

The Indian ponies that were left were driven toward the bottoms. Some horses would run back, and the soldiers would chase them, and head them the other way.

The soldiers would pass back and forth near the spot where I lay. As I turned sideways and looked, one soldier saw us, and rode toward where we lay. He stopped his horse, and stared at us. He did not say a word, and we wondered what would happen. But he left, and no one showed up after that. I suppose he pitied us, and left us alone.

Some of the women had remained in their lodges during the attack. Custer sent the scout Romero to round up the captives and herd them into a big lodge. The women thought that they were to be executed and made an attempt to escape into the hills south of the camp. They were spotted by the Osage scouts, who immediately went galloping after them. In Indian fashion, the Osages grabbed switches from tree limbs and whipped their victims back into camp.

The women now began singing their death songs, the wailing sounds casting an eerie shroud over the scene of death and destruction in the camp. All around lay the dead and dying—men, women, children, horses, and a few soldiers. One participant, writing just after the battle, described the scene: "The battle is over and the field covered with dead animals and savages, muddy and smeared, and lying upon each other in holes and ditches. The field resembles a vast slaughter pen."

During the initial charge, Major Hamilton had led his squadron in its headlong attack on the Indian encampment, and at some point in the charge he was struck by a bullet and killed. Accounts are in conflict as to where and how Hamilton was killed (see Appendix B). Custer claimed that he and Hamilton rode side by side until they reached the village. But Keim, who filed his story of the battle on December 1 after interviewing participants of the battle on their return to Camp Supply, described Hamilton's death differently: "It was as the centre column was charging down the preciptious bluffs to cross the river and take the village that Captain Hamilton was killed. When struck he gave one convulsive start, stiffened in his stirrups, and was thus carried a corpse for a distance of several yards, when he fell from his horse, striking his face, which was from this cause terribly lacerated and disfigured."

After the battle had slackened off, Hamilton's body was carried up and laid out near the makeshift hospital area. A guard of honor, chosen from his men, was placed over his body. The official report of Assistant Surgeon Henry Lippincott states: "Ball entered about five inches below left nipple and emerged near inferior angle of right scapula. Death was instantaneous." Likely, the bullet passed through Hamilton's heart.

Presently, Captain Barnitz was brought in on a blanket litter, a soldier at each corner. He had taken a bullet about three inches above and four inches to the left of his navel, just under the heart. It had ranged a little upward and emerged about three and a half inches from his spinal column, rupturing the case of his stomach and breaking a rib but not doing serious damage to any vital organs. A heavy pile of blankets and buffalo robes was put on the shivering Pennsylvanian, who told Lieutenant Godfrey: "Oh hell! they think because my extremities are cold I am going to die, but if I could get warm I'm sure I'll be all right! These blankets and robes are so heavy I can hardly breathe." Godfrey directed a detail to gather wood and build fires for Barnitz so the blankets and robes could be removed. Still Barnitz's situation looked serious if not fatal, and he delivered farewell messages for relatives and friends.

Barnitz was reported by Custer as having killed two Indians. The captain himself later wrote that he had not charged through the village, but by himself had ridden about three quarters of a mile up the hills to the south, where he engaged in a duel with a warrior with a Lancaster muzzle-loader. The rifle had an octagonal barrel and a brass-lidded patch box. A young Cheyenne warrior named Magpie, later to become a chief, told of being charged by a big man on a brown horse in the same area as Barnitz had described. The man wore a "chief's" insignia on his uniform, according to Magpie, indicating that it may well have been Barnitz whom he encountered.

Captain Benteen was also challenged by a young boy, mounted, who was attempting to escape to the east. Benteen, not wanting to kill the youngster, made signs indicating that he would not harm the boy if he came along peacefully. But the young warrior was pure Cheyenne. He charged Benteen with pistol leveled and, when closer, he loosed a shot that whizzed past the officer's head. The boy fired twice more, one of the bullets downing Benteen's horse and throwing the officer to the ground. Again the Cheyenne youth charged the cavalryman, but now Benteen realized the precariousness of his situation and the futility of trying to make peace. He killed the boy with his pistol, the youngster later proving to be Black Kettle's nephew.

As with most battles, there were many stories told in the aftermath. Lieutenant Smith claimed that as he was charging the village, followed by a bugler boy, he saw a figure wrapped in a blanket take refuge among the women. He ordered the bugler not to fire, thinking it was a woman; but just then the Indian, an old man, loosed an arrow which hit the bugler in the head. The arrow sliced the skin badly but did not penetrate the skull. The bugler killed the old man, later finding a bow and a quiver full of arrows under his blanket. Custer's version of the incident said that the arrow remained in the boy's head until the steel point was cut off and the shaft pulled out. He also said that the boy showed him the old man's scalp, which he had taken.

Another story was told by reporter Keim, of an Osage whose wife had been murdered earlier by the Cheyennes. Coming upon the already lifeless body of a Cheyenne, the Osage leaped upon it and started to take the scalp. But he discovered with great disappointment that the scalp had already been taken, whereupon he cut off the Cheyenne's head and smashed it against the ground. Custer's version is that the Osage did take the scalp, which he waved victoriously as he rode about.

One incident involved the murder of a child whom the soldiers took to be white. This story is told with varying details by Custer and others, though Keim is the most graphic, describing a savage who "with trembling fury, knife in hand, as if looking for an object upon which to avenge the loss of the day, rushed at the boy with one terrible shout, completely disemboweling him, his entrails, smoking, dropping upon the snow." However, Ben Clark later gave a more realistic account of the affair. He described how a group of Indians had taken refuge behind a pile of dirt caused by a cave-in of the riverbank. The soldiers were unable to dislodge them, but poured in a hail of bullets that finally killed all but one Cheyenne woman and her child.

> The warriors were dead. It was then that I saw a terrible example of a Cheyenne mother's despair. A squaw arose from behind the barricade holding a baby at arm's length. In her other hand was a long knife. The sharpshooters mistook the child for a white captive [Clark claimed that Cheyenne children were often as fair as white children] and yelled, "Kill that squaw. She's murdering a white child." Before a gun could be fired the mother with one stroke of the knife, disemboweled the child, drove the knife to the hilt in her own breast and was dead. A trooper poked his carbine over the embankment and shot her through the head but it was a needless cruelty.

It was about ten o'clock when Custer first began to notice the knots of warriors perched atop the surrounding hills. He had been engrossed in problems in the village, and at first merely supposed the hilltop Indians to be some who had escaped and found ponies. But then they became numerous enough to concern him, and he ordered a captive woman brought to him for questioning. The woman said through the interpreter Romero that her name was Mah-wis-sa, a Cheyenne, and she claimed to be Black Kettle's sister. Through her, Custer learned for the first time that this had not been a solitary Indian village, that below him were much larger villages of Cheyennes, Arapahoes, Kiowas, and others. Through his field glasses Custer could see a growing number of mounted Indians, as Benteen later described them:

"Savages on flying steeds, with shields and feathers gay, are circling everywhere, riding like devils incarnate."

About that time, the troopers who had been posted to guard the overcoats and haversacks came dashing into camp, having fled their posts when a force of Indians drove them off and captured the soldiers' accouterments. This was serious in itself, for the soldiers would be needing their coats and rations soon enough. Their ammunition was already running low, and the presence of a large hostile force about them was of much concern to Custer. The worst danger of all was that the Indians might discover and attack the wagons, which carried desperately needed supplies.

This danger had increased when regimental quartermaster Bell arrived with his seven wagons and one ambulance to pick up the coats and haversacks. The Indians spotted him and immediately drove between him and Custer's force in the village. But Bell acted quickly and decisively, heading his mules at top speed for the village down the long slope over which Custer had advanced earlier that morning. Several of his mules were killed in the galloping fight, and his tar-soaked wagon wheels became so hot they were set ablaze. But he and his men reached the village amid the cheers and shouts of their comrades, and the wagons were quickly jerked over by troopers who then grabbed handfuls of ammunition.

Lieutenant E. S. Godfrey had followed his orders to continue on through the village during the attack, driving about a mile below the encampment, where he found Indian ponies scattered about in groups. Sending his platoon to round up the horses, he rode to some high ground, from which he observed a group of Indians escaping on foot down the north side of the river valley. At about the same time, Lieutenant Edward Law came up with the second platoon of K Troop, and Godfrey turned the pony herd over to him to take back to the village while he gathered his platoon for a pursuit of the escaping Indians.

Crossing the stream, Godfrey struck an Indian trail which he followed to a wooded draw, where he found another large horse herd. The Indians ahead of him had mounted there and headed

on up the trail, which led alongside the hills north of the river.
Godfrey followed, and in about two miles he discovered a single
Indian tepee. Not far away, he could see two Indians circling
their horses as if they were signaling "Enemy!" to someone
behind the high ridge beyond the tepee. Godfrey's sergeants
warned him against continuing so far away from the main command. It was excellent advice, as other developments would
eventually prove, but Godfrey was still determined to know
what was on the other side of the ridge. Leaving his platoon
behind, he himself rode to the crest of the ridge and peered over.
There he beheld an amazing sight. All along the winding,
wooded valley of the Washita where it oxbowed northward were
hundreds of Indian lodges. It was the Arapaho encampment
under Little Raven, though Godfrey did not know it, and from
the villages swarmed mounted warriors ready for war.

Godfrey hurried back to his men and began a hasty retreat up
the river. He was soon overtaken by the Arapahoes, who opened
fire upon the troops. The young West Pointer dismounted his
men and returned the Indians' fire, driving them to cover. Now
deploying the troops as skirmishers, every fourth man leading
the horses of the other three, Godfrey retreated from ridge to
ridge. With the skirmishers divided into two groups, one would
halt and cover the retreat of the other. Finally the Indians left
them, and Godfrey returned to where the pony herd had been
found. In the herd, he was surprised to discover Captain Barnitz's horse, General, still saddled but without a bridle.

While making this retreat, Godfrey's platoon had heard the
sound of heavy gunfire across the river opposite them. Godfrey's
view of the south side of the river was obscured by the trees that
lined the valley, preventing him from knowing that what he was
hearing was in all probability Major Elliott and a small party of
troops fighting to their deaths against more of the Arapahoes.
When he returned to the battle site, Godfrey was quizzed by
Custer.

At that time many warriors were assembling on the high hills
north of the valley overlooking the village and the General kept

looking in that direction. At the conclusion of his inquiry, I told him that I had heard that Major Elliott had not returned and suggested that possibly the heavy firing I had heard on the opposite side of the valley might have been an attack on Elliott's party. He pondered this a bit and said slowly, "I hardly think so, as Captain Myers has been fighting down there all morning and probably would have reported it."

Custer was more concerned at the time with counting his spoils of war. He ordered Godfrey to take Troop K, scour the village, and bring in all the valuables. This was done, and the goods were heaped into piles and counted. Custer's report itemized 241 saddles, some of very fine and costly workmanship; 573 buffalo robes; 360 untanned robes; numerous hatchets; 35 revolvers and 47 rifles; 250 pounds of lead; some 4,000 arrows and arrow heads; 75 spears; 90 bullet molds; 35 bows and quivers; 12 shields; 300 pounds of tobacco; plus numerous lariats, bridles, and other items.

Additionally, the 7th had captured all the Indians' winter supply of dried buffalo meat, meal flour, and other provisions, including most of the Cheyennes' clothing. As critical as anything to the Indians was the loss of their lodges, fifty-one of them. A warrior might revere his horse, but it was his lodge that gave him and his family shelter and permitted survival on the open plains. One of the lodges was that of Black Kettle: "As evidence of his rank, his lodge was black and ornamented on the exterior in the highest style of Indian art and as became so great and powerful a chieftain."

Custer selected one of the lodges for his own personal souvenir and told Godfrey to burn the rest of them with the other goods. "I began destruction at the upper end of the village, tearing down tepees and piling several together on the tepee poles, set fire to them. As the fires made headway, all articles of personal property—buffalo robes, blankets, food, rifles, pistols, bows and arrows, lead and caps, bullet molds, etc.—were thrown in the fires and destroyed." Soon, huge clouds of black smoke began billowing skyward where the Cheyenne camp had sat so peacefully and serenely in the white snow the night before.

Shortly there was nothing left but a charred pile of blackened debris.

The cottonwood grove in which Black Kettle had made his camp now offered the troops good cover against the sniping of the Indians. Around noon, shortly after Bell had arrived with the wagons, an attack was made upon Custer's position by the Indians, but it and others of a similar nature were more attempts to draw out the troops than serious efforts to invade the area. Squadrons of the 7th would countercharge but pull up without going far from the battle site. Throughout the day, there were exchanges of gunfire between the troops and the Indians, who now encircled Custer's army. The warriors, having the security of knowing the cavalry horses could not catch their ponies, moved about freely just out of firing range, "circling around the village, after their custom—now dashing up and firing, now retreating in crooked circling movement behind hills and knolls." By three o'clock that afternoon, the fighting had ended.

In the afternoon, California Joe came jogging up to Custer's side and requested permission to round up a large herd of ponies and mules that had been discovered nearby. Custer agreed and assigned some men to help Joe. In about half an hour a herd of three hundred ponies came trotting into the village area, followed by two mounted Indian women. Joe had captured the women and forced them to herd in the ponies while he rode behind twirling his lariat. All together, some 875 Indian horses and mules were gathered in, and the white men discovered an interesting fact about them.

The Indian horses had an instinctive hostility to white men. Perhaps it was as Satanta had described it at Fort Larned when he complained that it "stink too much white man" there. The ponies would shy away from the soldiers, and when a rope was thrown over their heads they struggled violently to get away. Finally the Indian women were pressed into service, and they would walk up to the animals without causing the slightest disturbance. It was obvious from this that the animals could not be led or driven by the troops. Custer felt, too, that if taken with the command, the animals would offer too much temptation to the

Indians to try to recapture them. Nor did he intend to leave them for the warriors to have again.

The best animals in the herd were divided among the officers and scouts, who hoped to drive them back to the post and break them. Custer also allowed the women to pick out horses to ride. Then he ordered Lieutenant Godfrey to take four companies for a firing party to kill the remainder of the animals. As the Indians watched from the hilltops with furious dismay, the soldiers herded the horses to the southeast of the village and began executing nearly eight hundred of their most valued possessions.

> . . . the General ordered me to kill all the ponies except those authorized to be used by the prisoners and given to the scouts. We tried to rope them and cut their throats, but the ponies were frantic at the approach of a white man and fought viciously. My men were getting very tired so I called for reinforcements and details from other organizations were sent to complete the destruction of about eight hundred ponies.

Benteen described Custer's role in this with sarcastic bitterness:

> Our chief exhibits his close sharp-shooting and terrifies the crowd of frightened, captured squaws and papooses by dropping the straggling ponies in death near them. Ah! he is a clever marksman. Not even do the poor camp dogs of the Indians escape his eye and aim as they drop dead or limp howling away. But are not those our men on guard on the other side of the creek? Will he not hit them? "My troop is on guard, General, just over there," says an officer. "Well, bullets will not go through or around hills, and you see there is a hill between us," was the reply, and the exhibition goes on. No one will come that way intentionally—certainly not. Now commences the slaughter of the ponies. Volley after volley is poured into them by too-hasty men, and they, limping, get away only to meet death from a surer hand!

Concerning the number of Indians killed in the battle, Custer stated in his official report, written in the field on November 28:

"By actual and careful examination after the battle the following figures give some of the fruits of our victory:—the Indians left on the ground and in our possession the bodies of one hundred and three of their warriors. . . ." But in his book, *My Life on the Plains*, Custer tells of calling his officers together while on the way back to Camp Supply and asking each to give an account of his involvement in the battle and an estimate of the number killed in his sphere of action. Godfrey verified this, stating that "after supper in the evening, the officers were called together and each one questioned as to the casualties of enemy warriors, locations, etc. Every effort was made to avoid duplications. The total was found to be one hundred and three." Thus it is apparent that the number of Indian casualties given by Custer did not result from a count of the dead on the battlefield as Custer implied. (See Appendix C.)

Fifty-three Cheyenne women, young girls, children, and papooses were taken prisoner. Some of them had been wounded, all by gunshot. When interviewed by interpreter Dick Curtis at Camp Supply later, the captive women listed as being among those killed Black Kettle, principal chief; Little Rock, second chief; and eleven other headmen and war chiefs, plus two Sioux and an Arapaho who were in the camp. Among the captive women were Mah-wis-sa, Black Kettle's alleged sister; and Monah-se-tah, Little Rock's daughter.

In his official report on the battle, Custer makes two significant statements that he fails ever to mention again, either in his correspondence or in his book. His report states: "We also secured two white children, held captive by the Indians. One white woman who was in their possession was murdered by her captors the moment we attacked." Clarification of these matters has never been made or even attempted by historians dealing with the Washita conflict. Unexplained is a "Mrs. Crocker," whom a scout reported as having been rescued from the Cheyenne village though seriously wounded.

Four members of the 7th Regiment were killed or mortally wounded during the battle in the village. Captain Hamilton was killed instantly during the charge. Private Charles Cuddy of Troop B with Thompson's detachment was shot through the

WASHITA BATTLEFIELD PERSPECTIVE

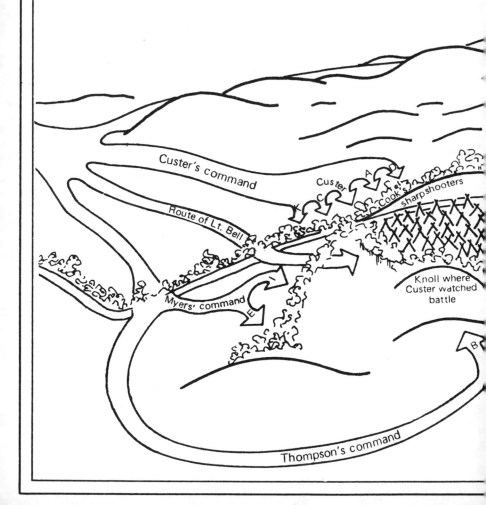

Custer's command

Custer

Cook's sharpshooters

Route of Lt. Bell

Knoll where Custer watched battle

Myers' command

Thompson's command

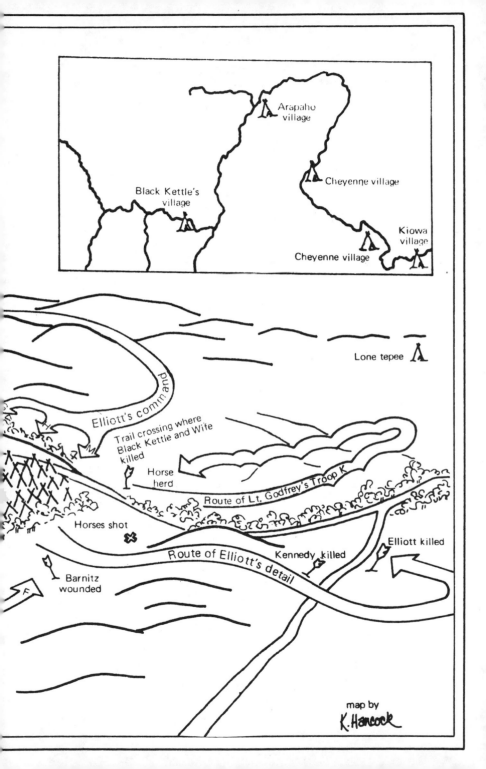

Arapaho village

Cheyenne village

Black Kettle's village

Kiowa village

Cheyenne village

Lone tepee

Elliott's command

Trail crossing where Black Kettle and Wife killed

Horse herd

Route of Lt. Godfrey's Troop K

Horses shot

Kennedy killed

Elliott killed

Route of Elliott's detail

Barnitz wounded

map by K. Hancock

head and died soon after. Private Augustus Delaney, also with Troop B, was shot in the chest and died some ten hours later the day of the battle. Private Benjamin McCasey, with Company H in Elliott's detachment, was hit by an arrow which penetrated the rib cage and entered his lungs. He died on November 30, the day before the regiment returned to Camp Supply. (See Appendix D.)

Eighteen men, including Major Elliott and Sergeant Major Walter Kennedy, were missing and presumed dead by Custer. In his official report, Custer chose to list all eighteen men as killed in battle, though he had no knowledge at all of what had happened to them. Reporter Keim's story of December 1 from Camp Supply tells what was known of Elliott and the others at the time:

> As the fight became general each man picked his antagonist and started for him. It was after this mode of fighting that Major Elliott, with a handful of men, started down the river after a small band of Indians. During the excitement of the fight the Major was not missed. At one time heavy firing was heard at a distance, which was supposed to be signals to the villages below. When the conflict lulled the question was carried along the line, "Where is Elliott? Where is Elliott?" The only reply was that he was last seen charging some fugitives fleeing down the river. There is no doubt that he and his party struck the approaching Kiowas and Arapahoes coming to the rescue of the Cheyennes and were cut off by them. There is no question that each man of this ill-fated band sold his life as dearly as possible and died at his post. For these unfortunate men there was no possibility of escape. Their alternative was death by some friendly bullet or death by the horrible fortune which the hellish ingenuity of the savage alone can invent.

With evening near and still no sign of Elliott and the missing men, Custer had several of his officers surveyed to see if they knew of the major's whereabouts. Lieutenant Owen Hale stated that he had seen Elliott and a number of troops headed down the valley to the east after some escaping Indians. As his detachment moved away, Elliott turned in his saddle and waved to Hale, yelling, "Here goes for a brevet or a coffin." One of the scouts recalled seeing the party in pursuit of Indians who were escaping in the avenue between Elliott's and Thompson's commands. Afterward he had heard some sharp firing in that direction, but it had lasted for only a few minutes. The scout was sent to accompany a search party in the direction he had indicated, but after looking fruitlessly for some two miles the party returned. This single effort by Custer was to cause considerable debate and resentment among the officers of the 7th.

The arrival of Bell with the ammunition earlier had prevented a potentially dangerous situation, but with night coming on the 7th's position was questionable at best. Many of the men were in shirt sleeves, and neither they nor their horses had had any food since the night before. The camp was completely surrounded by swarms of Indians on ponies less used than those of the troops. The command was now encumbered with both prisoners and their own wounded. It was not feasible to divide the command to provide a guard for the captives and wounded, and taking them along meant hampered operations. Nor was there any real assurance that the Indians, obviously in strength, had not discovered the supply train and taken it.

To merely retreat toward the wagon train was to draw attention to its whereabouts. Moreover, to attempt further action against the forewarned and numerous Indians down the river was by no means logical. The lessons of Indian fighting in Kansas would indicate the folly of such a move. Custer had his victory; his problem now was to get back to Camp Supply with it. He decided upon the strategy of a feinting movement.

Drawing his command up in full formation, banners flying, and the band again playing the gala and appropriate Civil War marching tune "Ain't I Glad to Get Out of the Wilderness," Custer displayed a forceful and confident front for the watchful Indians as he headed down-river toward their villages. He continued eastward for several miles until darkness had set in. The Arapaho, Kiowa, and Cheyenne warriors did the most natural thing for them. Leaving behind a small force to watch Custer's movement, they spurred their ponies back to protect their villages, which by now had been hurriedly dismantled by the women and moved toward some new place of safety.

When Custer felt his movements could no longer be seen by the Indians who were watching him, he gave the order to countermarch. The men, tired, hungry, and shivering in their saddles, were pleased to be moving toward the baggage train, where rations and clothing awaited them. By ten o'clock, the command had returned to the battlefield to snack at their limited food supplies, then pushed ahead on their own back trail up the Washita Valley until two o'clock, when Custer finally gave the command to halt and rest. Huge fires were built to give the frozen troops relief from the frigid night. One company was sent on to provide extra defense for the wagon train. At daybreak, the cavalrymen returned to their saddles and continued on until after ten that morning, when they were delighted to find the supply caravan, it having moved only sixteen miles from where Custer had left it at the foot of the Antelope Hills due to the roughness of the country and the melting snow.

Without halting even to allow for breakfast, the teams of the train were hitched to the wagons and the impatient Custer pushed his troops on. Finally, in the early afternoon he signaled for a halt and went into camp. The weary and hungry troops were allowed to eat a full meal from the wagon stores, then pitch their tents and get some much needed rest under the comfort of warm blankets. It was at this point that Custer called his officers together and informed them that, instead of having them write formal reports of their part in the battle, he wished each to merely tell briefly of his action. History thus lost the precise details of the various units of the 7th Regiment in the Washita battle. Custer wrote his report to Sheridan and dispatched California Joe and Jack Corbin to carry it to Camp Supply. He had them wait until dark to leave, fearing that Indians might be watching his movements.

No Indians were seen by the regiment during the next two days as it continued its march at a more leisurely pace and on a more direct route back to Camp Supply. Upon nearing Wolf Creek, the command was met by California Joe and Corbin, who were carrying a dispatch from Sheridan praising Custer and the 7th Regiment for the "efficient and gallant services rendered."

Custer was elated at this commendation and ordered the field order read to the entire command.

The wind had turned southerly now, bringing balmy temperatures and causing the snow to disappear quickly into the ground except for patches in shaded areas. The warm sunshine on their backs and the promise of a victorious return to Camp Supply had all in good spirits. At the last camp on Wolf Creek, some ten miles from the post, Custer again sent couriers to Sheridan, saying that the command would be pleased to march in review before Sheridan and his staff. It was a none too subtle hint that Custer would like a triumphant return with all the pageantry and pomp that could be mustered. It would be a grand present for a brevet major general whose twenty-ninth birthday was only four days off.

Chapter X
FOR A BREVET OR A COFFIN

Under a bright sun on the morning of December 1, General Phil Sheridan and his staff, in full uniform and flanked by all the officers and men of Camp Supply who were not otherwise on duty as well as the men of the 19th Kansas, waited expectantly for the returning conquerors of Black Kettle's village. Finally, a cluster of dark, almost indefinable objects appeared on a distant hilltop. The resulting pistol fire and shouts of welcome from the garrison troops sent the startled herd of horses and mules, which had been grazing in a nearby meadow, stampeding in alarm toward the fort. Sheridan and the others watched as the long columns of the 7th and its wagon train wound slowly down the hillside, disappeared from view, and then presently reappeared on a closer summit.

There Custer halted the command and carefully arranged his formation. At the front were the Osages in full war paint, shields and quivers over their shoulders, rifles in hand and lances held skyward to display the scalps of fallen Cheyennes, their own hair locks trailing silver ornaments looted from victims of the fight. Little Beaver rode with the stern dignity of a chief, but the other Osages whooped, sang war songs, and fired their rifles into the air. Conspicuous among them was the young warrior Trotter, who flaunted an elaborately decorated scalp lock which he claimed was that of Black Kettle, chief of the Cheyennes.

Next were the white scouts, led by California Joe, "mat of red whiskers hiding two-thirds of his face . . . a long, knotty head of hair, well powdered in a series of coats of dust . . . a suitable figurehead for this motley band of curiously-clad adventurers and rugged men." Behind them was Custer, riding his black stallion and wearing a short sack coat with fur collar and cuffs, an otter cap on his head, and accompanied by his staff.

Following were the prisoners, the fifty-three Cheyenne women, children, and papooses, wrapped in brightly colored blankets so that only their eyes were visible, some two or three to the pony, a mounted guard under Lieutenant Godfrey riding closely on both sides. The prisoners looked to neither the left nor the right, riding submissively and without the slightest sign that several of them were severely wounded. Next were the sharpshooters under Cook, and they were followed by "the bravest men of the different companies of the regiment in column by platoons under their proper officers." In a separate line of march were the wagons, led by the ambulances which carried the bodies of Hamilton, Cuddy, Delaney, and McCasey along with the wounded. The larger, canvas-topped supply wagons were in double columns, with the led horses between.

Sheridan directed two of his staff officers to ride out to conduct the command to the fort. As the column approached, the men of the 7th fired their guns over their heads and cheered wildly, and once more the regimental band struck up the rollicking notes of "Garryowen." Upon nearing Sheridan, Custer broke out of formation and spurred jubilantly up to his old commander and exchanged greetings. It was almost like the old days of glory in the Shenandoah. As each company passed, the troop commanders saluted Sheridan with their sabers, and he returned each salute by tipping his cap.

Following the review, the 7th marched on up the Beaver and went into camp in the cottonwood grove about a half mile from the fort, the encampment making a veritable village of white "A" tents, with Custer's Sibley tent at the center and the long lines of picketed horses fronting the cantonment. The remainder of the day was spent in celebration by the officers and men, who recounted the hardships and perils of the march and battle and displayed the trophies of war they had taken from the village before it was burned. That night, the Osages defied the freezing temperatures to celebrate the victory over their Cheyenne enemies with a scalp dance around a huge log fire on the banks of the river. Sheridan and Custer joined the other officers in watching as the Osages, blankets thrown off and wearing only the trophies taken in battle, stamped and chanted their songs of victory around the fire.

On the following day, Sheridan interviewed Mah-wis-sa, later claiming to have learned from her that the trail Custer had followed to Black Kettle's camp was that of a Cheyenne-Arapaho war party returning from a raid into Kansas during which it had killed and scalped three white men, one of them being a courier of Sheridan's. The general claimed, too, that the mail carried by the courier had been found in Black Kettle's camp, along with mules, photographs, and other articles taken in raids along the Solomon and the Saline. Mah-wis-sa also told of the presence of three white women in the other Indian camps, down the Washita.

The Indian prisoners were provided medical attention at the base hospital. At first they refused to go there, but once they saw they were to be helped, the women showed their gratitude by shaking the hand of the surgeon whenever he appeared. The children who were treated gave no sign of pain except for the suffering which showed in their eyes as the doctor probed deep into their bullet wounds. One girl had a bullet hole completely through her body.

Custer's souvenir lodge was unpacked, and the women were put to work erecting it. The whites were amazed at the speed with which the Indian women put the lodge poles in place, unfurled the heavy buffalo-skin cover, stretched it over the pole framework, and pegged it down. Hardtack, a luxury to the Indians, was distributed among the women, who devoured it with enthusiasm. A lame horse and a camp dog were killed for them, also. Charges were later made that the officers were allowed to choose from the young girl captives, but this has never been established. Keim commented only: "The well squaws are still encamped with the cavalry and seem to be contented with their lot."

On the afternoon of December 3, the four victims of the Washita fight were buried with military honors, the entire regular troops at Camp Supply turning out. The body of Hamilton, draped with a large United States flag, was carried in an army ambulance to a small knoll near the post. The ambulance was preceded by Hamilton's black-horsed A Troop, now commanded by Captain Weir, and followed by Hamilton's own ebony stallion. The mount was covered with a mourning sheet, with the dead officer's boots turned backward in the stirrups. Sheridan and Custer were among the pallbearers as the roll of drums and the volleys of rifle fire resounded over the sandy hills surrounding the camp. The enlisted men were buried nearby.

Later, the officers of the 7th Regiment were called together and, with Custer presiding, drafted a eulogy resolution in honor of Hamilton. In part, it read: "Resolved, that the death in battle of our late comrade, Captain Louis M. Hamilton, has bereft us of a dear and valued friend, whom while living we cherished as a rare and gifted gentleman of unsullied honor and spotless fame; that we miss the genial face, the sparkling wit, the well tried, warm and trusty heart of him whose loss we mourn more deeply than words can tell."

The eulogy was sent to Hamilton's parents in Poughkeepsie, New York, by Major West, who also later wrote a touching obituary sketch of Hamilton for the *Army and Navy Journal*. In January 1869, Hamilton's body was shipped under escort to Poughkeepsie for reburial. A similar eulogy was written for Elliott, curiously stating that the officer "fell in the attitude of defiant daring heroically rallying his men," though no one yet was even certain of his death.

Elliott, a native of Indiana, had served with the 7th Indiana Volunteer Cavalry during the Civil War, having enlisted as a private in September 1861. Distinguishing himself at the battle of Perryville, he received a commission in June of 1863 and was promoted to captain that same October. During the spring of 1864, he was involved in action in Tennessee, where he led strikes that destroyed three bridges on the Mobile and Ohio

California Joe, Custer's favorite guide, was with the 7th Cavalry throughout the Washita campaign. *Courtesy of Western Historical Collections, University of Oklahoma.*

Fort Cobb, Indian Territory, was originally established before the Civil War, in October 1859. Evacuated by U.S. troops when the war began, the post was reopened in 1868, supposedly as a central agency for all friendly Indian tribes in the region. *Courtesy of Oklahoma State Historical Society.*

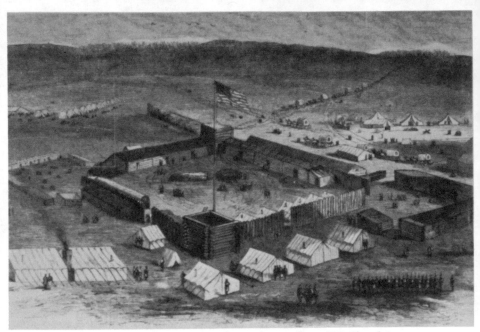

Newly constructed Camp Supply, at the conflux of Wolf and Beaver creeks in northwestern Indian Territory, now Oklahoma, in early 1869. *Courtesy of Kansas State Historical Society.*

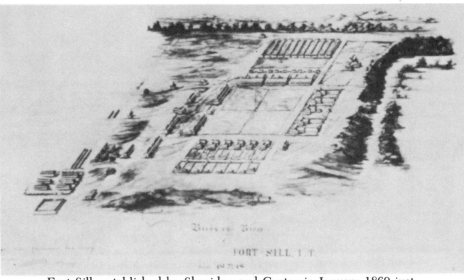

Fort Sill, established by Sheridan and Custer in January 1869 just east of the Wichita Mountains, in the Indian Territory. *Courtesy of Oklahoma State Historical Society.*

This photo, taken at Denver's Camp Weld in September 1864, shows a number of famous personalities of the frontier. Seated at center is Cheyenne chief Black Kettle. To his left is Bull Bear, Cheyenne Dog Soldier leader. Seated on the far left is Cheyenne chief White Antelope, who was killed at Sand Creek. Standing third from the left is frontiersman John Simpson Smith, while Major Edward Wynkoop, in dark hat, kneels in front of Black Kettle. *Courtesy of State Historical Society of Colorado.*

Some of the women and children captives taken at the Washita pose for a photograph at Camp Supply. *Courtesy of Oklahoma State Historical Society.*

These three Cheyennes were taken by Custer on the Sweetwater River in the Texas panhandle. Custer threatened to hang them if the Cheyennes did not release two white women they held captive. *Courtesy of Oklahoma State Historical Society.*

Railroad. In June of that year, he was shot in the lungs and shoulder and had his horse killed under him at White's Station on an expedition into Mississippi. He was wounded so seriously that he was left for dead on the battlefield. By January 1865, Elliott was back in action with the 7th Indiana and shortly commended for his untiring zeal and bravery in capturing a Rebel train during Grierson's famous raid.

After being mustered out of the service in February 1866, Elliott turned to schoolteaching for a time, becoming superintendent of the Toledo, Ohio, public schools. When the Union Army was being reorganized for frontier duty, he took the mental examinations required and made an exceptionally high score on them. Though he had anticipated a lieutenancy or, at the highest, a captaincy, his performance on the exams won him an appointment as the junior major of the 7th United States Cavalry and, eventually, as second in command of the unit.

Though he was not a West Pointer and had not held a major command during the war, Elliott was a hard-working, zealous officer. Likely, this zealousness was partially to blame for his going too far afield from the main command at the Washita.

The question of the young officer's fate was a cloud of uncertainty that still hung over Custer's victory. Already the fires of criticism were breaking out from officers such as Benteen, because Custer had chosen to abandon the field without ascertaining Elliott's condition. Sheridan had reservations about the matter also, but nevertheless he accepted Custer's annihilation of Black Kettle's village as the first victory in his campaign to conquer the wild tribes residing in the Indian Territory. Still, he felt it necessary to follow it up with another hard strike, this time against the Arapahoes, Kiowas, and Comanches as well. "If we can get in one or two more good blows," he wrote after the Washita battle, "there will be no more Indian troubles in my department."

A sizable military force was now gathered at Camp Supply. Garrisoning the post under the command of Captain John H. Page were three companies of 3rd Infantry, one of 5th Infantry, and one of the 38th Infantry. The twelve companies of the 19th Kansas were now all in camp, though many were dismounted, along with eleven companies of Custer's 7th Cavalry. On December 4, the 7th was inspected by Brevet Brigadier General J. W. Forsyth, Sheridan's adjutant, preparatory to another march. Private Harvey noted in his diary: "He condemned our old things, old horses, blankets, old tents, old swivel bores, also our old carbines. We are going to move soon."

On the day following, a two-hundred-fifty-wagon supply train under Captain Henry Inman, district quartermaster, arrived back at Camp Supply, having made the two-hundred-ten-mile round trip to Fort Dodge in twelve days. On his way to Dodge, at Mulberry Creek Crossing, Inman had discovered the massacre of two couriers whom Sheridan had dispatched from Bluff Creek on November 18 while on his way to join Custer at Camp Supply. First finding a piece of pantaloons covered with blood and a bullet-riddled coat, Inman searched farther. After chasing away a pack of some thirty wolves, he followed a line of spent cartridge shells and eventually found fragments of the couriers' bodies and a number of letters and dispatches strewn about, including one that reporter Keim had written on the eighteenth. On the return trip to Supply, Inman's escort pursued a small party of Indians without success.

Once Inman had arrived with the necessary supplies, Sheridan lost no time. Reveille was sounded at three o'clock on the morning of December 7, and by ten the expedition was under way, with Fort Cobb as its destination. Reporter Keim provides an excellent description of the expedition as it departed Camp Supply:

At an early hour on the morning of the seventh of December, the entire command was occupied striking tents and packing the camp equipage in the wagons. The day was clear, but intolerably cold and wintry. To break camp, with its few comforts, and set out on an extensive expedition in such weather was not a subject of agreeable contemplation. But wind and weather were entirely ignored in the catalogue of valid reasons for delay. Accordingly at the appointed hour, ten o'clock in the morning, the long dark lines of troopers and wagons were to be seen stretched across the snow covered plain awaiting the order to advance.

The expedition consisted of the eleven companies of the seventh cavalry, ten companies of the volunteers, Pepoon's scouts, and fifteen Osage and Kaw Indians, making a total of about seventeen hundred men. The supplies for men and animals for thirty days, together with shelter tents, cooking utensils and baggage, were conveyed in three hundred wagons. Three of the Cheyenne squaws were also taken with the expedition, to be used in giving information respecting the country.

When all was ready, Sheridan mounted his horse and attended by his staff, rode to the head of the column, and in person gave the order, "Forward." The scouts and Indians took the lead, and were followed by the seventh in front, the wagon train in the centre, and the volunteers as a rear guard. From the crest of the last range of hills, many an eye turned for a regretful gaze upon the little fort in the distant plain.

Two companies of the 19th had been withheld to provide escort for Inman's wagon train, which now returned to Fort Dodge with the Indian prisoners. They were to be taken on from there to Fort Hays. Those of the 19th who no longer had horses were to be left behind at Supply.

The route of Custer's original march southwestward up Wolf Creek was followed the first day, covering some ten or twelve miles before crossing the river and going into camp. It was at this camp that Private David L. Spotts of the 19th Kansas had his first look at the famous boy general of the 7th Cavalry, noting in his diary: "We got to see Gen. Custer today at close range. He is of medium size, light complexion, long curly golden hair, wears a light colored hat and buckskin suit, the same as scouts wear, with leather fringe on the seams of arms and legs. His men all like him."

California Joe was there, too, the wide brim of his dilapidated sombrero tied down over his ears with a cord, a bandanna around his neck which "looked very much as if it had originally served an Indian for a breech-clout," a cavalry overcoat, and a pair of monstrous Mexican spurs. The other white scouts were dressed in a wide variety of coonskin caps, buffalo leggings, and blankets to protect against the biting wind and cold.

The Osage and Kaw trailers were wrapped tightly in their blankets and buffalo robes, very unhappy with this winter campaigning of the white man. Hard Rope, an elderly Osage, commented that he was an old man and it was bad for an old man to be alone in cold weather. He hoped he could capture himself a Cheyenne woman to keep his back warm. Perhaps he was being envious in respect to the three captive women brought along by Custer: Mah-wis-sa; a Sioux woman who had been in Black Kettle's village and whom Mah-wis-sa wanted for company; and the comely Mo-nah-se-tah, daughter of the slain chief Little Rock.

At the first stop on the south bank of Wolf Creek, the cargoes of the wagons were readjusted and the command lined out in formation. The 7th rode the right flank of the train, and the 19th the left flank. One squadron rode as an advance guard, with the Indian and white scouts at the lead, while another troop rode in the rear-guard position. An important duty of the rear guard was to kill animals that gave out, so that they would not fall into the hands of the Indians. A line of flankers rode the outside perimeter some quarter of a mile off to signal if any war parties were spotted. The march began at four each morning and continued until dusk, based on the theory that sunrise and sunset were the favorite times for the Indians to make surprise attacks.

The second day's march was a long one, leaving the sandy, sagebrush country of Wolf Creek and crossing over a seemingly endless area which Keim aptly described as "forests of miniature oaks." This was the "shinnery" or blackjack area of present southern Ellis County, Oklahoma. Around noon, a small herd of buffalo was encountered, and two of the animals were killed. The expedition went into camp that night on a small creek which Sheridan named Hackberry Creek because of the abundance of hackberry trees along its banks.

As the command broke camp on the morning of December 9, a norther struck, driving temperatures as low as 10 or 15 degrees. The winter blast caused the men to suffer severely despite their buffalo boots and fur gloves. Many of the troops, finding it less painful to walk than to ride, dismounted and led their horses. As they approached the valley of the South Canadian, the countryside changed into an even more desolate condition, as described by Keim:

Bald hills rose on all sides, towering high over the plain, while the intermediate valleys could be followed away in the distance between the earth and the heavens. From some lofty eminence, gazing upon the extensive landscape, chaos and desolation alone conveyed the spirit and the reality of the scene. Countless hummocks of red gravel and rocks in every conceivable shape, from perfect cones to jagged boulders, covered the surfaces of the low grounds in every direction. Not a sign of animal life was visible, not a sound broke the awful stillness which prevailed.

The blizzard and the increasingly rough terrain slowed the columns so badly that the South Canadian was not reached in time that day to allow crossing to the other side, where there was more wood. That night as the storm howled furiously, its winds so fierce that the few fires made from green bushes could not be kept going, the troopers were forced to tramp up and down the camp to keep from freezing. The next morning, hardly anyone having slept, the half-frozen teamsters had to beat their suffering animals to get them to move.

Crossing the Canadian was an even more miserable experience. The river was frozen over, but not enough to support the horses or wagons. Troops with axes were sent to break up the ice, and then a company of cavalry went splashing through to break a path. The ice slashed the legs of the horses, causing some to fall and dump their riders into the frigid river. The temperature now having fallen to below zero, wagons froze in place while attempting to cross and had to be cut loose with axes. After five hours, the crossing was made, and the shivering men gathered around large fires built from dead tree limbs and buffalo chips to dry and thaw out.

Finally across, the command began its march on southward to the Washita, now able to see the Antelope Hills looming above the horizon to the west. By four o'clock that afternoon, the expedition reached the Washita, going into camp on its north bank at the top of the oxbow some eight miles below the battle site. Here a halt of one day in the march was ordered by Sheridan to rest troops and animals and give him a chance to visit the battlefield and learn, if possible, the exact fate of Elliott and the seventeen other missing men.

On the following morning, the eleventh of December, Sheridan and Custer, with an escort of over one hundred troops and scouts including one detachment of 19th Kansas and accompanied by Keim, followed the north bank of the river toward the battle site. After a ride of an hour and a half, they approached the battleground from the same direction and route by which Elliott's detachment had advanced upon the village, the tracks still clearly visible. As the search party rode down from the bluffs into the Washita Valley, huge black flocks of birds rose from their feeding while wolves and coyotes sulked away from their feasts. The offensive odor of death hung over the charred remains of Black Kettle's camp. Bodies were still scattered about the area. Some had been wrapped in blankets and tied with ropes for burial, and the surrounding trees held a few corpses already. The bodies of Black Kettle and his wife were gone. On the long hillside some two hundred yards southeast of the village were scattered the bloated carcasses of the Indian ponies that the troops had shot, and a number of Indian dogs were feeding there, snarling at the troops when approached.

Sheridan, Custer, and their party rode to a knoll on the south side of the battlefield. From there could be seen the circles of pins with black fire holes in the center, identifying the locations of the lodges on that fateful morning. Custer explained his battle strategy to Sheridan in detail, and after studying the field for a time, the party moved on eastward, crossing over a ridge. Search parties were spread out to scour the area for Elliott and the other missing troopers.

Beyond the ridge and near a dry tributary of the Washita, one of the parties discovered the naked corpse of a soldier, the torso replete with bullet holes, the skull crushed. At first this was thought to be Elliott, but eventually the body was identified as that of Sergeant Major Kennedy. Later the rivulet was named "Sergeant Major Creek" in his honor. Some two hundred yards on, in the center of a high-grassed, open prairie, they found more chalk-white bodies.

A scene was now witnessed sufficient to appall the bravest heart. Within an area of not more than fifteen yards, lay the sixteen

human bodies—all that remained of Elliott and his party! The winter air swept across the plain, and its cold blasts had added to the
ghastliness of death the additional spectacle of sixteen naked
corpses frozen as solidly as stone. There was not a single body that
did not exhibit evidence of fearful mutilation. They were all lying
with their faces down, and in close proximity to each other. Bullet
and arrow wounds covered the back of each; the throats of a number were cut, and several were beheaded. The body of one of the
horses only, which the men had ridden out, was lying at a distance
of fifty-yards. The other animals had evidently escaped and were
taken by the savages when the party found themselves hemmed in
and obliged to fight on foot.

Besides Elliott and Kennedy, the dead men included three
from Benteen's H Troop and five from Smith's M Troop, these
eight being in Elliott's original detachment. Two were from
Troop E and two from Troop I, making four from Myers' detachment. Three of the bodies could not be identified. Though Keim
stated, "All the missing bodies were found," this still left one 7th
Cavalry trooper who was never accounted for (see Appendix D).

Sheridan and Custer walked the field of action, attempting to
reconstruct the fight in which Elliott and the others were slain. It
will never be known precisely what occurred, but clues from the
field and accounts by Indian participants provide the essential
details. Basically, the contemporary accounts of the fight given
by Philip McCusker, Custer, and Keim—all of whom relied upon
Indian accounts—agree pretty well. McCusker's report of December 3, 1868, which preceded any information from Custer,
describes the fight this way:

> The Indians all fled towards some other camps of the Cheyennes,
> closely pursued by the troops. After the Indians had run a short dis-
> tance they separated in two parties, the braves and young women,
> who were fleet of foot, taking to the right, and the old and infirm
> taking to the left and running into the brush, where they were soon
> surrounded by the soldiers; the other party of Indians, who ran to
> the right, (and among them was one Kiowa,) were hotly pursued
> by a party of eighteen soldiers [which is exactly the number of
> missing men], who were all riding gray horses. They overtook and
> killed some Indians, when they were met by a large party of In-

dians who had rallied from the other camps. Here a sharp action took place, both parties fighting desperately, when one Arapaho brave rushed in, and with his own hands struck down three soldiers, when he was shot through the head and instantly killed. Here the soldiers all dismounted and tied their horses. About this time a Cheyenne brave rushed in and struck down two soldiers, when he was shot through the leg, breaking it and knocking him off his horse. The Indians then made a desperate charge, and succeeded in killing the whole of the party of eighteen men.

Keim's account tells of Elliott pursuing three warriors who attempted to break through his lines to go for help. Two of the three were killed but the third escaped and warned the other Indians, who struck Elliott's band several miles from the battlefield. Elliott began retreating, but the Indians occupied the ravine, Sergeant Major Creek, and forced him to make a stand.

Elliott gathered his men around him. The Indians now appeared on all sides, and with wild shouts gave vent to their savage determination. An Arrapahoe [sic] warrior, braver than the rest, in hopes of inspiring his people with courage, led off at a gallop, with the intention of riding down the party. As he came near, followed by one other warrior, a volley from the troops finished both. Confronted by the whole force of the Arrapahoes, and a large number of Kiowas, and having abandoned their horses, the party on foot made an effort to force their way down to the river and seek protection behind the trees, under cover of which Elliott, probably, hoped to fight his way back. Here, again, the savage warriors intercepted him. When all hope of rescue or escape was given up, the gallant band, evidently, determined to sacrifice their lives as dearly as possible. The grass, where they lay, was much trodden, and numbers of cartridge-shells, scattered on the ground, testified to the valor of the defence [sic], until some friendly, fatal bullet, afforded the only alternative of escape from the terrible torture awaiting them, if taken alive.

Brill, citing Indian sources many years later, tells how three women, three children, and two boys were spotted as they struggled through the snow east of the village. Hoping to draw the soldiers away, the two youths separated from the women and headed off in a southeasterly direction. Elliott, however, did not fall for the ruse and galloped in pursuit of the women and children, taking them prisoners. These he placed under the charge of Sergeant Major Kennedy with orders to take them back to the main force. He then led the other troopers in pursuit of the two Cheyenne boys. The crusted, often deep snow was more difficult for the boys than for the cavalry mounts, and Elliott's men quickly overtook and killed them.

Meanwhile, one of the women left with Kennedy had effected a delay by asking permission to wrap the feet of two of the children. Kennedy allowed his prisoners to stop, and the woman took purposely long in tearing off some strips of clothing for wraps. Suddenly the sound of horses behind him jerked Kennedy about in his saddle in time to see four mounted Indians bearing down upon him. Instantly realizing the perilousness of his situation, he threw one shot from his carbine in the direction of the Indians and jammed spurs to his horse. But it was too late. His mount was still struggling to gain momentum when the four warriors, all Arapahoes, dragged Kennedy from his horse and killed him with a blow of a battle-ax to his neck.

Kennedy's death was witnessed from a distance by Elliott's party. They also saw that many other warriors were coming up and that the whole area would soon be swarming with them. Wheeling their horses about, the group headed back toward the village battlefield, now some two miles away on the other side of a dividing ridge. But the Arapahoes, now nine in number, formed between them and the ridge for a charge. With his horses already spent, Elliott chose to employ the tactic of dismounting and taking up kneeling positions for more effective firing, every fourth trooper holding the horses of the other three.

The Arapahoes made their charge, driving head on at first, then suddenly splitting to either side, throwing themselves on the far side of their ponies and firing from under the animals' necks or rising up just long enough to get off a shot. They then went into an encircling movement around the beleaguered soldiers. Using the same tactics as had Custer's wagon train when attacked by Sioux near Fort Wallace, Elliott and his men began moving forward, fighting their way slowly toward the west, firing and reloading as they went. Evidently neither side did the other much real damage during this phase of the fight, except to kill a few horses.

But now the other Arapaho braves plus some Kiowas had come up and joined the fray, and this increasing force of swirling Indians, riding in ever closer, made it more and more difficult for the soldiers to advance. Ahead of them was the rivulet, whose banks could offer protection below the level of the prairie. But before the soldiers could reach it, a number of the Indians dismounted and took up positions there themselves, establishing a field of fire that Elliott could not penetrate. He tried to move toward the Washita; again he was cut off. His movement halted, there was no choice now but to utilize the tall grass. Tying their horses, the men took a prone position with their feet together and facing outward in a circle so as to defend themselves in all directions at one time.

Here Elliott and his men fought against the encirclement of mounted warriors. How long they might have held out is problematical. By this account the final coup was led by a Cheyenne named Tobacco, who charged Elliott's position and was killed. Nonetheless, his boldness led the others to make a rush against the embattled troopers, killing them all. The Arapaho Left Hand is cited as being with the attackers throughout the fight.

George Bent's account agrees with that of McCusker in that he tells of three Indians being pursued by Elliott:

She-Wolf, Cheyenne Indian, Little Rock, Cheyenne, and a Kiowa Indian were running down Washita river with squaws and children after Custer's attack on Black Kettle's village. She-Wolf, who is here now living, tells me this. He says they all came to a very deep hole of water, and high banks on each side of it, so they all had to get out of the creek bottom into open place to get around this deep hole. Soon as they came up in open view, Elliott and his men seen them, and charged towards them. Little Rock told the squaws and children to run back for the creek. These three men stayed behind the women and children to fight for them. Elliott and his men charged upon them, and commenced firing into them. Here Little Rock was killed. The Kiowa Indian, now living, ran to Little Rock and picked up his arrows (this Kiowa only had two arrows left), he picked up six arrows of Little Rock. Understand, these people were running from Black Kettle's camp or village. A Cheyenne woman called White-Buffalo-Woman, now living with her sister, had been running so long the girl gave out here. One soldier rode up to them and made motion to them to walk back towards the camp. The soldier got off his horse and walked behind them. Just in front of them a lot of warriors running from Black Kettle's village, rode up out of the creek timber. The soldier fired at the Indians as they were charging toward them [him]. This soldier, White-Buffalo-Woman says, shot at the warriors two times and then got cartridge fast in his carbine. Bob-Tail-Bear rode up to the soldier and tomahawked him.

Elliott and his men were still chasing She-Wolf and the women and children down Washita river when these warriors cut him off from Custer. Bob-Tail-Bear and his warriors pushed Elliott and his men right into a lot of warriors that were coming up from the big village of Cheyennes and Arapahoes. When Elliott saw he was surrounded they [he and his men] turned all their horses loose, then himself and his men got in among high grass and were all lying down when the Indians rode around them. Touching-the-Sky tells me he got off his horse and crawled up towards them in small ravine and could see them lying down. When he motioned to Indians to bring their guns he says several came running, stooping down. These opened fire on Elliott and his men and must have hit several of them as it was very close. Those Indians on horses commenced to close in on Elliott, and those in the ravine kept shooting at them [him]. In a little while Roman-Nose-Thunder, Cheyenne, now living, was first to ride over Elliott and his men. Then the Indians all made charge on them. Elliott and his men did not do much shooting for some reason, and Elliott and his men were all killed inside of two hours. She-Wolf and squaws then went to where Elliott and his men were killed. They had stopped in the creek soon as Elliott had left them, to rest up. The warriors after killing Elliott and his men went on up to where Custer's command was, and fought him again.

Some accounts give Left Hand credit for leading the Arapahoes in their annihilation of Elliott and his men. But a source much closer in time to the event disputes this. When a group of Quakers visited the Darlington agency in 1870, one noted in his diary the presence of some Cheyenne and Arapaho chiefs, including Big Mouth, who had been with Black Kettle when he met with Hazen prior to the battle: "Big Mouth, Arapahoe, commanded the Indian troop which slaughtered Major Elliott & command, perhaps the day after Black Kettle's camp was destroyed—Big Mouth has Major Elliott's horse yet."

When found, Elliott's body had two bullet holes in the head, plus numerous other wounds. Kennedy had a bullet hole in his right temple, and his head was partly severed from his body; he had seventeen bullet holes in his back and two in his legs. The others suffered similar wounds, many of them evidence that the Indians counted coup on them by riding up and shooting the bodies with bullets and arrows. Several of the men were scalped, some were beheaded, all were badly cut up.

Having found Elliott and his men, Sheridan and Custer continued on back along the south side of the river to camp. A detachment of the 19th Kansas followed more closely to the river's bank, and Doctor Bailey of that unit made another discovery. The bodies of a white woman and a small child of about two years of age were found. The woman, petite and exceptionally pretty, in her early twenties, was dressed in ordinary clothing and wore a pair of leather gaiters on her feet. A piece of corncake was found lying upon her breast, and the position of her hands made it appear she had been eating at the time of her death. She had been shot in the head, and the back of her skull was crushed. The child, who looked extremely undernourished, had only a single bruise on his face, giving rise to the speculation that he had been seized by the feet and bashed against a tree. (See Appendix E.)

The woman and child were taken back to camp and there laid out on a blanket, the boy on the woman's arm, and the men of the 19th Kansas were ordered to march by to see if they could identify the two. Eventually the woman was recognized as Mrs. Clara Blinn by one of the Kansans.

Wagons were detailed to bring in the bodies of Elliott and the others. It was nine o'clock before the wagons returned. Custer ordered Assistant Surgeon Lippincott to make a thorough examination of each body. Large fires were built, and several men from each company of the 7th came forward to help identify the victims. Each corpse was then wrapped in a blanket and carried to a trench that had been dug on a small knoll overlooking the Washita Valley just west of the camp site. It was midnight. With "death-like darkness and the mournful wintry wind" setting an eerie scene, the men of Elliott's lost detachment were buried by the flickering light of torches. The grave was covered over with logs and brush to keep the wolves from digging it up. The bodies of Elliott, Mrs. Blinn, and her child were placed in an ambulance to be taken to Fort Cobb and on to Fort Arbuckle for interment.

The matter of Custer's abandonment of the battlefield without making more effort to locate Elliott added fuel to the anti-Custer sentiments within the 7th's officer corps. It was brought to a head in a clash between Custer and Captain Frederick Benteen.

Benteen was a strapping Missourian who had served with the 10th Regiment of Missouri Cavalry during the Civil War. After seeing action as a captain with Bowen's battalion at the Battle of Pea Ridge, Arkansas, in 1862, Benteen was with the unit that fall, when it became a part of the 10th Missouri under Colonel Winslow. He was cited for his "gallant work" with the 10th in a number of raids into Alabama and Georgia and, like Elliott, was a part of Sheridan's Mississippi expedition. In 1864 the cavalry regiment was sent to the Missouri-Arkansas-Kansas area and took part in battles that blunted the invasion of General "Pap" Price and his Rebel army. During the battle of Little Osage Crossing, Winslow was wounded, and Benteen, now a lieutenant colonel, helped Major General Curtis drive Price back into the South. Benteen scoured southern Missouri, northern Arkansas, and the Indian Territory.

That same month, the 10th Missouri was ordered to Louisville, Kentucky, where it took part in Grierson's raid on the Mobile & Ohio Railroad and the capture of Veron and Egypt Station in late December—the same action in which Elliott participated. Benteen was recommended for the brevet rank of brigadier general for gallant and meritorious service, but this never received final approval.

That Benteen disliked Custer and that at least a portion of that dislike stemmed from jealousy is pretty well established Ben Clark contends that Benteen came to him after the Washita fight and asked him to make a statement to the effect that Custer had knowingly let Elliott go to his doom without trying to save him, a request that Clark refused.

A letter, scathingly critical of Custer's role in the Washita battle, appeared in the St. Louis *Democrat* and later in the New York *Times*. A copy of the St. Louis newspaper was sent to Custer while the regiment was in camp on Medicine Bluff Creek during January 1869. It read in part:

> But does no one think of the welfare of Maj. Elliott and party? It seems not. But yes! a squadron of cavalry is in motion. They trot; they gallop. Now they charge! The cowardly redskins flee the coming shock and scatter here and there among the hills scurry away. But is it the true line—will the cavalry keep it? No! No! They turn: Ah, 'tis only to intercept the wily foe. See! a gray troop goes on in the direction again. One more short mile and they will be saved. Oh, for a mother's prayers! Will not some good angel prompt them? They charge the mound—a few scattering shots, and the murderous pirates of the Plains go unhurt away. There is no hope for that brave little band, the death doom is theirs, for the cavalry halt and rest their panting steeds.

Much told is a story of how Custer called his officers together, the newspaper in one hand and his riding quirt in the other. He could tell, he said, that the article had been written by one of the officers, and if he found out who it was he would give the guilty one a sound thrashing. After a moment, Captain Benteen stepped forward and asked to see the paper.

Benteen read a few lines of the newspaper article. He recognized it as a letter he had written to a friend in St. Louis without intending for it to be published. The story goes that Benteen handed the newspaper back to Custer and at the same time adjusted his holster, saying that Custer could start in, because he, Benteen, was the author. Custer was nonplussed, his face turning scarlet. Finally, with a tight voice, he growled that he would see Benteen later, and stomped away. Nothing more was ever said about the matter between the two men. But the controversy over Elliott's death had reopened an old sore within the 7th Regiment, one that would fester all the way to the Little Bighorn.

Chapter XI
DELIVERANCE BY DECEPTION

Sheridan's expedition departed the Washita battlefield on December 12, heading down the river toward Fort Cobb. For nearly twelve miles along the river, they encountered the hastily abandoned camps of the other Indian tribes, finding lodgepoles still in place, wood stacked around burned-out campfires, and many items such as knives, kettles, moccasins, broken saddles, and other paraphernalia the Indians had left behind in their hurried exodus.

It was a miserable march, with yet another winter's blast hitting them, piling snow knee-deep and making the already difficult traveling even more so. Teamsters were forced to dig harness out of the ice and snow with frozen fingers in the morning darkness, and troopers were kept busy with picks, axes, and shovels to keep the wagons moving. "Pioneer parties" were put to building bridges across the ravine-slashed lands along the Washita. Though skies soon cleared and temperatures rose, the march was very hard on the horses, which floundered through the slush and red mud and daily became poorer due to the hard use and lack of forage. The men, who were forced by the officers to walk much of the way to save the horses, became footsore and weary. Still, a number of animals were lost on the march.

On the sixteenth, a small band of Indians was sighted, and Company C of the 7th charged after them, reportedly killing one. On the morning following, as the command was struggling to cross a ravine, one of the Osage scouts of the advance guard galloped back bringing a courier from Fort Cobb. The courier, a half-breed Comanche who had been ahead with a party of Indians bearing a white flag of truce, carried a dispatch addressed to the "Commander of troops in the field." It was from General Hazen at Fort Cobb, written on the day previous:

> Indians have just brought in word that our troops to-day reached the Washita some 20 miles above here. I send this to say that all the camps this side of the point reported to have been reached are friendly, and have not been on the war-path this season. If this reaches you, it would be well to communicate at once with Satanta or Black Eagle, chiefs of the Kiowas, near where you are now, who will readily inform you of the position of the Cheyennes and Arapahoes, also of our camp.

Another courier from Cobb, a man named Hart, was being held by Satanta, whose Kiowas were ahead. The Kiowa chief, upon learning of the military expedition approaching the vicinity of his camping grounds, had sent word to Hazen, who had promised that if the Kiowas camped near Fort Cobb and remained at peace, they would be protected.

Sheridan and Custer were thoroughly disgusted with Hazen for writing the letter. On the day after Custer's return to Camp Supply, Sheridan had complained to division headquarters, "Flour, sugar, and coffee, found in Black Kettle's village, was furnished by General Hazen. Something should be done to stop this anomaly. I am ordered to fight these Indians, and General Hazen is permitted to feed them." Here before them were the very Indians they had come to punish, for which they felt they had full justification. In one of the wagons were the bodies of Mrs. Blinn and her son, whom Mah-wis-sa said the Kiowas had murdered. But now came Hazen, talking like a peace advocate and telling them that Satanta was a friendly Indian and was not to be attacked. The same feeling was shared by the troops, especially the men of the 19th Kansas who had missed the Washita fight and who now saw their chance for the glory of battle. Still, Sheridan felt obligated to honor Hazen's position. He directed Custer to proceed to meet the Kiowas.

Somehow their trails had failed to cross in Kansas. Now here they were in the wilds of the Indian Territory, face to face, Custer and Satanta, both with their armies behind them. Custer, of the buckskins, bushy mustache, and blond hair curling long beneath his campaign hat; Satanta, hawkish, bronze face surrounded by straight black hair and fierce gaze. In Custer's party were several officers, the reporter Keim, and Lieutenant Pepoon's fifty-man force of scouts, while cresting the high ground a mile or so in the rear were the long, blue columns of the 7th Cavalry and the 19th Kansas. Satanta was accompanied only by Chief Lone Wolf, but to the left, among the trees that skirted the Washita, could be seen an indeterminable number of Indian warriors. On the hills behind the two chiefs was another force of Indians, estimated at around five hundred, riding about in battle array, brandishing their lances and rifles to indicate their willingness to fight.

Satanta and Lone Wolf sat their ponies in the center of a broad valley as Custer sent forward two interpreters to meet them. After a brief parley, a sign was given that the chiefs wished to talk with the "Big White Chief," and Custer then rode forward, accompanied by Sheridan's aide, Lieutenant Colonel J. Schuyler Crosby, and correspondent Keim, each with both pistol and rifle ready. Satanta, mistaking the uniformed Crosby as the ranking officer, rode forward to him and extended his hand with the usual greeting: "How!"

Crosby, however, refused to shake hands with Satanta, and the Kiowa chief drew back fiercely, striking his fist against his chest in angry indignation, exclaiming, "Me Kiowa!" For a dangerous second it appeared that Satanta was going to signal his warriors, who were milling about like angry hornets on the hilltops. But then the chief wheeled his pony to Custer's side and offered his hand to the long-haired cavalryman. Custer likewise spurned the Kiowa's gesture, explaining through his interpreter that he never shook hands with anyone "unless I know him to be a friend."

Satanta studied Custer for a long moment, then appeared to accept the explanation. Custer now called for the release of the white courier held captive by Satanta and issued Sheridan's demand that the Indians go immediately to Fort Cobb with their villages. Satanta signaled for the release of the courier, and then suggested that he and his other chiefs ride with Custer and Sheridan to the fort. This seemed to be reasonable to Custer, and he escorted Satanta and his party of about twenty Kiowa, Comanche, and Apache chiefs to where the troops of the 7th and 19th had waited expectantly with their carbines fully loaded and ready across their saddles. There Sheridan begrudgingly ordered rations distributed to the Indians, and soon the march was resumed, Satanta's army of warriors riding parallel to the troops at a distance.

On the morning following the meeting with Satanta, however, it was discovered that all but three chiefs had disappeared during the night. The remaining chiefs suggested that they, too, needed to go to their village to change horses and give directions to their people concerning the move to Fort Cobb. Custer states that he did let a lesser Kiowa chief go but placed Satanta and Lone Wolf under guard as hostages. Captain Thompson, however, tells it differently. He says that Custer allowed Satanta to leave. Around three that afternoon, the Kiowa chief returned with his son and from a hilltop beckoned for the others to join him. Custer and a party rode out to meet Satanta, who tried to escape before reaching the column. Keim agrees that Satanta tried to make a run for it but was caught by officers with faster horses after about a half-mile race. Following this, a squad of soldiers was placed as a guard over Satanta, Lone Wolf, and two Apache chiefs.

Fort Cobb was reached at dark on December 18, and the two chiefs were placed in leg irons and kept in a closely guarded Sibley tent. Sheridan, who was convinced that Satanta had merely ridden with them in order to allow his Kiowas to escape, was determined that he would "take some of the starch out of them before I get through with them." Though he himself refused even to talk with the Kiowas, Sheridan ordered Custer to tell them that if their families were not in by sunrise of the next day, December 20, he would hang the two chiefs. Satanta was allowed to send word to his people by his son Tsalante. Moore of the 19th Kansas described Satanta's reactions:

He would wrap his blanket around himself and come out and sit down by the side of the tent, then swaying back and forth, chant the most doleful and monotonous death-song. Then stooping over he would scoop up sand and dirt and put into his mouth. Then he would go around to the south and west side of the tent and, shading his eyes with his hand, would sweep the horizon to discover if possible the approach of his people.

The results were immediate. On the morning following, a number of other Kiowa chiefs arrived to assure Custer that their villages were on the way to Cobb. Within two days they arrived, a small party of chiefs led by Black Eagle followed by the warriors and then the women and children, their goods piled on travois and accompanied by their camp dogs and, in the rear, the horse herds. All of the Kiowas came in except Kicking Bird's band, establishing their camp a mile below the fort, on the north bank of the Washita. Sheridan, convinced as to the Kiowas' guilt for depredations and murders in both Kansas and Texas, later wrote: "I shall always regret, however, that I did not hang these Indians; they had deserved it many times; and I shall also regret that I did not punish the whole tribe when I first met them."

Efforts were also being made to talk in the Arapahoes and Cheyennes. On December 20, Custer dispatched an Apache chief, Iron Shirt, and Mah-wis-sa as emissaries to carry a message of friendship to the two tribes. When Iron Shirt returned, Mah-wis-sa was not with him, she reportedly having been ordered by the chiefs not to return. However, Iron Shirt did carry promises from Little Robe of the Cheyennes and Yellow Bear of the Arapahoes that, being anxious for peace, they would bring in their villages shortly.

At midnight of December 31, 1868, a delegation of twenty-one Cheyenne and Arapaho chiefs arrived at Fort Cobb. They were afoot, their horses being too weak to carry them. Their ponies were all dying, they said. There was no buffalo where they were now forced to hide for the protection of their families, and even their camp dogs were all eaten up. They asked permission to bring in their people, who were starving. On January 2, Sheridan

and Custer held a long council at Fort Cobb with the chiefs of
the Apaches, Kiowas, Comanches, Cheyennes, and Arapahoes,
during which the tribes agreed to maintain peaceful relations
with the government.

Meanwhile the other two prongs of Sheridan's winter campaign had been in operation. A command of seven companies of
5th Cavalry under Major (Brevet Major General) Eugene A.
Carr left Fort Lyon, Colorado, in December and scouted
southeastward to the North Canadian and down the river,
finding no Indians. On December 30, Carr established a supply
depot just north of the Texas panhandle, then penetrated on
southward to Skull Creek, in the northern Texas panhandle.
Company L of the 7th Cavalry served as a wagon-train escort to
Skull Creek before Carr finally returned battle-less to Fort Lyon.

Somewhat more successful was a force of 3rd Cavalry and
37th Infantry under Major (Brevet Lieutenant Colonel) A. W.
Evans. Leaving Fort Bascom, New Mexico, on November 18,
Evans drove eastward along the South Canadian River across the
Texas panhandle. On December 7 he established a supply
redoubt on Monument Creek. From there he again took up his
march on December 18, striking an Indian trail that led him to
the west side of the Wichita Mountains. There, on Christmas
Day on the North Fork of the Red River, he discovered and attacked a Comanche village, which he burned. Twenty to twenty-
five Indians were reported killed, with the loss of one soldier.
Carr continued his hunt to within twenty miles of Fort Cobb,
where couriers from Sheridan brought orders for him to return to
Fort Bascom. On January 13, 1869, Carr reached his supply
depot on Monument Creek, having lost 172 horses and over sixty
mules by starvation on the long march.

Fort Cobb being anything but a satisfactory post, Sheridan
looked to the establishment of a new base of operations farther
to the south, where the military could keep closer surveillance on
the tribes ranging in the vicinity of the Wichita Mountains. On
the morning of December 28, he had dispatched Colonel Benjamin H. Grierson of the 10th Cavalry (Colored)—the same
Grierson who led the famous Civil War raid into Mississippi—to
reconnoiter a potential site for a new post near the juncture of

Medicine Bluff Creek and Cache Creek, some forty miles south of Fort Cobb and just to the east of the Wichita Mountains.

On January 3 and 4, two large wagon trains loaded with much-needed supplies arrived at Fort Cobb, and by the sixth both the 19th Kansas and the 7th regiments had moved out of Cobb toward the new location, going into camp there on January 8. At first the new post was called "New Fort Cobb" by some, and the officers of the 7th recommended naming it "Fort Elliott" in honor of their fallen comrade. Most of the soldiers merely referred to it as the "camp on Medicine Bluff Creek." Eventually Sheridan designated the post as "Fort Sill," in honor of an old West Point classmate, Joshua W. Sill, who had been killed during the Civil War. The site was an ideal one, offering grassy meadows, good water, wood supply, stone for building, and wild game in abundance. The area was, in fact, a veritable hunter's paradise.

Concerned that the Cheyenne and Arapaho villages had not come in, Custer decided to go out with a minimum-size force of forty men—large enough to defend itself but not so big as to frighten the Indians—and visit the Indian camps. Cheyenne chief Little Robe and Arapaho chief Yellow Bear agreed to accompany him as guides. Going along also were Tom Custer, Lieutenant Robbins, Surgeon Renick, Romero, California Joe, another Indian guide named Neva, and young Daniel Brewster. Brewster was the brother of Mrs. Morgan, who had been captured by the Indians during the Solomon raids of the previous fall.

Brewster had shown up at Camp Supply and approached Custer about being allowed to go along with the command. Custer at first refused, but when the boy explained about his sister, whom he hoped to rescue, Custer relented and gave him a job as a substitute teamster. Originally from New Jersey, the young man had had his father and a brother killed in the war, and his mother had died soon after, leaving only him and his sister. Though barely twenty years of age, the youth journeyed to Kansas, where he took up a claim on the Solomon River. After building a cabin, he sent for his sister to come out and keep house for him, which she did until she married a carpenter named Morgan and moved onto a homestead—only a month before her capture.

Traveling westward along the northern foot of the Wichitas, Custer eventually contacted Little Raven's band of Arapahoes, who received him in friendly fashion and promised to move in to the new fort. With his command destitute of supplies by this time, Custer dispatched California Joe to contact a preplanned supply cortege under Lieutenant Cook. When Cook arrived with his dozen men and pack animals, Custer proceeded southward to the Red River. Meanwhile, Brewster and Neva made a search westward to the Red River, hoping to contact the Cheyenne band that held captive a white girl answering to his sister's description. Locating only a weak trail that led on farther west, Brewster and Neva returned to rejoin Custer. The expedition made it back to Medicine Bluff Creek on February 7. It had been a rough trip, as Custer told his wife in a letter written to her on the eighth. They were ". . . gone sixteen days, without wagons or tents. Our provisions became exhausted, there was no game, and officers and men subsisted on parched corn and horseflesh. . . ."

Conditions at the post were not much better. The officers, who had their own supply chests and were allowed to stock canned goods, had a difficult time keeping their food stuff from being stolen by the hungry men. One soldier, who was caught stealing a ham from an officer of the 19th Kansas, was left bound and gagged on the parade ground and almost suffocated before the matter was reported to another officer, who demanded the soldier's release. On another occasion, a soldier was tied spread-eagled on the ground for a similar offense.

Desertions were still a problem. Three men deserted in early February, taking with them a horse belonging to Captain Pliley, who had gained a reputation for not losing a horse during the entire march. Pliley requested the loan of an Osage scout from Custer and with another officer went after the deserters. The three returned later with the horses and guns of the men but with no prisoners, saying only that the last time they saw the men in question they were lying "looking at the sun."

But desertions in both the 7th and the 19th continued, the men usually heading for Texas, which lay just across the Red River, to the south. In late February there was a mutiny by men of the 19th Kansas who complained because they had not been paid and were being fed so poorly that it was beginning to show in their faces. In fact, provisions for payment of the expense of the 19th had been cut out of a House bill. On February 14, Crawford resigned his commission in order to go to Washington to see about getting pay for the volunteers. Command of the unit went to Lieutenant Colonel Moore.

Sheridan had decided to return to Kansas, and on February 23 he set out for Camp Supply with his staff, Keim, and an escort of Pepoon's scouts. It was determined also that the garrison at the new fort would be turned over to Grierson and the 10th Cavalry. Custer would lead the 7th and 19th back to Fort Hays via Camp Supply but would conduct an Indian-hunting expedition on the way. On February 16, Satanta and Lone Wolf were finally released from their imprisonment.

Custer left Medicine Bluff Creek on March 2, 1869, with a command of eleven troops of 7th Cavalry and ten of 19th Kansas, driving westward around the south side of the Wichitas to the crumbled site of old Camp Radziminski, which had been established in 1858 as an outpost for troops of the 2nd Cavalry and abandoned prior to the Civil War. There Custer divided his command, selecting some eight hundred men from both units and placing Captain Myers in charge of the remainder with orders to proceed with the wagon train to the vicinity of the Washita battleground, there to wait further orders. Major Inman was to meet them there with a train of supplies.

Not all were aware as they camped at Radziminski on March 4 that another Civil War hero, Ulysses S. Grant, was on that day being inaugurated as President of the United States. Few cared, for it was cold, snowy, and windy, and many of the 19th were nursing blistered feet. Before leaving Medicine Bluff Creek, the horses of the 19th had been taken from them and turned over to the 7th, the spent ones being sent to Fort Arbuckle, where Sheridan had leased a cornfield for them. The men of the 19th, bitter but determined to prove they could keep up with the mounted 7th, were thereafter referred to by the Indians as "wakaheaps."

Custer soon struck a fresh trail, made by about fourteen mounted Indians and a single travois. With the Osage trailer running ahead to read the trail, Custer followed in hot pursuit. On the third day, they overtook the Indians, who had gone into camp because of an approaching storm. A company of the 7th charged the camp and quickly captured it, only to find that the Indians had heard the barking of Custer's dogs and escaped. Custer himself attempted to cut off the escape of an Indian woman, but she eluded him, causing the 7th to receive some hearty joshing from the men of the 19th that they could not even catch a single squaw. All the 7th could claim from the action was one lodge, eleven ponies, cooking utensils, and a few provisions.

Custer now called his officers together. The command was already seriously low on provisions, and it seemed inadvisable to push the hunt any farther. Custer had originally intended to drive a beef herd along with him, but to his disgust the commissary failed to deliver the cattle. Despite the difficulty of their situation, most of the officers accepted Custer's intuition that success lay ahead, and it was agreed to push on.

On the morning of the ninth, the march was continued westward, crossing the Texas border, but on the following day Custer turned directly south and went into camp on the Salt Fork of the Red River. From there he moved southwestward until the main stream of the Red River was reached. There a trail, judged to be nearly a month old and of only one lodge, was discovered. It led northward, and, with no better prospects in sight, Custer decided to follow it in hopes it would lead to something bigger. After a time the command had the satisfaction of seeing the trail joined by another eleven lodges, still headed northward. On March 12 it was seen that even more lodges had enlarged the trail, it now consisting of some one hundred or more.

The march became increasingly difficult, and the men of the 19th began to discover what the 7th's troops already knew: that Custer had a penchant for long, hard marches:

> The pace was that of the forced march of light cavalry. From the first of dawn till dark, with a few minutes' stop two or three times a day, the march was steady. Always scores of men hobbled in the

This post-Washita photo taken at Camp Supply includes Custer's interpreter Romero (standing third from left), John Simpson Smith (standing fourth from left), and agent Brinton Darlington (standing fifth from left). The identities of the others are an intriguing mystery, particularly the two Indians standing at center, one of whom is holding a military saber. *Courtesy of Division of Manuscripts, University of Oklahoma.*

Photographed during an 1871 visit to Washington were (seated) Little Raven; Cheyenne chief Bird Chief; Cheyenne chief Little Robe; and Buffalo Goad, Wichita chief. Standing are Edmund Guerrier, who served as guide for Custer on his first campaign against the Indians; Kaw agent Mahlon Stubbs; long-time Cheyenne interpreter and frontiersman John Simpson Smith; and Philip Mc-Cusker, Comanche interpreter who was at Fort Cobb when the Washita fight occurred. *Courtesy of Smithsonian Institution.*

This photo, taken at Fort Dodge by William Soule, includes Arapaho chief Little Raven, William Bent of Bent's Fort, and Raven's daughter and two sons. The one on the far right, Shield, was reportedly a leader in the Solomon and Saline raids. *Courtesy of Bureau of American Ethnology.*

Kicking Bird, though known to be a peaceful Kiowa chief, refused to come in to Fort Cobb with his band. *Courtesy of Western History Collections, University of Oklahoma.*

Arapaho chief Left Hand was reported by many to have been one of the leaders of the Indian counterattack after Custer's massacre of Black Kettle's village. *Courtesy of Bureau of American Ethnology.*

Kiowa chief Satanta was taken prisoner by Custer and Sheridan and was threatened with hanging if the Kiowas did not come in to Fort Cobb. *Courtesy of Western Historical Collection, University of Oklahoma Library.*

It was reported that Big Mouth, an Arapaho chief who had been with Black Kettle during his conference with Hazen before the Washita fight, had killed Elliott during the battle and later rode Elliott's horse. *Courtesy of Smithsonian Institution.*

rear, staggering into camp during the night only to limp off with the others at early dawn. The mules were starving, but having been in fairly good flesh at the start, they kept their feet pretty well till the 10th. As long as one could be got into the next camp its life was sacred—none might touch its tempting quarters. On the 10th, coffee and sugar, met at rare intervals hitherto, disappeared from society. Tobacco was a dream. On the 12th the worst calamity of all befell—the salt gave out. Day and night it was bitter cold. A bitter wind penetrated the threadbare and ragged clothing, while an increasing number became barefooted daily. The short sleep at night was broken by cold.

At last the mules began to fall. Every morning, when it became evident that rest had not restored an animal, its throat was cut and it was used for food, while the remaining mules were "doubled" into complete teams, and the extra wagons and all belonging to them were burned. At first awakening the fatigue, soreness and cold of the night made it seem impossible to move. As there was no breakfast to cook, the command moved out at once.

The order went out now that no bugle calls or firing of guns would be permitted. That night, in camp on the Salt Fork, no fires were allowed until after dark, when smoke could not be seen at a distance. Light marching orders were issued and, though the nights were freezing, all blankets but one per man were burned along with tents and all clothing not being worn. A number of wagons, many of which were already empty and whose animals had worn out, were likewise destroyed. The men were now on the severest of rations, many of them eating steaks from the horses and mules shot by the rear guard. The horses themselves were long since out of corn, and they were fed upon armfuls of cottonwood bark cut for them by the troopers.

For two more days the small army moved forward as rapidly as the spent horses and weary men could follow behind the lead of Hard Rope, the Osage who ran the trail ahead. The course was northward along the one hundredth meridian, on the Texas side, heading for the Washita River. On the morning of the fifteenth an abandoned camp site on the North Fork told them that the Indians were now only a short distance ahead. Custer pushed on rapidly, and around noon, as the command

approached the Sweetwater River, the Osage trailer came on a
herd of Indian ponies grazing, watched over by two Indians,
who saw Custer's advance at about the same time.

The Indian herdsmen at once drove the ponies off toward a
timbered stream. Custer's command was strung back along the
trail for several miles, and he immediately sent word for the columns to close up. After moving forward for about two miles with
only Romero and his orderly with him, Custer spotted a number
of Indians partially concealed by some sand hills ahead. Through
Romero he indicated his wish to parley until finally eight of the
Indians came forward. From them Custer learned that a large
Cheyenne village lay ahead, numbering around two hundred
lodges. It was Medicine Arrow's band, while not far away was
the camp of Little Robe. Custer requested that Medicine Arrow
be sent for.

In a few moments a party of about forty Indians came galloping up, led by Medicine Arrow, who, after a brief parley, invited
the yellow-haired general to visit his village, saying that it would
reassure the Cheyennes, who would otherwise be greatly
alarmed upon seeing such a large body of troops approaching.
Custer, now joined by Lieutenant Cook and Assistant Surgeon
Lippincott, accepted Medicine Arrow's invitation, believing that
the threat his force offered against the security of the Indian village was enough to provide him safety. Leaving instructions for
his command with Lippincott, Custer allowed himself and Cook
to be escorted into the Cheyenne village, seeing Mah-wis-sa
among the women as he passed.

Custer was ushered into Medicine Arrow's lodge, and there he
sat through an ordeal of ceremonies by a medicine man, even
sharing a smoke of the potent kinnikinnick, which the Indians
smoked in lieu of tobacco. It was about all that the nonsmoking
Custer could stomach, but he managed to endure, explaining the
purpose of his march as being to get the Cheyennes to come in
to their reservation at Camp Supply. Medicine Arrow agreed to
call his chiefs together, talk about the matter, and let Custer
know their decision.

Meanwhile, outside the lodge, the camp had been thrown into
a turmoil by the arrival of the columns, which surrounded the

village with arms ready. A herd of ponies had been quickly driven into the camp, and almost all the Indians were mounted and riding about excitedly. Private Hadley wrote of the reaction of the Kansas volunteers who had made this torturous march to meet the Cheyennes:

> As the men gripped their repeating carbines and saw that they each had a cartridge in the barrel and seven others in the magazine, an officer came from Custer with the order to Colonel Moore: "Don't fire on those Indians." The men, stupid with wonder, hardly realized what it meant, before another aide brought Moore the orders for his position. The Nineteenth was marched into the valley at the upper end of the village and halted in column of troops to "rest in place." The men of the Nineteenth, not knowing the reason for this, and fearing their general had been tricked, as had so often been the case, were angry. Neither Custer nor Moore ever knew what a critical time it was for about ten minutes. It looked, at one time, like they could not be restrained. The line officers argued, begged and cursed. The accidental discharge of a carbine, or the shout of a reckless soldier, would have precipitated a killing that could not have been stopped, and would have entailed consequences impossible to estimate.

Another member of the 19th, trooper Rodgers, gave a vivid description of the situation in the Indian camp:

> The warriors were all mounted coming out of the timber, hundreds of them, riding in a circle in a threatening way, swinging their rifles over their heads, with one war whoop after another, as that was their mode of doing before a charge. Their bonnets painted up, fringed and beaded leggings, and once in a while one with a gaudy blanket over his shoulder. The troops stood there, anxious for the order to fire. The officers were watching every soldier to see that he did not fire. Our troops faces [were] black, with smoke from the camp-fires, their eyes sunk, and their teeth standing out like skeletons, their cheeks sunk in.

Finally Custer came out of the village and withdrew the troops some three quarters of a mile up the Sweetwater, where they went into camp. On the day following, Medicine Arrow and some of his headmen arrived in the soldiers' camp, stating that in a gesture of friendship some of their young men would like to perform for them. Around a dozen warriors, themselves and their horses bedecked with ornaments, put on a dazzling display of horsemanship, galloping around in ever smaller circles while making sounds on a reedlike instrument.

While this show was in progress, an officer came to Custer and reported that the Indian village was decamping. Custer gave the word for his officers to mingle with the visiting Indians and upon his signal to pull their revolvers and take prisoner the chiefs then seated around the campfire. Having learned by now from Mo-nah-se-tah that two captive white women were in Medicine Arrow's village, it was Custer's intention to use the Indians as hostages to secure their release. He was apparently unconcerned that on the day previous the Indians could have betrayed their hospitality and done the same to him when Custer visited their camp, but had not.

To show he did not wish to fight, Custer stood up and un-buckled his side arm, allowing it to fall to the ground. At the same time, he informed the chiefs that his men had them surrounded and asked them to submit to capture quietly.

The Cheyennes immediately reacted, springing to their feet, grabbing their weapons and horses in readiness to defend themselves. Some of the younger ones wished to fight then and there, but the older chiefs restrained them. Custer described the scene in his book, *My Life on the Plains:*

> Even at this date I recall no more exciting experience with Indians than the occasion of which I now write. Near to me stood a tall, gray-haired chief, who, while entreating his people to be discreet, kept his cocked revolver in his hand ready for use, should the emergency demand it. He was one of the few whom I had determined to hold. Near him stood another, a most powerful and forbidding-looking warrior, who was without firearms, but who was armed with a bow already strung, and a quiver full of iron-pointed arrows. His coolness during this scene of danger and excitement was often the subject of remark afterward between the officers whose attention had been drawn to him. He stood apparently unaffected by the excitement about him, but not unmindful of the

surrounding danger. Holding his bow in one hand, with the other he continued to draw from his quiver arrow after arrow. Each one he would examine as coolly as if he expected to engage in target practice. First he would cast his eye along the shaft of the arrow, to see if it was perfectly straight and true. Then he would with thumb and finger gently feel the point and edge of the barbed head, returning to the quiver each one whose condition did not satisfy him.

For a moment, the situation was volatile and deadly. The Cheyennes made a sudden dash for freedom. Custer called out to his men not to fire but to grab the older chiefs. As it turned out, all of the Cheyennes escaped Custer's trap except four men: Dull Knife (not the famous northern Cheyenne chief Dull Knife; probably his name was Lean Face, as George Bent claims), Big Head, Fat Bear, and another. None of them were, as Custer claimed them to be in his official report, chiefs of consequence. Even so, the soldiers had a difficult time convincing the four Cheyennes to give up their weapons without bloodshed.

The captives were placed under heavy guard. Later, one of them was released to carry Custer's demands to the Cheyenne chiefs. These demands were the unconditional release of the two white women and a promise by the Cheyennes to proceed to Camp Supply and remain on the reservation there. He also sent a messenger to Little Robe, promising him safe conduct to come for a council.

Shortly before dark that night, several Cheyenne warriors came within calling distance of the soldier camp for the purpose of learning the fate of the three prisoners. When they, not too surprisingly, seemed reluctant to accept Custer's offer to come into camp and talk, Mo-nah-se-tah was sent out to persuade them to come in. She was successful, and Custer talked with the warriors, repeating his demands. On the next day, another group of Indians, led by Little Robe, arrived at the camp. Little Robe admitted that the two women were in the Cheyenne camps but said it would be difficult to secure their release without buying them from their owners, as was the Indian custom. Custer, however, was determined not to pay what he looked upon as ransom.

Little Robe returned to his camp, and another day passed before a Cheyenne chief who had been with Little Robe on the previous visit returned to say that the Cheyennes wanted Custer to first release his hostages before talking about the matter of the two girls. Custer refused. After some time had passed without further word from the Cheyennes, Custer ordered his troops to move some ten miles down the Sweetwater, closer to where the Cheyenne camps were now located. The same chief contacted him once more, but still would make no promises regarding the captive women, and Custer was just as unbudging regarding his prisoners.

Becoming more and more exasperated at the delay and knowing that time was not on the side of his starving command, Custer called in a delegation of the Cheyenne chiefs to his tent. They were, he accused them, trying to stall matters. If the white girls were not turned over to him by sunset of the next day, he would hang the three prisoners and on the following day attack the Cheyenne camp. Just how far he went to convince them is not clear. Custer states in his report: "The ropes were ready, and the limb selected. . . ." Moore, Rodgers, and Hadley all agree that the chiefs were taken to a cottonwood tree, a rope was thrown over a limb, and one of the Cheyennes, Dull Knife, was pulled up until his toes barely touched the ground.

There was considerable suspense in the camp following Custer's ultimatum, no one knowing if the Indians would respond as demanded, attempt to escape, or attack. All day, the troops waited without any sign from the Indians. It wasn't until around three that afternoon that a party of about twenty horsemen was spotted on a far hilltop. Romero was sent forward to parley with them. Indistinguishable at first, they were studied by Custer through his field glasses, and soon he was able to discern that one pony carried two figures. Even as he watched, the two figures slid to the ground and began walking down the long slope of the hill toward the troops, clinging to one another.

One was a short, heavy figure; the other, tall and slender. The only clothes of both were flour sacks, the insignia of the mill still showing, and Indian moccasins and leggings. Their hair was also Indian style, hanging down in braids over their shoulders, and they wore numerous brass wire bracelets on their arms, a variety of rings on their hands, and Indian beads around their necks. Both were several months pregnant.

In deference to the Kansas volunteers, Custer appointed Lieutenant Colonel Moore and two of his officers to go forward and meet the two girls. As the entire body of the 7th and 19th watched, the officers met the women at the foot of the hill and, putting their coats around the scantily clad captives, escorted them back to the lines. Moore told of the meeting:

> I met them at the foot of the hill, and taking the elder lady by the hand asked if she was Mrs. Morgan. She said she was, and introduced the other, Miss White. She then asked, "Are we free now?" I told her they were, and she asked, "Where is my husband?" I told her he was at Hays recovering from his wounds. Next question: "Where is my brother?" I told her he was in camp, but did not tell her that we had to put him under guard to keep him from marring all by shooting the first Indian he saw. Miss White asked no questions about her people. She knew they were all dead before she was carried away.

Now Dan Brewster was released, and he rushed forward to throw his arms around his sister. This burst the restraint of the Kansas volunteers, who now crowded around the girls also, cheering jubilantly. Custer still had with him one "A" tent, and this was made available to the women. With the command was another white woman, a cook, who attended to the two girls. Previously, a scouting party had chased a lone Indian, causing him to drop a bundle of goods that included calico cloth, beads, thread, and needles. The cook now put these to good use and made dresses for the ex-captives. The girls told distressing stories of being sold back and forth among the Indians, of beatings from the women of the tribes, of countless hardships and abuses, and of ill-fated attempts to escape. That night at retreat, Custer ordered the 7th Regiment band to serenade the two with "Home, Sweet Home."

Before dark, a delegation of Cheyenne chiefs came to Custer and asked that he now release the prisoners he held. But Custer refused. He told them that he would do so only when they had brought their bands into Camp Supply. The chiefs, feeling they had bargained for the release of the three Cheyennes when they had freed the girls, were forced to leave without their tribesmen. Custer moved his camp three miles upstream, to where the Indian village had stood until evacuated in fear of an attack by the troops. There he burned the poles of approximately two hundred lodges, plus much other material of the Indians, taking possession of numerous ponies, bows, arrows, shields, and firearms. This left the tribe in a destitute condition. That night, Custer penned a lengthy report of his excursion into the Texas panhandle, saying he would have attacked the Cheyennes had not his supplies been exhausted. Still he considered his success in rescuing the two women and capturing the three Cheyennes as "the termination of the Indian war."

In an interview with Colonel Grierson at Fort Sill later, Little Robe and other Cheyenne chiefs gave their version of the affair:

> General Custer told the chiefs to bring in two white women who were in their camp, or he would hang the three young men. They brought him the two white women, and then expected that he would release the three young men; but he would not do so. Sometimes he would talk good and sometimes bad to them; they could not understand him. He staid near them only a little while, and started for Camp Supply. He told them he wanted them to follow him on to Camp Supply; but he talked so strangely to them they would not trust him.

On March 22, Custer put his haggard army in motion toward the Washita battlefield, where its other half waited along with Inman's supply train. After two more days of painful march, during which many of the men were so badly crippled and weak from hunger that they were near collapse, the Washita was reached. Hadley, who had to be helped along by his comrades of Company A of the 19th, described the reunion with the other forces:

> About noon, rounding a point of timber, a sentinel was encountered, and in the river bend were the tents, horses, wagons and men of a big camp. In the eyes of the pilgrims that sentinel, personally, was a monstrosity. His body appeared to be swollen, his cheeks

were puffed, his eyes bulged, his face was white, his lips were large, loose and covered his teeth altogether, while his clothes were a gaudy blue. He had a sickly, bloated and dropsical look generally. I was astonished to see that all the men at Inman's camp had the same peculiarities, and it was some time before I understood that this was the normal man. We didn't realize that it was our appearance that had changed. It had come about gradually, and as all were alike there was no contrast to attract attention. When we turned to the left of the first line of tents and saw the bright mess-fires with clean cooking utensils at the side, hard-bread boxes partly filled, and sides of raw bacon banking them around, the ranks were broken without ceremony, and officers and men without a word began to eat hard bread and raw bacon.

Inman's men stood gaping in silent astonishment while their rations were consumed. Among those looking on were at least thirty men of this troop, some of whom had left it only nineteen days before at Gypsum creek, Texas, but not one recognized a face among us—not even their captain's and first sergeant's. They supposed it was a party of starving Mexicans, wrecked somewhere on the plains. As the clothing was black and brown and hanging in rags and tatters it was little wonder.

The troops rested and recuperated on the Washita until the twenty-seventh, when they marched for Camp Supply. From there they continued on toward Kansas and Fort Hays, whooping and cheering as they went into camp there on April 10. Six months' pay was placed in the hands of the officers and men of both regiments, and for some time thereafter nearby Hays City, already wild, saw even wilder times. Trouble erupted not only between the 7th and the 19th, where animosity had already grown intense, but within the units themselves.

One fracas involved two soldiers of the 7th who had robbed a member of the 19th. A squad of the 19th caught the two and recovered part of the money, killing one of the two 7th Cavalry men when they broke and tried to escape. Rumors floated about that three other members of the 7th had been killed earlier in troubles growing out of an old feud between the two regiments.

Another situation developed when a lieutenant of the volunteers, who was holding some money for his men, disappeared.

One of the men, who had lost $250, followed the lieutenant's trail as far as St. Louis but lost it there.

Second Lieutenant Charles Brady of the 19th's Company E, whose favorite sport prior to enlistment was beating up Negroes in Topeka, was exceedingly drunk when time came for him to catch a train out of Hays. When he refused to board the train, the 19th's Sergeant Major Gunning tried to get him on a car. Brady told Gunning to let him go by the count of three or he would kill him. He counted, then shot Gunning in the head and killed him. A month later, a body was found in an empty boxcar at State Line Depot of the Kansas Pacific Railroad. The throat was cut, and the victim had been shot in the hip and head. It proved to be Brady.

Racial troubles, too, had been flaring between the white soldiers and the black troops of the 38th Infantry then stationed at Fort Hays. When some of the black soldiers supposedly went to a Hays City "house of ill repute to break it open," a party of whites, led by ex-Forsyth scout and member of Troop M of the 19th Jim Curry began firing on the soldiers. Over five hundred rounds were exchanged, with several killed on both sides. Curry, later known as "Kid" Curry, was shot in the head and arm.

This wave of violence also invaded the premises of Fort Hays, where Custer's three Sweetwater prisoners had been placed in the compound with the other Cheyenne captives from the Washita battle. When it was decided to move the three Cheyenne men into an adjoining guardhouse on May 9, a sergeant and a guard entered the prisoner compound with guns in hand. They had no interpreter with them. Unable to make the prisoners understand what they wanted, the guards tried to physically force the three Cheyennes into the guardhouse. Thinking the men were to be executed, an Indian woman pulled a knife from under her blanket and drove it into the back of the sergeant of the guard. Others followed suit, and in the melee that followed, Big Head was killed, Dull Knife received a bayonet wound from which he later died, and Fat Bear was knocked unconscious.

Prior to this, in late April, the commanding colonel at Fort Hays, Colonel Nelson A. Miles, had been ordered to take two boys from the Indian captives. Evidently these were the two boys Custer had reported he had rescued from the Indians. But Chief Little Raven, who had brought his Arapahoes into Camp Supply, demanded the return of one of the children, an Arapaho boy of twelve years who was blind in one eye. The other was the subject of a letter written by Miles on April 30:

> I have the honor to report that I have had taken from the Indian prisoners at this Post and placed in the Post Hospital one white child apparently about two years of age. Said child is, in my opinion, the son of white parents. The color of his hair is light, his features and complexion indicate very strongly that he belongs to the white race.
>
> The Indians assert that he is a quarterbreed but from their cruel treatment of him I judge he must have been one of their captives or the child of some settler. His health is much impaired, owing to this improper treatment.
>
> His history is and must be a mystery. While he remained with the Indians he was placed in the most exposed part of their quarters and his food and clothing taken from him and thrown away.
>
> I would earnestly recommend that in view of these facts, he be sent to Govt. Hospital or asylum where he can receive proper care and attention. As if he is compelled to remain with the savages, he will die from exposure and ill treatment.

On June 4 the Arapaho boy was returned to Camp Supply with an Inman supply train, and eight days later the rest of the fifty-three Cheyenne captives were returned likewise. The men of the 19th Kansas were mustered out and the regiment ceased to exist. Custer and the 7th Cavalry returned to duty in Kansas, where once again the Dog Soldiers were striking, the Indian war being far from over. The invasion of the Indian Territory had annihilated Black Kettle, the most peaceful of the Cheyenne leaders, and the Indian Territory had been broken open for eventual settlement by the white man. Already, the nation was debating the propriety of the Sheridan-Custer campaign and the Battle of the Washita.

Chapter XII
A QUARREL OF CONSCIENCE

Even as the conflict on the plains was being waged with weapons and tactics, another war—a war of charges and countercharges—was being carried on throughout the nation. At stake were the will and conscience of the United States in resolving the great dilemma of the American Indian. It was an issue in which no middle ground was begged, and one for which history offered no definitive answer concerning the rightness or wrongness of one society and people overcoming and displacing another. At hand was not only the question of human morality but also the march of empire and the inevitable contest between barbarism and civilization.

On the one side were the forces of those who insisted that the Indian could be dealt with ultimately only through the use of force. It was the Indian, these men claimed, who broke the treaties, committed depredations and unspeakable crimes against the frontier whites, and who refused the help of the United States Government in settling down to an agrarian life. It had been demonstrated time and again, those of the "sword" claimed, that compassion and understanding were wasted upon the plains savage. Let those who believed so strongly in the "olive branch" come live on the raw frontier for a time, they said, and test their faith when their homes and families were endangered.

Principal proponents of this view were the frontier settler, who had been invited to settle upon land that the government claimed no longer belonged to the native Indian; the military leader, who was trained to see solutions to such problems in terms of force of arms and whose profession was enlarged by war; the business entrepreneur, whose vested interests were at stake; and the politician, who was busy shaping the destiny of a new and powerful nation.

Against these momentous forces stood the Indian Bureau, whose assigned purpose was the welfare of the Indian but whose trader system was bloated with corruption and graft; the eastern humanitarian, whose concept of the American Indian was often naïvely Cooperish; and a few men such as Commissioner of Indian Affairs Taylor, peace commissioner Tappan, and Agent Wynkoop who were willing to speak out openly in defense of the Indian. These men, whom Sherman once referred to as "Tappan, Taylor and Co.," were considered by Sherman and Sheridan to be at the head of a conspiracy identified only as the "Indian Ring." The "Ring" was meant to encompass an organized conspiracy of men who sought to profit from the Indian problem. It supposedly headed, as one newspaper put it, "a crew of sharks, sharpers, runners, traders, sutlers, swindlers, and Indian agents generally" who "took care to let as little as possible of the worth of any money set apart to the use of the Indian reach them." There was indeed enough such chicanery to give credence to the charge, though there was no evidence for Sherman's charge of involvement by Taylor, Tappan, or Wynkoop.

These two forces had locked in battle long before Custer's attack on the Washita. The peace commission, which had signed the Medicine Lodge Treaty and then gone on to treat with the northern tribes at Fort Laramie, was severely split on the question of dealing with the tribes. Largely, it was the generals opposed by Taylor and Tappan. Meeting at the Tremont House in Chicago in October of 1868, General Sanford submitted a resolution that the Indians who would "locate permanently on their agricultural reservations" should be fed, clothed, and protected, but that military force should be used to compel the removal of all who refused to go. The motion was passed, providing tacit support of the campaign then being organized by Sheridan.

General Terry submitted a resolution to the commission that
the August raids along the Saline and Solomon justified the government in abrogating those clauses in the treaty made at Medicine Lodge "which secure them the right of roaming and hunting
outside of their reservations. . . ." This, too, was adopted. Terry
then submitted another resolution, which would lead to the
transfer of the Indian Bureau to the War Department. This was
an idea originally suggested by Sheridan, who wrote to Sherman
on October 15, 1868:

> The motive of the peace commission was humane, but there was
> an error of judgment in making peace with these Indians last fall.
> They should have been punished and made to give up the plunder
> captured, and which they now hold, and, after properly submitting
> to the military, and disgorging their plunder, they could have been
> turned over to the civil agents. This error has given many more vic-
> tims to savage ferocity.
>
> The present system of dealing with the Indians, I think, is an
> error. There are too many fingers in the pie, too many ends to be
> subserved, and too much money to be made; and it is the interest of
> the nation, and of humanity, to put an end to this inhuman farce.
> The peace commission, the Indian department, the military, and the
> Indians make a "baulky team." The public treasury is depleted, and
> innocent people murdered in the quadrangular management, in
> which the public treasury and the unarmed settlers are the greatest
> sufferers.
>
> There should be only one head of the government of Indians.
> Now they look to the peace commission, then to the Indian depart-
> ment, both of which are expensive institutions, without any system
> or adequate machinery to make good their promises. Then the In-
> dian falls back on the military, which is the only reliable resort in
> case he becomes pinched from hunger.
>
> I respectfully recommend, in view of what I have seen since I
> came in command of this department, and from a long experience
> with Indians heretofore, that the Indian Bureau be transferred to
> the War Department, and that the Lieutenant General, as the com-
> mon superior, have sole and entire charge of the Indians; that each
> department commander and the officers under him have the sole
> and entire charge of the Indians in his department.

When this idea was submitted to the commission, Tappan countered with a move to make the Bureau of Indian Affairs a separate department or bureau, rather than being under either the Department of the Interior or the Army. Only Tappan and Taylor voted for the latter, the generals all voting to support army control over the Indians.

Tappan now moved to recognize that while individual members of the Cheyenne and Arapaho tribes deserved to be punished for crimes they had committed, there was no justification for a declaration of war against all Cheyennes and Arapahoes. This motion created strenuous debate before it was finally rejected, Tappan casting the only vote in favor of his resolution. He defended his position later in a long letter to Commissioner Taylor. The letter, which was carried by several frontier newspapers, argued in part:

> We complain of their atrocities (which cannot be justified or even excused), forgetting that our own people have for generations and for centuries committed as cruel and disgusting barbarities upon the Indians, giving them, as the weaker party, the advantage of a plea of doing all they do only in retaliation. We repeat the fatal error of underrating the capacity of the Indians for a protracted and successful guerrilla warfare, and persist in pursuing and punishing the innocent instead of the guilty, more intent on attacking the villages containing the women and children, than the active war parties, which of course is considered by the Indians not a war against a single tribe, in punishment for real or fancied outrages, but a war for the extermination of their race. Can they by any known process of reasoning come to any other conclusion from what has happened to them during the last few years? Can they from the treatment of their ancestors for the last 300 years? The Cheyennes cannot forget the assassination and mutilation of 120 of their own women and children at Sand Creek in 1864 while in the employ and under the protection of the Government; they cannot fail to remember their acceptance of an invitation in the Spring of 1867 to come to Fort Larned, Kansas, with their families, to confer with a prominent officer of the army, and the advantage taken of their confidence to destroy their village and force them to war.

From Philadelphia on October 7, 1868, Wynkoop outlined the causes of the war as he saw them:

> Undoubtedly this war could have been prevented, had Congress made an appropriation for the purpose of continuing the supply of subsistence to these Indians, thus following the dictates of Humanity and justice. The expenditure of a few thousands would have saved millions to the country; would have saved hundreds of white men's lives; have saved the necessity of hunting down and destroying innocent Indians for the faults of the guilty; of driving into misery and starvation numbers of women and little children, not one of whom but now mourns the horrible massacre of Sand Creek, and who still suffer from the loss of their habitations and property, wantonly destroyed by Major General Hancock.
>
> Had each member of Congress seen what I have of these injustices practiced toward these Indians, they would imagine that there was not sufficient money in the United States Treasury to appropriate for their benefit.

Even as Custer was marching toward Camp Supply, Wynkoop received orders to proceed to Fort Cobb in the Indian Territory and there to congregate all the Indians of his agency who were in that vicinity. But upon arriving at Leavenworth on November 29—before the first couriers from Camp Supply had carried the news of the Washita battle to the telegraph lines at Fort Dodge —Wynkoop learned that troops were already in the field and that their destination was the same as where he had been ordered to assemble the Indians. In this he saw the makings of another Sand Creek affair, and in a letter to Taylor, Wynkoop resigned his agent's post:

> Since I have started on my journey thither, I have learned of some five different columns of troops in the field, whose objective point is the Washita River. The regular troops are under control, commanded by officers who will not allow atrocities committed; but there are also in the field, under sanction of the Government, volunteer troops and Ute and Osage Indians, the deadly enemies of all Plains Indians, and whom nothing will prevent from murdering all, of whatever age or sex, wherever found. The point to which that

portion are marching who have expressed their determination to kill under all circumstances the Indians of my agency, is the point to which I am directed to congregate them at. They will certainly respond to my call, but I most certainly refuse to again be the instrument of the murder of innocent women and children. While I remain an officer of the Government, I propose to do my duty—a portion of which is to obey my instructions. All left me under the circumstances, with the present state of feelings I have in this matter, is now to respectfully tender my resignation, and return the commission which I have so far earnestly endeavored to fulfill the requirements of.

Wynkoop now determined to go to Washington, where he could fight for the Indians on a public level. But even before he left Leavenworth, the news arrived that Custer had struck down the village of Wynkoop's close friend Black Kettle—the same village Chivington had struck at Sand Creek almost exactly four years to the day earlier! It was precisely what Wynkoop had predicted. As he passed through St. Louis, he angrily expressed his opinion that Custer's "battle" was nothing more than another "massacre" and that "Black Kettle and his band were friendly Indians, and were on their way to the reservation when attacked."

Wynkoop's letter of resignation and charges of another massacre were printed in the New York *Times* on December 19. On the twentieth, the paper published a report from Sheridan concerning the Washita affair in which he cited the testimony by Mah-wis-sa, who he said had admitted that it was Cheyennes and Arapahoes who committed recent depredations on the Arkansas River. Sheridan saw this as proof that the trail followed by Custer had been that of a Cheyenne war party. Also, Sheridan claimed, mail was found in Black Kettle's camp linking the village with the killing of two couriers earlier. Based upon this evidence, the *Times* ran an editorial in its December 22 issue entitled "The End of the Indian War and Ring," in which Black Kettle was castigated as a troublemaker:

The most serious of these,—the charge that Gen. Custer had attacked and massacred a band of peaceful Indians in the late battle on the Washita,—has already been disproved by the statements of captured Indians themselves, and by not less significant indications and arrangements found in their camp. The truth is, that Gen. Custer, in defeating and killing Black Kettle, put an end to one of the most troublesome and dangerous characters on the Plains. Black Kettle was one of the most active Chiefs in stirring up the tribes to war,—and on account of this influence he was one of the most useful accessories of the "ring" which now so loudly deprecates his taking off. From the beginning of the war in 1864, this Black Kettle, of the Cheyennes, aided by Santanté [sic], of the Kiowas, and Little Raven, of the Arapahoes, has been always most active in mischief, and it was a fortunate stroke which ended his career and put the others to flight.

The *Times* went on to state that Sheridan would doubtless "continue to march until the Indian question, as far at least as the tribes living near the lines of the Pacific Railroads are concerned, is finished and forever settled." In a letter read to the United States Indian Commission in Washington, D.C., the Reverend H. B. Whipple of Minnesota answered the *Times* and others by expressing the view that "even if there had been several acts of hostility by individual Indians of peaceable bands, and by hostile bands, this shameless disregard for justice has been the most foolhardy course we could have pursued. . . . Congress will whitewash it all over; the Press and people and army will act on the principle 'dead men tell no tales.' Human kind like to throw mud on people they have wronged." Wynkoop appeared before the commission on December 23 and delivered an eloquent defense of Black Kettle:

His innate dignity and lofty bearing, combined with his sagacity and intelligence, had that moral effect which placed him in the position as a potentate. The whole force of his nature was concentrated in the one idea of how best to act for the good of his race; he knew the power of the white man, and was aware that thence might spring most of the evils that could befall his people, and consequently the whole of his powers were directed toward conciliating the whites, and his utmost endeavors used to preserve peace and friendship between his race and their oppressors.

Sheridan was quick to respond to charges that Custer's fight was another Sand Creek Massacre. He pointed to the interview between Hazen and Black Kettle in which the officer refused to allow the Cheyennes to come in to Fort Cobb and cited testimony from an army guide that Black Kettle "had many scalps dangling to his belt of white women and men." The same scout also claimed that "Black Kettle was among the first who committed the depredation on the Solomon, and then crossed the Arkansas River for the border of Texas, there to carry on a murderous war with tribes of peaceful Indians which are now recognized as citizens of the United States."

In Topeka a joint resolution of the Kansas legislature was passed to thank Sheridan, Custer, and Forsyth for their services in the Indian war and declaring "want of sympathy" for the peace commissioners and the eastern philanthropists in trying to "cast odium on these gallant officers." At Fort Cobb, General Hazen read Wynkoop's statements regarding the battle and counterattacked by blaming the agent for the fate of Black Kettle's village:

"Wynkoop," Hazen wrote, "in place of coming here when he was ordered, where he could have saved the life of Black Kettle, whose death he now mourns so bitterly, resigned, as it were, in the face of duty, and his people are without any civil agent." Hazen went on to stress that Black Kettle was not on his way to the reservation as Wynkoop had said, that he had been refused asylum at Fort Cobb, and that he had been duly warned that Sheridan was in the field.

Writing to Sherman from Fort Cobb on December 31, 1868, Hazen gave a slanted account of his meeting with Black Kettle: "In his talk with me some five or six days before he was killed, Black Kettle stated that many of his men were then on the war path, and that their people did not want peace with the people above the Arkansas. His people were then engaged in the troubles on the Solomon and their Reservation was not in this section of the country at all."

This letter, forwarded by Sherman to Secretary of War Schofield, was in turn relayed to the United States Senate as proof of Black Kettle's villainy and justification for Custer's attack:

> The Secretary of War has the honor to submit to the Senate of the United States (and House of Representatives) the accompanying copy of a communication from [Major] General W. B. Hazen to the Lieutenant General of the Army, as to the hostile character of the band of Indians lately attacked and defeated by General Custer on the Washita River.

In his annual report of the military operations of the Department of the Missouri, dated November 1, 1869, Sheridan continued to justify the strike against the Cheyennes and to vilify Black Kettle:

> It was this band that, without provocation, had massacred the settlers on the Saline and Solomon, and perpetrated cruelties too fiendish for recital. Black Kettle, the nominal chief—a worn out and worthless old cipher—was said to be friendly; but when I sent him word to come into Dodge, before any of the troops had commenced operations, saying that I would feed and protect him and family, he refused, and was killed in the fight. He was also with the band on Walnut creek when they made their medicine, or held their devilish incantations previous to the party setting out to massacre the settlers.

To support his charges against Black Kettle, Sheridan pointed to evidence he said was found on the field of battle when he visited it on December 10:

> . . . found in Black Kettle's village, photography and daguerreotypes, clothing and bedding, from the houses of the persons massacred on the Solomon and Saline. The mail which I had sent by the expressmen, Nat Marshal and Bill Davis, from Bluff creek to Fort Dodge, who were murdered and mutilated, was likewise found; also a large blank book with Indian illustrations of the different fights which Black Kettle's band had been engaged in, especially about Fort Wallace and on the line of the Denver stages, showing when the fight had been with the colored troops, when

with whites, also when trains had been captured, and women killed in wagons.

These claims were later questioned by former Commissioner of Indian Affairs George W. Manypenny, who pointed out that neither Custer, who had itemized carefully the captured items from the village, nor reporter Keim, who was with Sheridan practically every step when he revisited the Washita battlefield and described the entire visit in detail, made mention of the above discoveries:

> As to the evidences offered that Black Kettle and his band were guilty of the excesses on the Solomon and Saline, it is submitted that Gen. Sheridan overdoes the matter. How did he know that the Indians ravished women forty and fifty times in succession? And as to the illustrated book, how did he know that it represented the operations of Black Kettle's band?

Manypenny pointed out further that there was considerable question as to the Sheridan claim that the war party trailed by Custer to the Washita was even a Cheyenne group:

> Black Eagle, a Kiowa Chief, gave McCusky [McCusker] the first information he had "concerning the action that recently took place on the Washita river, near the Antelope hills," between a column of United States troops and the Cheyenne Indians. This chief stated that a party of Kiowa Indians, returning from an expedition against the Utes, saw, on the 25th of November, on nearing the Antelope hills, on the Canadian river, a trail going south toward the Washita. On their arrival at the Cheyenne camp, they told the Cheyennes about it, but the Cheyennes only laughed at them. One of the Kiowas concluded to stay all night at the camp, and the rest of them went on to their own camps. About daylight the next morning the camp was attacked by the troops. The Kiowa who was a guest made his escape, and bore the news to the villages below. . . . It seems pertinent here to ask the question, if Custer did strike a trail, whether it was not the trail of this war party of Kiowas, who were returning from an expedition against the Utes?

Manypenny also argued that, one way or another, Custer had no idea just whose camp he was attacking at the Washita, and that by no means were Sheridan's indications of guilt on Black Kettle's part known *prior* to the attack. Charges and countercharges continued to fly in the public press and in Congress even as Custer was still on his Indian hunt in the Indian Territory and the Texas panhandle. Custer, Sheridan, and the frontier army in general looked hopefully to the new President, their own Ulysses S. Grant, for a change of direction in the nation's Indian policy.

But the change that came was not at all what they hoped for. In December the move to place the Bureau of Indian Affairs under the Army had been defeated in Congress. And when Grant took over as President, he responded favorably to a suggestion that had been made several years earlier to President Lincoln: that the Society of Friends, or Quakers, be given the responsibility of implementing a new policy of peace and friendship among the Indians. A former Grant aide-de-camp, Ely S. Parker, was named as Commissioner of Indian Affairs, and a special commission of Friends was appointed to the task of inspecting the Indian reservations.

Many Quakers were placed in positions in the Indian Bureau; one of them, Brinton Darlington, arrived in the Indian Territory in July 1869 to take charge of the Upper Arkansas Agency for the Cheyenne and Arapaho Indians. The nation's conscience could sigh in relief, for now the problems of the Plains Indian had been placed at the bosom of Christian morality.

Custer, now sporting his new reputation as an Indian fighter, would continue to conduct forays against the Indians of the plains. Much the same as his comparison of General Sully to the forces of France, he would march up the hill and down again until that fateful day of June 25, 1876, at the Little Bighorn. It would be a day of redemption for the Cheyennes against Custer and the 7th Cavalry.

Following the Sheridan-Custer campaign, the Cheyennes in the Indian Territory would begin a gradual and reluctant acceptance of reservation life, though their fierce warrior spirit was far from conquered. It would be twenty years after Custer's attack that the white man would make the first mass settlement of what is now Oklahoma with the Run of 1889. But it was at the Washita that the land of western Indian Territory was conquered.

APPENDIX A

*Organization of the 7th Cavalry
at the Battle of the Washita*

Custer's Attack Unit: Lieut. Col. (Bvt. Maj. Gen.) G. A. Custer,
comdg. unit & regiment (approximate
strength: 300)

Hamilton's Squadron:
Troop A   Capt. Louis M. Hamilton, comdg. (60)
Troop D   Capt. (Bvt. Lieut. Col.) Thomas B. Weir, comdg. (60)
First Lieut. (Bvt. Lieut. Col.) Thomas W. Custer
First Lieut. Samuel M. Robbins, aide-de-camp

West's Squadron:
Troop C   First Lieut. (Bvt. Capt.) Matthew Berry, comdg. (60)
Troop K   Capt. (Bvt. Col.) Robert M. West, comdg. (60)
First Lieut. Edward S. Godfrey
Second Lieut. Edward Law

Cook's Sharpshooters: First Lieut. (Bvt. Lieut. Col.) W. W.
Cook, comdg. (40)

Others with Unit:
First Lieut. (Bvt. Capt.) Myles M. Moylan, reg. adj.
Second Lieut. Henry Lippincott, asst. surgeon
Second Lieut. William Renick, actg. asst. surgeon
Second Lieut. (Bvt. Capt.) A. E. Smith, actg. reg.
commissary
Sgt. Maj. Walter Kennedy

White and Indian scouts
Regimental band

Elliott's Attack Unit:　Major Joel H. Elliott, comdg. unit and second
in command of regiment (approximate
strength: 180)

Troop G　Capt. (Bvt. Lieut. Col.) Albert Barnitz, comdg. (60)
Troop H　Capt. (Bvt. Lieut. Col.) Frederick W. Benteen, comdg. (60)
Troop M　First Lieut. Owen Hale, comdg. (60)
Second Lieut. T. J. Marsh
Second Lieut. H. Walworth Smith

Myers' Attack Unit:　Capt. (Bvt. Lieut. Col.) Edward Myers, comdg.
(approximate strength: 120)

Troop E　First Lieut. John M. Johnson, comdg. (60)
Troop I　First Lieut. (Bvt. Capt.) Charles Brewster, comdg. (60)

Thompson's Attack Unit:　Capt. (Bvt. Lieut. Col.) William
Thompson, comdg. (approximate
strength: 120)

Troop B　Capt. (Bvt. Lieut. Col.) William Thompson, comdg. (60)
Troop F　Capt. George W. Yates, comdg. (60)
First Lieut. D. M. Wallingford
Second Lieut. Frank M. Gibson

Advance Supply Wagons:　First Lieut. (Bvt. Maj.) James M. Bell,
comdg. & reg. qm. (approximate
strength: seven wagons with small
escort)

Supply Train in Rear:　Second Lieut. Edward G. Mathey, comdg. &
officer of the day (approximate strength: 80)

APPENDIX B

Statements Concerning
Hamilton's Death

The suggestion has been offered by Brill in *Conquest of the Plains* that Hamilton was killed by a bullet that struck him in the back, this being based upon the evidence of Hamilton's coat, which was later donated to the Oklahoma Historical Society by Hamilton's brother. The coat bears a bullet hole in the back but none in the front, prompting the supposition that Hamilton was shot in the back by a trooper rather than by an Indian. Brill looked to the possibilities that the officer may have caught a bullet intended for Custer or merely a misdirected shot. He supports his contentions with a statement by Ben Clark, who supposedly said that Hamilton was shot before the Indians opened fire, though two known accounts by Clark do not say this.

It is true that Hamilton's tunic bears only one bullet hole, that in the approximate position of his right shoulder blade. (There are several moth holes in the tunic, but the heavy lining of the coat is punctured only adjacent to the hole in its back.) The bottom button hole, however, is torn. The tunic itself is cut much like the Eisenhower jacket, barely reaching to the waist. It is a possibility that the jacket may have been pulled up or worn open in front at the time the bullet hit Hamilton in the front part of his body and angled upward to come out near the shoulder blade. This is, of course, just as hypothetical as Brill's argument.

History will never completely resolve this matter, but it seems that in the face of virtual total agreement of those involved in the battle that Hamilton was killed by an Indian bullet, better proof to the contrary is required to refute their statements. Following are the most creditable statements concerning Hamilton's death:

"Hamilton, who rode at my side as we entered the village . . . was among the first victims of the opening charge, having been shot from his saddle by an Indian rifle" (Custer, *My Life on the Plains*, p. 246).

"Thus charging and marshalling his squadron in splendid style right up to the enemy's lodges, the heroic Hamilton fell dead from his horse, shot by a bullet from a Lancaster rifle in the hands of a savage, who was concealed in his wigwam" (Captain West, *In Memoriam*, p. 374).

"It was as the centre column was charging down the precipitous bluffs to cross the river and take the village that Captain Hamilton was killed. When struck he gave one convulsive start, stiffened in his stirrups and was thus carried a corpse for a distance of several yards, when he fell from his horse, striking his face, which was from this cause terribly lacerated and disfigured" (Keim, New York *Herald*, December 24, 1868).

"Hamilton was shot through the heart while gallantly leading his squadron into the hostile village, and it is said he remained mounted and rode many yards after his death" (Lieutenant Gipson, in Chandler, *Garryowen*, p. 21).

"Captain Louis M. Hamilton, whom I knew well, was shot off his horse as he charged through the village at the head of his company. He was killed in front of Cranky Man's lodge and both Red Shin and Medicine Elk Pipe tell me that Cranky Man rushed out of his lodge and shot Hamilton" (George Bent in Hyde, *Life of George Bent*, p. 317).

Ben Clark was quoted as saying that Hamilton was with Barnitz below the Indian village and "was shot squarely between the eyes and killed," in the Kansas City *Star*, December 3, 1904. This is obviously incorrect. In another newspaper account, in 1899, Clark was quoted as saying that "Hamilton was also killed at the beginning of the fight, being shot from his horse" (New York *Sun*, May 14, 1899).

It could be that neither the whites nor the Indians wished to admit to the unromantic truth: that Hamilton may well have ridden into the line of fire of an overanxious trooper. Until other evidence is offered, however, Assistant Surgeon Lippincott's report (Appendix D) must be accepted.

APPENDIX C

Number of Indians
Killed at the Washita

As with most Indian battles, there has arisen a great deal of question concerning the number of Indians killed by Custer at the Washita. As Sully openly admitted, it was not uncommon for officers to make undue claims in order to dramatize their military successes. Custer implied in his official report that someone had gone around the battlefield and counted the dead Indians, but this was not the case. Though there was a precise listing of captured goods, there was no actual battlefield count of the dead made. Instead, Custer depended upon the memories and calculations of his officers some twenty-four hours after the battle to estimate the number of Indians killed.

Custer later upped his original claim, in a report from Fort Cobb on December 22, writing, "The Indians admit a loss of 140 killed, besides a heavy loss of wounded. This, with the Indian prisoners we have in our possession, makes the entire loss of the Indian in killed, wounded, and missing not far from 300" (*Senate Executive Document No. 40,* p. 9).

This would mean that if each of the fifty-one lodges held an average of seven persons, virtually all were killed or captured. Reporting from Fort Cobb prior to the arrival of Sheridan and Custer, Captain Alvord wrote on December 7, 1868: "The Indians lost five chiefs and distinguished braves, Black Kettle among them, and about 75 of their ordinary fighting men were killed" (*Executive Document No. 18,* p. 37).

J. S. Morrison, one of Custer's scouts with obvious sympathies for the Indians, said in his letter of December 14, 1868, that "The other scouts all agree in stating that the official reports of the fight were very much exaggerated, that there was not over twenty Bucks killed, the rest, about forty, were women and children" (Brill, *Conquest,* p. 313). Ben Clark in 1899 is reported to have said: "I estimate the Cheyenne loss at seventy-five warriors and fully as many women and children killed" (New York *Sun,* May 14, 1899).

Realistically, large casualties must be accepted in view of the surprise nature of the attack, the overwhelming superiority of fire power by the troops, and the tactical advantage of being mounted and having surrounded the Indians prior to the attack. Even though the number 103 was not arrived at by a precise battlefield count, it is a definite figure which has already been placed on historical markers of the battlefield. Since it will likely never be proved absolutely incorrect, the figure will undoubtedly remain accepted as the number of Indians killed by Custer at the Washita. History should make it clear, however, that the dead were by no means all warriors who were met in open battle and defeated.

APPENDIX D

*Custer's Killed and Wounded
at the Washita*

Confusion has long existed concerning Custer's killed and wounded at the Battle of the Washita. The most precise information is to be found in Assistant Surgeon Henry Lippincott's reports, File F, 421, Old Military Records, National Archives. The following lists provide the basic data on the casualties.

Special Report of Enlisted Men Killed and Wounded at the Battle of the Washita, Indian Territory, November 27, 1868.

	Surname	Christian Name	Rank	Troop	Remarks
1.	Kenedy (Kennedy)	Walter	Sergt. Maj.		Body not recovered.
2.	Cuddy	Charles	Private	"B"	Ball entered about an inch above upper lip and a little to the left of nose, passed upwards and back-

	Surname	Christian Name	Rank	Troop	Remarks
					wards, and emerged behind and a little above left ear.
3.	Mercer	Harry	Corporal	"E"	Body not recovered.
4.	McClernan	John	Private	"	" " "
5.	Christie	Thomas	Private	"	" " "
6.	Carrick	William	Corporal	"H"	" " "
7.	Clover	Eugene	Private	"	" " "
8.	Milligan	William	"	"	" " "
9.	George	John	"	"	" " "
10.	Williams	James F.	Corporal	"I"	" " "
11.	Downey	Thomas	Private	"	" " "
12.	Vanousky	Irwin	Sergeant	"M"	" " "
13.	Fitzpatrick	Thomas	Farrier	"	" " "
14.	Lineback	Ferdinand	Private	"	" " "
15.	Myers	John	"	"	" " "
16.	Myers	Carson D. J.	"	"	" " "
17.	Sharpe	Cal	"	"	" " "
18.	Stobacus	Frederick	"	"	" " "

This report would indicate that only Charles Cuddy, of the enlisted men, was killed during the charge or died immediately thereafter.

Official Report of Officers Killed at the Battle of the Washita, November 27, 1868.

	Surname	Christian Name	Rank	Remarks
1.	Elliott	Joel H.	Major	Maj. Elliott was last seen pursuing some Indians about a mile and a half from the Indian village in which the battle of the Washita was fought. There can be no doubt of his death. Body not recovered.

Surname	Christian Name	Rank	Remarks
2. Hamilton	Louis M.	Captain	Was killed in action at the battle of the Washita, I.T., Nov. 27th, 1868. Ball entered about five inches below left nipple, and emerged near inferior angle of right scapula. Death was instantaneous.

Special Report of Recovery and Condition of bodies of Enlisted Men Killed at the Battle of the Washita, Indian Territory, on the 27th day of November, 1868.

Surname	Christian Name	Rank	Troop	Remarks
1. Kenedy (Kennedy)	Walter	Sergt. Major		Bullet hole in right temple, head partly cut off, seventeen bullet holes in back, and two in legs.
2. Mercer	Harry	Corporal	"E"	Bullet hole in right axilla, one in region of heart, three in back, eight arrow wounds in back right ear cut off, head scalped, and skull fractured, deep gashes in both legs, and throat cut.
3. Christie	Thomas	Private	"E"	Bullet hole in head, right foot cut off, bullet hole in abdomen, throat cut.

	Surname	Christian Name	Rank	Troop	Remarks
4.	Carrick	William	Corporal	"H"	Bullet hole in right parietal bone, both feet cut off, throat cut, left arm broken. Penis cut off.
5.	Clover	Eugene	Private	"H"	Head cut off, arrow wound in right side, and both legs terribly mutilated.
6.	Milligan	William	Private	"H"	Bullet hole in left side of head, deep gashes in right leg, penis cut off, left arm deeply gashed, head scalped and throat cut.
7.	Williams	James F.	Corporal	"I"	Bullet hole in back, head and both arms cut off, many and deep gashes in back, penis cut off.
8.	Downey	Thomas	Private	"I"	Arrow hole in region of stomach, thorax cut open, head cut off, and right shoulder cut by a tomahawk.
9.	Fitzpatrick	Thomas	Farrier	"M"	Scalped, two arrow and several bullet holes in back, and throat cut.
10.	Lineback	Ferdinand	Private	"M"	Bullet hole in left parietal bone, head scalped, one arm broken, penis cut off, and throat cut.

	Surname	Christian Name	Rank	Troop	Remarks
11.	Myers	John	Private	"M"	Several bullet holes in head, scalped, skull extensively fractured, several arrow and bullet holes in back, deep gashes in face, and throat cut.
12.	Myers	Carson D. J.	Private	"M"	Several bullet holes in head, scalped, nineteen bullet holes in body, penis cut off, and throat cut.
13.	Sharpe	Cal	Private	"M"	Two bullet holes in left side, throat cut, one bullet hole in left side of head, one arrow hole in left side, penis cut off and left arm broken.
14.	Unknown				Head cut off. Body partially destroyed by wolves.
15.	Unknown				Head, right hand, and penis cut off, three bullet and nine arrow holes in back.
16.	Unknown				Scalped, skull fractured, six bullet and thirteen arrow holes in back, and three bullet holes in chest.

This list accounts for all of the missing soldiers except McCleman, George, Vanousky, and Stobacus. Three of these can be accredited to the bodies which could not be identified, but this leaves one 7th Cavalry trooper not accounted for in any way.

Special Report of Recovery and Condition of the body of an Officer Killed at the Battle of the Washita, Indian Territory, on the 27th Day of November, 1868.

	Surname	Christian Name	Rank	Remarks
1.	Elliott	Joel H.	Major	Two bullet holes in head, one in left cheek, right hand cut off, left foot almost cut off, penis cut off, deep gash in right groin, deep gashes in calves of both legs, little finger of left hand cut off, and throat cut.

List of Wounded in the 7th U. S. Cavalry, under command of Bvt. Maj. Gen. Custer, U.S.A., at the Battle of the Washita, Indian Territory, on the 27th day of November, 1868.

	Surname	Christian Name	Rank	Troop	Missile or Weapon	Seat of Injury	Slight or Severe	Remarks
1.	Barnitz	Albert	Captain		Bullet	Abdomen	Severe	Ball entered about three inches above and about four inches to the left of navel, ranged a little upwards and emerged about 3½ inches from center of spinal column.
2.	Custer	Thomas W.	1st Lieut.		Bullet	Right hand	Slight	
3.	March	Thomas J.	2nd Lieut.		Arrow	Left hand	Slight	
4.	Eastwood	William	Corporal	"A"	Bullet	Right elbow	Severe	Ball entered elbow joint at internal surface and emerged at external side.
5.	Gale	Mortimer	Private	"A"	Bullet	Right arm	Slight	
6.	Delaney	Augustus	Private	"B"	Bullet	Thorax	Severe	Ball entered one inch below and one inch external to left nipple, passed downwards and inwards into abdominal cavity, but did not emerge. Lived about 10 hours. Died November 27th, 1868.

	Name		Rank	Co.	Missile	Location	Severity	Remarks
7.	Zimmer	George	Private	"D"	Bullet	Left arm	Compound fracture	Ball entered at external surface of arm about two inches above elbow joint and emerged at internal side about three inches above joint. Humerus was considerably fractured.
8.	Klink	Frederick	Private	"E"	Bullet	Left arm	Slight	Spent shot.
9.	Brown	William	Private	"F"	Bullet	Left arm	Slight	Spent shot.
10.	Martin	August	Saddler	"G"	Bullet	Right forearm	Compound fracture	Radius fractured about three inches above wrist joint.
11.	Morrison	Daniel	Private	"G"	Arrow	Right temple	Flesh wound	
12.	McCasey	Benjamin	Private	"H"	Arrow	Thorax	Severe	Arrow entered left side at intercostal space passing backwards and upwards into lung. Patient expectorated a good deal of blood. Died November 30th, 1868.
13.	Strahle	Conrad	Private	"I"	Bullet	Left ankle	Flesh wound	
14.	Morgan	Hugh	Private	"I"	Bullet	Right arm	Severe flesh wound	
15.	Murphy	John	Bugler	"M"	Arrow	Thorax	Severe flesh wound	Arrow entered right side about four inches from nipple on a line nearly corresponding with the latter.

The number of Custer's men killed at the Battle of the Washita, therefore, was twenty-two: two officers and twenty enlisted men. They were:

Major Joel Elliott	Private William Milligan
Captain Louis Hamilton	Private Eugene Clover
Sergeant Major Walter Kennedy	Private John George
Sergeant Irwin Vanousky	Private Thomas Downey
Corporal Harry Mercer	Private Ferdinand Lineback
Corporal William Carrick	Private John Myers
Corporal James F. Williams	Private Carson D. J. Myers
Farrier Thomas Fitzpatrick	Private Cal Sharpe
Private Charles Cuddy	Private Frederick Stobacus
Private John McClernan	Private Augustus Delaney
Private Thomas Christie	Private Benjamin McCasey

Hamilton, Cuddy, Delaney, and McCasey were mortally wounded during the battle in the village, seventeen of the others died in the Elliott fight, and one trooper is unaccounted for. This missing man and the three unidentifiable bodies found with Elliott would be troopers McClernan, George, and Stobacus, and Sergeant Vanousky.

APPENDIX E

Reports on the Discovery of
Mrs. Blinn and her child

An unresolved mystery surrounds the death of Mrs. Blinn and her two-year-old son, resulting from contradictory reports of where their bodies were found and whether or not they were scalped. Charges were made that they were actually killed by Custer's troops during the attack. Former Comanche-Kiowa agent Colonel Jesse Leavenworth testified before a Senate committee on Indian affairs that Mrs. Blinn was shot by troops as she started to run toward them when the firing commenced (*Kansas Daily Tribune*, February 14, 1869). He did not give the source of his contention, but the statement in Custer's official report regarding a white woman who was supposedly killed by her captors lends some credence to the charge.

Keim, in his New York *Herald* story (December 8, 1868), which was written on November 29, stated: "A white woman and a boy ten [sic] years of age, held by the Indians, were killed when the attack commenced." However, he does not mention this in his December 1 account. It is possible to support the argument further by citing a few lines of Benteen's accusative letter concerning the battle: ". . . we slowly pick our way across the creek over which we charged so gallantly in the early morn. Take care! do not trample on the dead bodies of that woman and child lying there" (New York *Times*, February 14, 1869).

Surgeon Lippincott reported from Fort Cobb on December 20 that "the bodies of a white woman and child, were found on the 11th of this month, near the ground on which the Battle of the Washita, was fought." Major Moore indicated that Mrs. Blinn and her child were found by men of the 19th Kansas. Captain Jenness of that unit, writing in retrospect, placed the discovery at the battlefield site: "In the timber, by the river, were the ashes and remains of the Indian wigwams, burned by Custer's men, and at this point, Black Kettle was killed. Here were the bodies of five or six squaws and that of Mrs. Blinn and her child, lying some rods apart" (Jenness, *History of the 19th Kansas*, p. 38).

Sheridan and Custer—neither of whom were with the party that found Mrs. Blinn and did not see their corpses until they were brought into camp—both contend that the bodies were found several miles down-river, in the deserted camp of the Kiowas. Custer wrote to his wife on December 19, the day he reached Fort Cobb: "Five miles below the battle-ground, in a deserted Indian village, the bodies of a young and beautiful white woman and her babe were found, and I brought them away for burial at Arbuckle" (E. B. Custer, *Guidon*, p. 46). His report of December 24 states: "On returning from the battle-ground to the camp of my command, and when in the deserted camp which . . . was lately occupied by Satanta with the Kiowas, my men discovered the bodies of a young white woman and child . . ." (*Senate Executive Document 40*, p. 5).

Sheridan, in his report from Fort Cobb on December 19, related about the same story: "We also found the body of Mrs. Blinn and her child in one of the camps about six miles down the river . . ." (*House Executive Document 18*, p. 40). Both Sheridan and Custer cited Mah-wis-sa as having told them the camp in which Mrs. Blinn was found was a Kiowa camp, and they used this to establish the hostility of the Kiowas and justify action against the tribe in the face of Hazen's defense of them as having been peaceful.

Keim, who filed a story from the December 11 bivouac, said: "During the journey to the battlefield this morning a detachment moving along the river found, near the recent camp of the Kiowas, the body of a white woman and child" (New York *Herald*, January 4, 1869).

Comanche-Kiowa agent A. G. Boone wrote on January 12, 1869, from Fort Cobb: ". . . I have thoroughly investigated all the facts, as I have several friends (officers) in the fight, and feared she had been accidentally killed by our own troops; but she was in a party some ten or twelve miles from the main fight, and from the fact of her being scalped shows it was done by the infernal savages" (New York *Times*, March 21, 1869).

Surgeon Lippincott's report lists Mrs. Blinn's wound as being "one bullet hole above left eyebrow, head scalped, and skull extensively fractured." Of the child he said, "The child's head and face presented evidences of violence" (Office of the Adjutant General, File F, 421). This is contradicted in some degree by Keim's report of December 11, 1868, which says nothing of either body being scalped: "The body was brought into camp and examined. Two bullet holes penetrating the brain were found; also the back of the skull was fearfully crushed as if by a hatchet. The body of the child presented the appearance of starvation, being reduced to a perfect skeleton. There were no marks on the body except a bruise on the cheek" (New York *Herald*, January 4, 1869).

Even further mystery is provided by a statement in a letter from scout J. S. Morrison, who wrote to Lieutenant Colonel Wynkoop from Fort Dodge on December 14, 1868. Stating that he had just arrived at the fort with some other scouts who had been in the battle, Morrison wrote: "The prisoners have got in today. They consist of 53 women and children. One boy is an Arapahoe. The rest are all Cheyennes. Mrs. Crocker is amongst them. She is badly wounded. She says that her child is killed" (Brill, *Conquest*, pp. 313–14).

Perhaps this is the woman to whom Custer referred in his report. One must logically assume she was known to Wynkoop as well as Morrison, and it is possible, of course, that she was an Indian woman married to a white man named Crocker. No further information concerning this woman has come to light.

FOOTNOTES

Chapter I   A Certain Impetuosity

Page 1
several staghounds . . . Jay Monaghan, *Custer, the Life of General George Armstrong Custer,* pp. 279–80.

Page 1
"hero of Shenandoah" . . . New York *Times,* December 7, 1867, quoting St. Louis *Republican* story from Fort Leavenworth, November 29, 1867.

Page 2
"circus rider gone mad" . . . Mark Mayo Boatner III, *The Civil War Dictionary,* p. 216, citing R. Agassiz, ed., *Letters of Colonel Theodore Lyman from the Wilderness to Appomattox.*

Page 4
"abandon the war-path" . . . E. B. Custer, *Tenting on the Plains,* p. 484.

Page 4
"principal characteristics". . . Henry M. Stanley, *My Early Travels and Adventures in America and Asia,* I, 86. Stanley's presence on the Kansas plains is a unique fact of western history. Having run away from a school workhouse in England and gone to sea as a cabin boy, he ended up in New Orleans, where he worked for and was eventually adopted by Henry Morton Stanley, who left him only his name in death. When the Civil War broke out, the penniless Stanley enlisted in the Confederate Army, was captured by Union forces, and then was released to serve briefly in the U. S. Navy, later becoming a "descriptive writer" for various newspapers. He was successful at this, and ". . . in my twenty-fifth year I was promoted to the proud position of a Special Correspondent, with the very large commission to inform the public regarding all matters of general interest affecting

the Indians and the great Western plains" (Stanley, *My Early Travels*, I, v). Davis described Stanley as a "sufficiently characteristic figure to attract attention," with his loose-fitting felt cap, stout lumberman's-style boots, jockey's spurs, and "unmilitary" horse equipage (Theodore Davis, "Henry M. Stanley's Indian Campaign in 1867," in *The Westerner's Brand Book, 1945–46*, p. 113).

Page 4
light of the campfire . . . Stanley, *My Early Travels*, I, 29.
Page 4
over to the chiefs . . . George Hyde, *Life of George Bent*, p. 257. The St. Louis *Republican* of October 4, 1867, gave Sherman the credit for finding the boy and paying the ransom to get him back. One Cheyenne girl, according to the *Republican* account, was carried off by the circus. Another girl was being cared for by an Episcopal minister of Central City, Colorado, and she refused to go back to the tribe (New York *Times*, October 7, 1867). Stanley, writing from Medicine Lodge later, told of the boy, Wilson Graham, whose acrobatic feats, knowledge of English, and many-bladed jackknife were the sources of admiration among his people (*Missouri Democrat*, October 25, 1867). George Bent says the boy's name was Wilson Graham, having been in the Wilson & Graham Circus, and that he was later known as Tom Whiteshirt (Hyde, *Life of George Bent*, p. 257).
Page 5
well taken care of . . . Theodore Davis, "A Summer on the Plains," *Harper's New Monthly Magazine*, XXXVI, No. 213 (1868), pp. 294–95.
Page 5
"would be exterminated" . . . Donald Berthrong, *The Southern Cheyennes*, p. 274, citing *Major General Hancock upon Indian Affairs and Accompanying Exhibits*, pp. 45–48.
Page 6
in the morning sun . . . George Armstrong Custer, *My Life on the Plains*, pp. 33–34.
Page 6
excited and disturbed . . . Stanley, *My Early Travels*, I, 37–38. George Bent claimed that Roman Nose wanted to kill Hancock but Bull Bear stopped him (Hyde, *Life of George Bent*, p. 259).
Page 6
guns of the soldiers . . . Stanley, *My Early Travels*, p. 38.
Page 6
"envelop its victim" . . . Custer, *My Life on the Plains*, p. 37.
Page 7
where both soon died . . . Custer and Hancock said the girl was a white captive who had been brutally raped by the Indians. Wynkoop, George Bent, and Tall Bull insisted the girl was a half-witted Cheyenne whom the soldiers ravished. Cheyenne chief Grey Head said the girl was a Cheyenne who was not in her right mind, and when asked if he was sure

she was a Cheyenne, he said, "Did I not know her parents; did I not see her as she grew up, day by day?" Stanley, who had been pro-Hancock on the issue, was convinced of Grey Head's sincerity. "A British Journalist Reports the Medicine Lodge Peace Councils of 1867," *Kansas Historical Quarterly,* No. 3 (Autumn 1967), p. 302.

Page 7
as scouts and guides . . . The following account is based upon Custer, *My Life on the Plains;* Davis, "A Summer on the Plains"; Lawrence A. Frost, *The Court-Martial of General George Armstrong Custer;* Lieutenant Henry Jackson, *Itinerary of the March of the United States Seventh Cavalry —1867;* Marguerite Merinton, *The Custer Story,* pp. 204–5; and Minnie Dubbs Millbrook, "Custer's First Scout in the West," *Kansas Historical Quarterly,* XXXIX, No. 1 (Spring 1973), pp. 75–95.

Page 7
belonged to Roman Nose . . . George Bent stated that Roman Nose and Guerrier were friends, the wife of Roman Nose being a cousin of Guerrier (Hyde, *Life of George Bent,* p. 260).

Page 7
"not one is seen" . . . Frost, *Court-Martial of Custer,* p. 18, citing "Difficulties with Indian Tribes," 41 Cong., 2d sess., *House Executive Document 40,* p. 131. Bent said that Guerrier, who had been sent ahead by Custer, helped the Indians escape by leading Custer in another direction (Hyde, *Life of George Bent,* p. 262).

Page 8
on an Indian hunt . . . Custer, *My Life on the Plains,* pp. 49–52.

Page 8
"destroyed this camp" . . . Frost, *Court-Martial of Custer,* p. 22, citing "Difficulties with Indian Tribes," p. 66.

Page 9
destroyed Indian lodges . . . Stanley, *My Early Travels,* I, p. 46.

Page 9
"a general war" . . . Frost, *Court-Martial of Custer,* citing "Difficulties with Indian Tribes," pp. 130–31. See *Indian Affairs, 1867,* 310–14, Wynkoop, September 14, 1867.

Page 9
hunting was good . . . E. B. Custer, *Tenting on the Plains,* pp. 527–28, Custer to Mrs. Custer, April 8, 1867.

Page 10
found a hot trail . . . Minnie Dubbs Millbrook, "The West Breaks In General Custer," *Kansas Historical Quarterly,* XXXVI, No. 2 (Summer 1970), p. 123.

Page 11
for personal reasons . . . *Report of the Secretary of War, 1867, House Executive Document No. 1,* 40th Cong., 2d sess., p. 35.

Page 14
"*Bring none back alive*" . . . Tom Custer, Cook, and Elliott all gave testimony to these verbal orders (Frost, *Court-Martial of Custer,* pp. 151, 159, 178).

Page 14
actually shot Johnson . . . Ibid., pp. 151–52.

Page 15
with the courier group . . . George Bent stated that there were both Sioux and Cheyennes in the war party, that one of them was the Cheyenne Yellow Horse, whose sister was married to frontiersman John Simpson Smith (Hyde, *Life of George Bent,* pp. 274–75).

Page 15
could get them out . . . It was during this fight that Sergeant Frederick Wyllyams was killed, and a photographer was on hand to take a picture of his mutilated corpse, a sketch of which ran in the July 27, 1867, issue of *Harper's Illustrated Weekly* (p. 468).

Page 15
"*turns during the day*" . . . Millbrook, "The West Breaks In General Custer," p. 130, citing *Memorial of Lieut. Frederick Henry Beecher, U.S.A.,* p. 31.

Page 15
while Custer was there . . . Ibid., p. 137.

Page 16
to infect Fort Wallace . . . Ibid., p. 138.

Page 17
"*of hunting the Indians*" . . . Ibid., p. 140, citing *Western America in Documents,* Catalogue 161, p. 41.

Page 18
and Leavy . . . Frost, *Court-Martial of Custer,* p. 91, letter from Charles Brewster to G. A. Custer, September 7, 1867.

Page 18
strong bias against him . . . New York *Times,* December 31, 1867, quoting letter from Custer to Colonel A. B. Nettleton, December 21, 1867, as published in Sandusky (Ohio) *Register.*

Page 19
parade ground . . . New York *Times,* November 30, 1867, quoting St. Louis *Republican* story from Fort Leavenworth, November 25, 1867.

Page 20
pay for two months . . . Other accusations were made against Custer in a Kansas newspaper: "Rumor says that a certain officer who was recently tried by court martial, not a hundred miles from Fort Leavenworth [the trial was originally set for Fort Riley] will have to undergo another siege of the same description, for there is positive evidence that he starved his men one-half of the time, and wantonly fed them on bad food the other half;

that he forced them to work, without extra pay, on the homes and lands of citizens, and compelled them, at the same time, to perform all the duties of a soldier; that he obliged them to destroy their clothes, and yet demanded that they should always appear neat and clean; that he encouraged murder, rape and arson, but punished his men for unintentionally omitting to salute him; that he suffered his worse ruffians to maltreat his best men in camp or garrison, but ordered his best men to do all the roughest fighting when before the common ememy; that he shaved the heads of men and "ducked" them for going a few rods beyond the camp to get a mouthful of food, when there were no orders to the contrary." *Kansas Daily Tribune* (Lawrence), November 22, 1867, citing the Leavenworth *Bulletin.*
Page 20
for the presidency . . . Kansas Daily Tribune, December 8, 1867.

Chapter II   Treaty by Trickery

Page 22
beyond those rivers . . . "C.H.," New York *Times,* July 2, 1867.
Page 23
Department of the Platte . . . Members of the commission were characterized by one reporter thusly: "When Harney talks, Sanborn doesn't like it and Harney backs out quietly. Terry is a gentleman and calmly dumb. Taylor yields to Sanborn. Sanborn is 'all talk.'" New York *Times,* October 26, 1867. Tappan was a quiet stick-whittler; Terry, stylish and neat; Augur, a cigar smoker with muttonchop side whiskers; Sanborn, a legal mind; Taylor, a philanthropist; Henderson, the public-relations spokesman for the group.
Page 23
Apaches to attend the council . . . "O.," Leavenworth *Democrat Conservative,* September 9, 1867; "Frontier," Chicago *Tribune,* September 30, 1867.
Page 24
Wynkoop on September 8 . . . Berthrong, *The Southern Cheyennes,* p. 292. George Bent said that Black Kettle first met with Leavenworth before going on to Fort Larned (Hyde, *Life of George Bent,* pp. 280–82).
Page 24
sixty miles south of Larned . . . Brown, Cincinnati *Commercial,* October 21, 1867, letter, Murphy to Commission, Medicine Lodge Creek, October 5, 1867. Sherman attempted to prevent the train of treaty presents from reaching the Indians: "In case Wynkoop or Leavenworth try to move goods towards the Indian country Hancock has orders to escort the goods to Larned and there held" (Fort Larned, Letters Received, Sherman to Major Leet, July 19, 1867).

Page 24
safety of Fort Larned . . . Brown, Cincinnati *Commercial,* October 21, 1867; Milton Reynolds, Chicago *Times,* October 22, 1867; Leavenworth *Democrat Conservative,* October 3, 1867; Fayel, *Daily Missouri Republican,* October 18, 1867.

Page 25
council in the West . . . These included George C. Brown of the Cincinnati *Commercial;* John Howland, artist correspondent for *Harper's Illustrated Weekly;* Solomon T. Bulkley of the New York *Herald;* William Fayel of the *Missouri Republican;* H. J. Budd of the Cincinnati *Weekly Gazette;* S. F. Hall of the Chicago *Tribune;* Henry M. Stanley, reporting for the *Kansas Weekly Tribune* (Lawrence), the *Missouri Democrat,* and other papers; James E. Taylor, son of the Indian Commissioner, who represented *Frank Leslie's Illustrated Newspaper;* and Milton Reynolds of the Lawrence *State Journal* and the Chicago *Times.* Additionally, there was a correspondent for the New York *Times* who signed his copy "C.H."; another, besides Hall, who reported for the Chicago *Tribune,* accompanying Leavenworth into the Indian Territory and signing his copy "Frontier"; and a Leavenworth *Daily Conservative* correspondent who signed his copy "O."

Page 26
"we are, off again" . . . Brown, Cincinnati *Commercial,* October 21, 1867.

Page 26
"stink too much white man here" . . . Fayel, *Daily Missouri Republican,* October 18, 1867; Reynolds, Chicago *Times,* October 22, 1867; Brown, Cincinnati *Commercial,* October 21, 1867; Stanley, New York *Tribune,* October 23, 1867; New York *Times,* October 19, 1867.

Page 26
"all intent on buffalo" . . . Brown, Cincinnati *Commercial,* October 21, 1867.

Page 27
"whooping and yelling" . . . Reynolds, Chicago *Times,* October 25, 1867.

Page 27
"among the commissioners" . . . Brown, Cincinnati *Commercial,* October 24, 1867.

Page 27
operations against the Indians . . . Fayel, *Missouri Republican,* October 24, 1867; Stanley, *Daily Missouri Democrat,* October 23, 1867.

Page 28
other appropriate symbols . . . Stanley, New York *Tribune,* October 23, 1867.

Page 28
take several more days . . . Ibid.

Page 28
goods were even delivered . . . Reynolds, Chicago *Times,* October 29, 1867.

Page 28
"*stay for improper purposes*" . . . Hall, Chicago *Tribune*, October 24, 1867.
Page 28
stabbed twice in the ribs . . . Stanley, *Kansas Weekly Tribune*, November 24, 1867.
Page 29
throughout the meeting . . . Brown, Cincinnati *Commercial*, October 26, 28, 1867; Reynolds, Chicago *Times*, October 29, 1867.
Page 29
"*which I can't see*" . . . Stanley, *Kansas Weekly Tribune*, October 31, 1867.
Page 30
the Kiowas did not . . . Hall, Chicago *Tribune*, October 29, 1867.
Page 30
by the interpreter . . . Stanley, *Kansas Weekly Tribune*, November 14, 1867.
Page 30
and Min-im-mic . . . Budd, Cincinnati *Gazette*, November 4, 1867.
Page 31
bringing back some scalps . . . Brown, Cincinnati *Commercial*, November 4, 1867; Henry M. Stanley, "A British Journalist Reports the Medicine Lodge Peace Councils of 1867," *Kansas Historical Quarterly*, XXXIII, No. 3 (Autumn 1867), p. 292.
Page 31
"*dozens of butcher knives*" . . . Brown, Cincinnati *Commercial*, November 4, 1867; *Missouri Democrat*, November 2, 1867; Stanley, "A British Journalist Reports the Medicine Lodge Peace Councils of 1867," op. cit., p. 293. Several of the guns blew up when the Indians tried to fire them.
Page 32
Poor Bear and others of his tribe . . . Brown, Cincinnati *Commercial*, November 4, 1867; Stanley, New York *Tribune*, November 6, 1867.
Page 32
"*treaty stipulations*" . . . Reynolds, Chicago *Times*, October 12, 1867.
Page 32
Monday, the twenty-eighth . . . Brown, Cincinnati *Commercial*, November 4, 1867.
Page 32
uneasiness of the whites . . . The following description is based on a number of accounts, principally Stanley, New York *Tribune*, November 8, 1867, *Kansas Weekly Tribune*, November 11, 1867, and *Daily Missouri Democrat*, November 2, 1867; George C. Brown, Cincinnati *Commercial*, November 4, 1867; S. F. Hall, Chicago *Tribune*, November 4, 1867; William Fayel, *Daily Missouri Republican*, November 2, 1867; and General E. S. Godfrey, "Medicine Lodge Treaty 60 Years Ago," *Winners of the West*, VI, No. 4 (March 30, 1929), p. 8. Though original newspaper

sources were used throughout this chapter, Douglas C. Jones's *The Treaty of Medicine Lodge* was a helpful guide.

Page 33
"*Indians of our day*" . . . Brown, Cincinnati *Commercial*, November 4, 1867.

Page 34
"*masters of the Plains*" . . . Ibid.

Page 34
Harney to the center . . . Hall, Chicago *Tribune*, November 4, 1867; Stanley, New York *Tribune*, November 8, 1867; Stanley, *Kansas Weekly Tribune*, November 11, 1867.

Page 35
"*that provokes war*" . . . Stanley, New York *Tribune*, November 8, 1867.

Page 35
conduct clearly implied . . . Ibid.

Page 36
returning to their seats . . . Hall, Chicago *Tribune*, November 4, 1867.

Page 36
back to the treaty table . . . Stanley, New York *Tribune*, November 8, 1867.

Page 36
made his mark on the paper . . . Brown, Cincinnati *Commercial*, November 4, 1867; Stanley, New York *Tribune*, November 8, 1867; Stanley, *Kansas Weekly Tribune*, November 11, 1867.

Page 37
"*The commissioners*" . . . Stanley, Kansas *Weekly Tribune*, November 11, 1867.

Page 37
"*warriors of the plains*" . . . Hall, Chicago *Tribune*, November 4, 1867.

Page 37
throughout the encampment . . . Ibid.

Page 38
belligerent Dog Soldiers . . . Jones, *The Treaty of Medicine Lodge*, pp. 143, 179–80. In a story filed later, while with the commission at North Platte, Nebraska, Stanley declared that the commissioners ". . . have been criminal in more ways than one. After witnessing the Cheyennes' signature to this mock treaty, they then distributed *seven hundred Springfield rifles, one hundred and ten Colt's revolvers, ten kegs of powder, and a wagon load of fixed ammunition*" (*Kansas Weekly Tribune*, November 4, 1867). The *Missouri Democrat* answered: "In some mysterious way, the Kansas people seem entirely incapable of getting at the truth about Indian matters. No Springfield muskets at all were delivered to any Indians, and no muskets or revolvers to the tribes who have been at war" (*Missouri Democrat*, as cited by *Kansas Daily Tribune* (Lawrence), November 21, 1867). The *Democrat* contended that only old, worthless pistols were is-

sued, and the *Tribune* deplored this as a "shameless confession" of openly
cheating the Indians in the issuance of worthless goods (*Kansas Daily Tribune,* November 17, 21, 1867).

Page 38

hunt and secure food . . . Stanley, "A British Journalist Reports the Medicine Lodge Peace Councils of 1867," op. cit., p. 314.

Chapter III   In Search of an Enemy

Page 39

Medicine Lodge meeting . . . Central Superintendency, Letters Received,
Murphy to Snow, Lawrence, November 28, 1867; Murphy to Snow,
Atchison, December 9, 1867; Snow to Murphy, Neosho Falls, December 4,
1867; Murphy to Mix, Atchison, December 11, 1867.

Page 39

interpreter along, just in case . . . Ibid., Wynkoop to Murphy, Fort Larned,
December 18, 1867; Browning to Taylor, Washington, D.C., April 13,
1868.

Page 40

potential trouble . . . Upper Arkansas Agency, Letters Received, Smith to
Murphy, February 5, 1868.

Page 41

command of Colonel A. J. Smith . . . Rister, *Border Command,* p. 35. Major
General Philip Sheridan, who stood only five feet five inches tall, had been
one of the outstanding Union generals of the Civil War. Known to his men
as "Little Phil," he was a graduate of West Point, where he risked court-
martial by threatening a sergeant with a bayonet and then going after him
with his fists. His military career had a slow and inauspicious beginning,
Sheridan holding mostly minor administrative posts and almost being court-
martialed for violations of regulations as chief quartermaster in Curtis' Army
of the Southwest. His break came in May of 1862, when he was appointed
commanding colonel of the 2nd Michigan Cavalry. Beginning that July with
Booneville, where he won his first star only thirty-five days after becoming a
colonel, Sheridan rocketed from one success to another. By December he
had won his second star. Then came engagements at Winchester and at
Chickamauga, the Chattanooga campaign, and Missionary Ridge. In May
1864 Sheridan's Richmond raid resulted in the defeat and death of the
South's outstanding cavalryman Jeb Stuart, at Yellow Tavern. During the
winter of 1864–65 he conducted the devastating Shenandoah Valley campaign, defeating Early's army at Waynesboro and Picket at Five Forks and
then blocking Lee's withdrawal, leading to the surrender of the Confederate

Army and the end of the Civil War. Following the war, he led some fifty thousand veterans to the Texas border in a show of strength in connection with the Maximilian affair. Serving as military governor of Texas and Louisiana, Sheridan was so severe and uncompromising that President Johnson recalled him after several months.

Page 41

available for them to hunt . . . This may have been the meeting between Sheridan and the Cheyennes referred to by George Bent: "I was present as interpreter. At the council, Wynkoop asked General Sheridan if he could issue arms to the Indians. Sheridan said, 'Yes, give them arms and if they go to war the soldiers will kill them like men.' This I interpreted to the Cheyennes, and Stone Calf, a Cheyenne chief and a great warrior, replied to Sheridan, 'Let your soldiers grow long hair, so that we can have some honor in killing them.' Sheridan smiled and said he was very sorry but he could not accommodate him as the soldiers would get lousy" (Hyde, *Life of George Bent*, p. 290). Sheridan was not present August 10, when the guns were issued, as Bent remembered it. See *Report of Secretary of War, 1868*, p. 12.

Page 41

northwest of Fort Wallace . . . Berthrong, *The Southern Cheyennes*, p. 302, citing Captain E. P. Miller to AAAG, District of Upper Arkansas, April 11, 1868.

Page 42

by Agent Wynkoop . . . Ibid., p. 301. "Ned" Wynkoop had come to Kansas as early as 1856, a young American seeking adventure, and he found his share. Catching the notice of Governor Denver of Kansas, he was appointed as the first sheriff of "Arapahoe county," then encompassing the gold-rush region of the Rocky Mountains. As a member of the third gold-rush group to reach Cherry Creek, the Leavenworth-Lecompton group, Wynkoop helped initiate the Denver Town Company. Not only was he the one who suggested the name of "Denver," but he and another man made a heroic trek over the Platte Trail in the dead of winter to carry the Denver town charter back to Kansas. He took part in Denver's early history as a gold miner, as a bartender in Charley Harrison's famous Criterion Saloon, and as an officer in the Colorado 1st Cavalry, playing a major role in the defeat of the Texas Confederate Army at La Glorieta Pass, New Mexico. Later, as commanding officer of Fort Lyon, Wynkoop led a daring expedition into the heart of hostile Indian country in a successful effort to persuade Black Kettle and the Cheyennes to make peace. When Black Kettle, with whom he became fast friends, was betrayed by Chivington, Wynkoop risked army censure in demanding an inquiry into the infamous massacre at Sand Creek.

Page 42
Fort Wallace by Indians . . . Berthrong, *The Southern Cheyennes*, p. 303, citing Beecher to Sheridan, May 28, 1868.
Page 43
"to clean out the Kaws" . . . *Kansas Daily Tribune*, June 6, 1868.
Page 44
"let white man go and do it" . . . *Commissioner of Indian Affairs, 1868*, pp. 64–65, Boone to Taylor, June 4, 1868; *Kansas Daily Tribune*, June 6, 7, 8, 11, 1868; *Emporia News*, June 5, 12, 1868. Stover's son later wrote a humorous poem about the fracas. *Kansas State Historical Collections*, Vol. XVI (1923–25), pp. 548–49.
Page 44
"be given them at present" . . . *Commissioner of Indian Affairs, 1868*, p. 66, Taylor to Murphy, June 25, 1868.
Page 44
ammunition they expected . . . Ibid., pp. 66–67, Wynkoop to Murphy, July 20, 1868.
Page 44
units from Harker . . . *Report of Secretary of War, 1868–69*, p. 10, Sheridan to Sherman, September 26, 1868.
Page 44
Indians in check . . . *Kansas Daily Tribune*, July 21, 1868.
Page 45
"had been promised them" . . . *Commissioner of Indian Affairs, 1868*, pp. 66–67, Wynkoop to Murphy, July 20, 1868.
Page 45
used against the whites . . . Ibid., pp. 68–69, Murphy to Taylor, August 1, 1868. Little Raven was still laboring under the delusion that the Treaty of Medicine Lodge would allow him and his tribe to return to Colorado as he had requested.
Page 45
"their treaty pledges" . . . Ibid.
Page 45
agency during that season . . . Ibid., p. 70, Wynkoop to Murphy, August 22, 1868. Historians who have condemned Wynkoop on the grounds that the very arms issued to the Indians were used in the raids on the Saline and Solomon have failed to note that the raids began on the day following the issuance of the weapons and occurred some eighty miles away. While it is within the realm of possibility that the Indians overnight dashed the distance to the Saline, it is not at all logical. Even Sheridan accepted the assertion by Little Rock that the war party left Walnut Creek on August 2 or 3.
Page 46
essentially what happened . . . *Kansas Daily Tribune*, August 14, 16, 18, 1868; *Emporia News*, August 21, 1868.

Page 47
died in early September . . . *Kansas Daily Tribune*, August 27, September 13, 1868; *Report of Secretary of War, 1868*, p. 11, Sheridan to Sherman, September 26, 1868; *Record of Engagements with Hostile Indians with the Military Division of the Missouri from 1868 to 1882*, p. 8.

Page 47
"day of the outbreak" . . . Rister Collection, University of Oklahoma Division of Manuscripts, Hazen to Sherman, Fort Cobb, November 10, 1868.

Page 50
"I will protect you" . . . "Report of an Interview between Col. E. W. Wynkoop, U. S. Indian Agent, and Little Rock, a Cheyenne Chief, Held at Fort Larned, Kansas, August 19, 1868," Bureau of Indian Affairs, Cheyenne and Arapaho Indians.

Page 51
Colonel Bankhead at Fort Wallace . . . *Kansas Daily Tribune*, August 20, 1868; *Report of the Secretary of War, Executive Document 1*, p. 11, Sheridan to Sherman, September 26, 1868; Berthrong, *The Southern Cheyennes*, p. 309, citing *Harper's Weekly*, XII, No. 612 (September 19, 1868), p. 606, and Fort Wallace, Letters Sent, Bankhead to AAAG, District of the Upper Arkansas, August 19, 1868. One account has it that Grover played dead and, after looking them over, the Indians rode off.

Page 51
"fairly enter into it" . . . *Commissioner of Indian Affairs, 1868*, p. 71, Wynkoop to Murphy, August 19, 1868.

Page 51
"those who do not" . . . Ibid.

Page 52
war on the Cheyennes . . . Ibid., pp. 75–76, Murphy to Mix, September 19, 1868.

Page 52
"confined to that locality" . . . Ibid., p. 74, Sherman to Townsend, August 22, 1868.

Page 52
"war path with the Cheyennes" . . . Ibid., p. 75, Murphy to Mix, September 19, 1868.

Page 52
in the Indian Territory . . . *Emporia News*, May 29, 1868.

Page 52
cared for by his wife . . . Central Superintendency, Letters Received, Tappan to Murphy, July 13, 20, 1868; Wynkoop to Murphy, August 4, 1868; Murphy to Taylor, August 6, 1868; *New York Times*, August 14, 1868.

Page 52
"make them very poor" . . . *Report of Secretary of War, 1868*, p. 12, Sheridan to Sherman, September 26, 1868.

Chapter IV   The Solomon Avengers

Page 54
requested the assignment . . . Leavenworth *Times and Conservative*, September 30, 1868.

Page 55
an accomplished gymnast . . . New York *Times*, October 4, 1868.

Page 55
taken on with the unit . . . Forsyth, *Thrilling Days in Army Life*, pp. 12–15.

Page 56
a good opportunity . . . Scout Sigmund Shlesinger, "The Beecher Island Fight," *Collections of the Kansas State Historical Society*, 1919–22, XV, p. 540.

Page 56
the Solomon and the Saline . . . New York *Herald*, October 12, 1868.

Page 57
pack train of four mules . . . Forsyth, *Thrilling Days in Army Life*, p. 11.

Page 58
large masses of Indians . . . Scout John Hurst, "The Beecher Island Fight," *Collections of the Kansas State Historical Society*, 1919–22, XV, p. 531; Forsyth, *Thrilling Days in Army Life*, pp. 23–24.

Page 58
"Indians!" went up . . . Davis, "A Summer on the Plains," p. 295; General George A. Forsyth, *Thrilling Days in Army Life*, p. 56. The following relies upon various sources as cited, but especially upon two long-overlooked accounts—one by a scout who had been with Carpenter's relief column, written from Fort Wallace on October 1, 1868, and appearing in the New York *Tribune*, October 16, 1868; the other taken from Forsyth's scouts themselves at Fort Wallace on October 8, 1868, and appearing in the New York *Herald*, October 12, 1868. The *Tribune* account may have been written by chief scout L. L. Howe, who first brought the news to Fort Wallace on September 27 and who is mentioned in a New York *Times* story on September 28, 1868.

Page 60
"insignia of command" . . . New York *Herald*, October 12, 1868.

Page 60
agreed to do so . . . Hyde, *Life of George Bent*, pp. 302–3.

Page 62
near the Beecher home . . . (New York *Tribune*, October 5, 1868). Beecher's obituary in the September 28, 1868, issue of the *Tribune* stated: "He had just been ordered to duty in the Signal Office but was killed before he could obey the order."

Page 62
sundown when he died . . . Ibid.; Forsyth, *Thrilling Days in Army Life,*
pp. 54–55.
Page 62
"last damned horse is gone" . . . New York *Herald,* October 12, 1868.
Most of the scouts thought this was George or Charlie Bent, but one writer
suggests that it was one of two renegades, Nibsi or John Clybor, who was
there. It was Nibsi, he states, whom Roman Nose ordered to blow the
bugle, not as a signal but simply as martial music (Hurst, "The Beecher Island Fight," p. 533).
Page 62
"Indians will be charging us" . . . Hurst, "The Beecher Island Fight," p.
534.
Page 63
"speak right straight" . . . New York *Herald,* October 12, 1868.
Page 64
for the Indians to find . . . George M. Heinzman, " 'Don't let them ride
over us,' " *American Heritage,* Vol. XVIII, No. 2 (February 1967), p. 87.
An often-told but unsubstantiated story of their trip relates how the two
men, traveling only by night, hid from Indians in the carcass of a buffalo,
where they discovered a rattlesnake, and how Stillwell spat tobacco juice in
the snake's eyes, running it off.
Page 65
"Have you deserted us?" . . . Chauncey B. Whitney, "Diary," *Collections of
the Kansas State Historical Society, 1911–12,* XII, pp. 296–99.
Page 65
a day after Carpenter . . . New York *Daily Tribune,* October 12, 1868.
Special report written from Fort Wallace, October 1, 1868, by a scout with
Colonel Carpenter.
Page 65
"is seldom witnessed" . . . Whitney, "Diary," p. 298.
Page 65
trappings of an Indian warrior . . . This was first reported by Chief Scout
L. L. Howe, from Fort Wallace on September 27, 1868, having returned
ahead of the others (New York *Times,* September 28, 1868). It is repeated
in the New York *Daily Tribune* story of October 12.
Page 66
"eagle feathers down the back" . . . Shlesinger, "The Beecher Island
Fight," p. 546. E. A. Brininstool ("The Rescue of Forsyth's Scouts," *Collections of the Kansas State Historical Society, 1926–28,* XVII, p. 849) states
that five of the scaffold burials reported were found first, then an Indian
tepee was discovered, and inside it was the body of an Indian lying on a
small platform, wrapped in buffalo hides. He had been killed by a bullet
wound and was thought to be a chief of importance. Brininstool does not
give his source of information.
Page 66
energy in relieving Forsyth . . . New York *Times,* January 14, 1869;

Brevet Colonel L. H. Carpenter, "Story of a Rescue," *Winners of the West,* II, No. 3 (February 1925), pp. 6–7.

Page 66
hands over his chest . . . Letters Received, Fort Wallace, December 28, 1868.

Page 66
scout named Mooney . . . *Army and Navy Journal,* 1869, p. 450.

Page 67
other Indian equipment . . . David L. Spotts, *Campaigning with Custer and the Nineteenth Volunteer Cavalry on the Washita Campaign, 1868–69,* E. A. Brininstool, ed., pp. 207–15.

Page 67
meet in a Cheyenne camp . . . *Record of Engagements,* p. 12. Letter, Captain William Penrose to AAAG, Department of the Missouri, October 15, 1868, Fort Lyon Letters Sent.

Page 68
Satanta among them . . . Penrose to AAAG, Department of the Missouri, October 8, 11, 15, 1868, Fort Lyon Letters Sent.

Chapter V   Return of the Beau Sabreur

Page 69
"protection of their own families" . . . Samuel J. Crawford, *Kansas in the Sixties,* p. 296, citing letter, Sheridan to Crawford.

Page 70
"Sully, District Commander" . . . Godfrey, "Some Reminiscences," *Cavalry Journal,* XXXVII, No. 153 (October 1928), p. 481. The following account also relies upon Report of Brevet Brigadier General Alfred Sully to Brevet Brigadier General Chauncey McKeever, Camp on Bluff Creek, Kansas, September 16, 1868, Records of the U. S. Army Commands – N.A., Selected Letters, 1868–72; Winfield Scott Harvey, "Campaigning with Sheridan: A Farrier's Diary," ed. by George Shirk, *Chronicles of Oklahoma,* XXXVII, No. 1 (1959), pp. 68–105; and Melbourne C. Chandler, *Of Garryowen in Glory—The History of the Seventh United States Cavalry Regiment,* pp. 26–27, quoting Official Record of Events written by Captain Albert Barnitz.

Page 70
"crossed the Rubicon" . . . Brigadier General E. S. Godfrey, "Some Reminiscences," *Cavalry Journal,* XXXVI, No. 148 (July 1927), p. 421.

Page 71
"two Indians and one pony" . . . Sully to McKeever, Report, September 16, 1868.

Page 72
7th Cavalry officers . . . Custer, *My Life on the Plains,* pp. 160–61;

Godfrey, "Some Reminiscences," *Cavalry Journal*, XXXVI, pp. 423–24. The 7th Regiment was highly incensed at Sully over this, as it was considered a strong principle to rescue comrades in distress.

Page 73
"marched down again" . . . Custer, *My Life on the Plains*, p. 190.

Page 73
mules were lost . . . Sully to McKeever, Report, September 16, 1868.

Page 74
"man or beast" . . . Carl Coke Rister, *Border Command*, p. 92.

Page 74
reverberating through Congress . . . A lengthy Congressional "Memorial" to Sand Creek, chastising Chivington in the severest terms, appeared in the New York *Times* on October 20, 1868.

Page 75
"application will be successful" . . . Custer, *My Life on the Plains*, p. 183, citing letter, Sheridan to Custer, September 24, 1868.

Page 75
"swallows on the wing" . . . Elizabeth B. Custer, *Following the Guidon*, p. 7.

Page 75
about the situation at once . . . Custer, *My Life on the Plains*, p. 12.

Page 76
"desires to be done" . . . Custer, *My Life on the Plains*, p. 205.

Page 76
"this part of the territory" . . . E. B. Custer, *Following the Guidon*, p. 14.

Page 77
mounted on grays . . . Godfrey, "Some Reminiscences," *Cavalry Journal*, XXXVII, p. 483. Hamilton, with Troop A, was given first pick and he chose the blacks ("In Memoriam: Louis McLane Hamilton," *Chronicles of Oklahoma*, XLVI, no. 4 [Winter 1968–69], p. 381, citing New York *Evening Post*). Barnitz, Troop B, took the chestnuts and browns (Brill, *Conquest of the Southern Plains*, p. 305). Troop K rode the sorrels (Harvey, "Campaigning with Sheridan," p. 81). Troop M had the odds and ends: roans, piebalds, etc. (Godfrey, "Some Reminiscences," *Cavalry Journal*, XXXVII, p. 483).

Page 77
for the Indian Territory . . . New York *Herald*, December 12, 1868, DeB. Randolph Keim from Camp Supply, I.T., November 22, 1868.

Page 78
between the flanking troops . . . Godfrey, "Some Reminiscences," *Cavalry Journal*, XXXVII, p. 485.

Page 79
"graze until retreat" . . . *Army and Navy Journal*, January 2, 1869, p. 310.

Page 80
"thus engaged in" . . . Custer, *My Life on the Plains*, p. 212.

Page 80
confluence of the two streams . . . New York *Herald,* December 12, 1868. Though Custer undoubtedly did not know it, the site of the new supply camp at the juncture of Beaver and Wolf creeks had been the camping site some eight years earlier of his famous Rebel counterpart the dashing cavalryman J. E. B. Stuart. Then Major John Sedgwick and Lieutenant Stuart had led an Indian-hunting expedition into the Indian Territory, their command lying in camp on June 9, 1860, at the confluence of the two streams. Sedgwick moved up the Beaver while Stuart scouted up Wolf Creek, chancing to meet with a government party then surveying the northern boundary of Texas (W. Stitt Robinson, ed., "The Kiowa and Comanche Campaign of 1860 as Recorded in the Personal Diary of Lt. J. E. B. Stuart," *Kansas Historical Quarterly,* XXIII [1957], pp. 394–95).

Page 80
upright walls, rafters, etc. . . . Godfrey, "Some Reminiscences," *Cavalry Journal,* XXXVII, p. 485.

Page 81
brevet-major-general rank . . . Ibid., p. 487.

Page 81
about twenty wagons . . . DeB. Randolph Keim, *Sheridan's Troopers on the Borders,* p. 94.

Page 82
"in honor of the occasion" . . . Ibid., p. 100.

Page 82
six inches deep . . . E. B. Custer, *Following the Guidon,* pp. 16–17.

Page 82
"all women and children" . . . Keim, *Sheridan's Troopers,* p. 103.

Chapter VI   Forbidden Sanctuary

Page 84
Texas and even Mexico . . . *Report of Commissioner of Indian Affairs, 1857, 1858, 1859, 1860, 1861, 1862, 1863, 1864, 1865, 1866,* and *1867;* Report of Special Commissioner C. F. Garret, 1868, *Report of Commissioner of Indian Affairs, 1868;* Annie Heloise Abel, *The Slaveholding Indians,* 3 vols.

Page 85
refuge at Fort Arbuckle . . . LeRoy R. Hafen and Carl Coke Rister, *Western America,* p. 300.

Page 86
western Indian Territory . . . Rister, *Border Command,* pp. 51–52.

Page 87
Hazen to Fort Cobb . . . W. B. Hazen, "Some Corrections of 'Life on the Plains,'" *Chronicles of Oklahoma,* III, No. 4 (December 1925), p. 301.

Page 87
"known hostile bands" . . . Ibid., p. 300, citing letter, Sheridan to Hazen, In the Field, Fort Larned, September 19, 1868.
Page 87
tribes in his district . . . Ibid., p. 303, citing letter, Sherman to Hazen, St. Louis, November 23, 1868.
Page 88
arrival at Cobb . . . Ibid., pp. 301–2.
Page 88
companies of 10th Cavalry . . . Marvin Kroeker, "Colonel W. B. Hazen in the Indian Territory, 1868–69," *Chronicles of Oklahoma,* XLII, No. 1 (Spring 1964), p. 60.
Page 88
"traps for them at both places" . . . Rister Collection, University of Oklahoma Division of Manuscripts, Captain Henry E. Alvord to Major James E. Ray, Old Fort Cobb, November 5, 1868.
Page 88
"for lasting peace" . . . Ibid., Alvord to Ray, Old Fort Cobb, October 30, 1868.
Page 88
provisions and ammunition . . . Ibid., Alvord to Ray, Old Fort Cobb, November 5, 1868.
Page 89
Kiowa-Comanche agent . . . Kroeker, "Colonel W. B. Hazen," p. 65.
Page 89
pick up her effects . . . Rister Collection, Papers of General W. T. Sherman and P. H. Sheridan, letter, W. T. Walkley to Hazen, Eureka Valley, October 10, 1868.
Page 90
"north of the Arkansas" . . . Office of the Adjutant General, Letters Received, Report of Conversation Held Between Colonel and Brevet Major General W. B. Hazen, U.S.A., on Special Service, and Chiefs of the Cheyenne and Arapaho Tribes of Indians, at Fort Cobb, Indian Territory, November 21, 1868.
Page 90
"we wish for peace" . . . Ibid.
Page 91
"rendezvousing at Fort Cobb" . . . Hazen, "Some Corrections," p. 303, citing letter, Sherman to Hazen, St. Louis, October 13, 1868.
Page 91
"avoid the war" . . . Central Superintendency, Letters Received, Sherman to Schofield, Telegram, St. Louis, October 20, 1868.
Page 92
"make peace with you" . . . Report of Conversation, Fort Cobb, November 21, 1868.

Page 92
"peace with these parties" . . . Office of the Adjutant General, Letters Received, Hazen to Sherman, Fort Cobb, November 22, 1868.
Page 93
"will probably develop" . . . Ibid., Hazen to Major J. P. Roy, November 26, 1868.
Page 93
"spoke for all the Cheyennes" . . . New York *Times,* letter, Hazen to James A. Garfield, February 21, 1869.
Page 93
"deaf, and cannot hear" . . . Ediger and Hoffman, "Some Reminiscences," p. 138.
Page 93
"but a short distance off" . . . Hazen, "Some Corrections," p. 310, citing letter, McCusker to Murphy, Fort Cobb, December 3, 1868.
Page 94
Comanches and Apaches . . . The precise order of the tribal camps has never been fully agreed upon. Wolf Belly Woman, a Cheyenne who was ten or eleven at the time of the Washita attack, stated: "Black Kettle's camp was the farthest west on the Washita; thus it was the one that was attacked. Next to it was an Arapaho camp, then another Cheyenne, then my father's, then a Kiowa camp." Theodore A. Ediger and Vinnie Hoffman, "Some Reminiscences of the Battle of the Washita," *Chronicles of Oklahoma,* XXXIII, No. 2 (Summer 1955), p. 141. Mah-wis-sa told Dick Curtis that "eight miles downstream were all the Arapahoes, and seventy additional lodges of Cheyennes, the Kiowas, then the Apaches and Comanches" (Sheridan to Nichols, Junction of Beaver Creek, December 3, 1868). The location of the Kiowa camp has an important bearing on which camp it was in which the body of Mrs. Blinn and her child were found and the Sheridan-Custer use of the incident to prove the Kiowas were then hostile.
Page 95
offered them shelter . . . In his rebuttal to Custer's *Life on the Plains,* Hazen attempted to establish the innocence of the Kiowas and justify his note to Sheridan, which halted hostilities against the tribe, claiming that on the night of November 26, Satanta, Satank, Lone Wolf, and most of the Kiowa chiefs slept in his tent at Fort Cobb, and left on the twenty-seventh ("Some Corrections," p. 306). But Hazen's letter from Cobb on November 26, 1868, states: "The Kiowas and Apaches have all been in, taken ten days' rations, and to-day gone back to their camps some thirty miles up the Washita, some of them, particularly Sa-tan-ta, grumbling because they could not have everything there is at the post." Office of the Adjutant General, Letters Received, Hazen to Roy, Fort Cobb, December 26, 1868.
Page 95
"murdering in Texas" . . . Office of the Adjutant General, Letters Received, Hazen to Sherman, Fort Cobb, November 22, 1868.

Page 95
"*happy hunting grounds*" . . . Rister Collection, Walkley to Hazen, October 10, 1868. George Bent described Cheyenne Jennie as a fine woman who "had often succeeded in recovering white captives from the Comanches, Kiowas, and other tribes." As an invalid, she was forced to travel in an army ambulance her husband had purchased for her (Hyde, *Life of George Bent*, p. 279).

Page 96
"*baby is very weak*" . . . Office of the Adjutant General, Letters Received, enclosure to letter, Hazen to Nichols, November 25, 1868.

Page 97
"*reclaim these parties*" . . . Office of the Adjutant General, Letters Received, Hazen to Nichols, Fort Cobb, November 25, 1868. Griffenstein (or Greiffenstein) had originally operated a trading post at the site of present Wichita, and later he was to become that town's first mayor. Eventually he moved to Burnett, in Indian Territory, and became involved in oil exploration.

Chapter VII   March of the 19th Kansas

Page 98
ranges of western Kansas . . . James Albert Hadley, "The Nineteenth Kansas Cavalry and the Conquest of the Plains Indians," *Transactions of the Kansas State Historical Society, 1907–08*, X, pp. 425–29. Numerous accounts of the 19th Kansas march appear in issues of the *Winners of the West*. Old-timers of the unit were holding reunions in Topeka as late as the 1930s.

Page 99
Major George B. Jenness . . . Samuel J. Crawford, *Kansas in the Sixties*, pp. 421–22.

Page 99
proclamation call to arms . . . Ibid., pp. 319–20.

Page 99
end of the war . . . Ibid., pp. 104–38.

Page 100
Marmaduke and Cabell . . . Ibid., p. 102.

Page 100
"*barbarians*" *of the plains* . . . Ibid., p. 231.

Page 100
until the treaty council . . . Ibid., p. 251.

Page 101
"*cavalry from this State*" . . . Ibid., p. 426.

Page 101
heard for some distance . . . Hadley, "The Nineteenth Kansas Cavalry," p. 431.
Page 102
Oklahoma lands to settlement . . . Ibid., p. 430; Crawford, Kansas in the Sixties, pp. 428–32.
Page 102
by Kansas newspapers . . . Kansas Daily Tribune (Lawrence), October 22, 1868.
Page 102
into three battalions . . . Ibid., October 29, 1868; Captain George B. Jenness, "History of the 19th Kansas Cavalry—Indian War of 1868–69," extracts from private diary, Kansas State Historical Society unpublished manuscript, p. 14.
Page 102
some one hundred fifty miles distant . . . Hadley, "The Nineteenth Kansas Cavalry," p. 433; Spotts, Campaigning with Custer, pp. 44–45.
Page 103
colds and sore throats . . . Hadley, "The Nineteenth Kansas Cavalry," p. 434; Kansas Weekly Tribune, December 24, 1868; Joseph Phelps Rodgers, "A Few Years of Experiences on the Western Frontier," Kansas State Historical Society unpublished manuscript, p. 4.
Page 103
"sticky, Kansas mud" . . . Hadley, "The Nineteenth Kansas Cavalry," p. 434.
Page 103
"felt sorry for it" . . . Ibid.
Page 103
planned to name El Dorado . . . Spotts, Campaigning with Custer, p. 49.
Page 103
belonging to some Kaw Indians . . . Jenness, "History of the 19th Kansas Cavalry," p. 15.
Page 104
Apache Bill Seaman . . . Hadley, "The Nineteenth Kansas Cavalry," p. 435. Seaman, who had lived among the Apaches for six or seven years, had been employed by Hancock as a scout, captured by the Kiowas and escaped, and afterward appointed chief of scouts at Dodge. Apache Bill was often in trouble with the law, including a charge of stealing a mule, of which he was acquitted (Kansas Daily Tribune, May 23, 1869). Sheridan eventually dismissed "Patchy," who was later killed in a gun fight at Ellsworth (Kansas Daily Tribune, August 7, 1869).
Page 104
"Dutch Henry's Trail" . . . Jenness, "History of the 19th Kansas," pp. 17–19. Dutch Henry was the leader of a horse-thief gang that operated in the territory.

Page 104
"*South of the Arkansas River*" . . . Rodgers, "A Few Years of Experiences," p. 5.

Page 104
"*land of silence and desolation*" . . . Hadley, "The Nineteenth Kansas Cavalry," p. 436.

Page 104
"*makes them homesick*" . . . Ibid.

Page 105
"*had not broken loose*" . . . Rodgers, "A Few Years of Experiences," p. 5. Most accounts blame the trooper. Jenness says the stampede was started by a wagon mule team ("History of the 19th Kansas," p. 21).

Page 105
a few miles at a time . . . Spotts, *Campaigning with Custer*, p. 57.

Page 106
their last for forty hours . . . Jenness, "History of the 19th Kansas," p. 25.

Page 106
grumbling was heard . . . Horace L. Moore, "The Nineteenth Kansas Cavalry," *Transactions of the Kansas State Historical Society, 1897–1900*, VI, p. 38; *Kansas Weekly Tribune*, December 24, 1868.

Page 106
quiet the nervous animals . . . Hadley, "The Nineteenth Kansas Cavalry," p. 437.

Page 106
"*in spite of the cold*" . . . Ibid., pp. 437–38.

Page 107
"*in the entire command*" . . . Jenness, "History of the 19th Kansas," p. 25. One man reported seeing another offer five dollars for a piece of buffalo meat the size of a dollar ("A. L. Runyon's Letters from the Nineteenth Kansas Regiment," *The Kansas Historical Quarterly*, Vol. IX [1940], p. 66).

Page 107
"*'till the guard interfered*" . . . Hadley, "The Nineteenth Kansas Cavalry," p. 438.

Page 107
"*sick to see them begging*" . . . Rodgers, "A Few Years of Experiences," p. 6.

Page 108
"*circulation of the blood*" . . . Captain George B. Jenness, "Lost in the Snow at Old Camp Supply," *Sturm's Oklahoma Magazine*, V, No. 4 (December 1907), p. 53.

Page 108
remainder of the march . . . Jenness, "History of the 19th Kansas," p. 25.

Page 108
"*wise to keep still*" . . . Spotts, *Campaigning with Custer*, p. 60.

Page 108
assistance to Sheridan . . . Hadley, "The Nineteenth Kansas Cavalry," p. 439.

Page 108
"1–1000th part of a buffalo" . . . Spotts, *Campaigning with Custer*, p. 60.

Page 109
"castor oil and salts" . . . Rodgers, "A Few Years of Experiences," p. 7.

Page 109
"Camp Starvation" . . . Gus Johnston, "Memorandum of Trip from Topeka, Kansas, to the Indian Country," Kansas State Historical Society unpublished manuscript; W. R. Smith, "Camp Starvation," *Winners of the West*, III, No. 7 (March 30, 1926), p. 7.

Page 109
until they could be rescued . . . Moore, "The Nineteenth Kansas Cavalry," p. 39.

Page 110
from Camp Supply later . . . *Kansas Weekly Tribune*, December 24, 1868.

Page 110
"making forty-five miles" . . . Ibid.

Page 110
a treat for the men . . . Hadley, "The Nineteenth Kansas Cavalry," p. 440.

Page 110
"not five miles away" . . . Ibid.

Page 111
"filled the whole valley" . . . Ibid.

Page 111
tent for bedding . . . Ibid., p. 441.

Page 111
miss their share . . . Spotts, *Campaigning with Custer*, p. 71.

Page 111
"horse in the command" . . . Jenness, "History of the 19th Kansas," pp. 31–32. A letter written from Cow Skin Creek on November 14 by E. P. Russell stated: Governor Crawford is with us, and is universally liked, as is also Col. H. Moore of Lawrence" (Emporia *News*, November 27, 1868). But another letter, written from Fort Dodge on December 15 by a member of Company M, indicated a change in temper among the 19th: ". . . if the regiment had the choosing of a commander to-day, S. J. Crawford would not get any votes; also in time to come said S. J. will get but few votes from the 19th for any position in civil life" (Emporia *News*, January 8, 1869). Ironically, in 1889 Crawford would come to Oklahoma Territory to represent the Cheyennes and Arapahoes in selling their claims to the Cherokee Outlet, the very land where he had become lost on a campaign against those tribes.

Chapter VIII   Custer's Luck

Page 112
"*a fluke or a frolic*" . . . Chandler, *Of Garryowen in Glory*, p. 14. The following account relies upon Godfrey, "Some Reminiscences"; E. B. Custer, *Following the Guidon;* Chandler, *Of Garryowen in Glory*, which contains an account written by Second Lieutenant F. M. Gibson of Troop A; Harvey, "Campaigning with Sheridan"; New York *Herald*, December 8, 24, 1868, accounts of march and battle; New York *Daily Tribune*, December 29, 1868, account of march and battle.

Page 112
cartridges and caps . . . Godfrey, "Some Reminiscences," pp. 488–89.

Page 112
"*cloud of mystery*" . . . Chandler, *Of Garryowen in Glory*, p. 14.

Page 113
warmth of his blankets . . . Rister, *Border Command*, p. 101; Custer, *My Life on the Plains*, p. 215.

Page 114
the Wichita Mountains . . . E. B. Custer, *Following the Guidon*, p. 16.

Page 114
"*Custer's Crossing*" . . . Fort Supply Letters Sent, Medical History, November 23, 1868, entry.

Page 114
through the saddle leather . . . Godfrey, "Some Reminiscences," p. 488.

Page 114
"*to keep us warm*" . . . Harvey, "Campaigning with Sheridan," p. 85.

Page 114
"*the travellin' was good overhead*" . . . Custer, *My Life on the Plains*, p. 147.

Page 116
"*despatch him with my pistol*" . . . Custer, *My Life on the Plains*, p. 220.

Page 116
toward the Antelope Hills . . . Custer, *My Life on the Plains*, states that the command camped three nights in the Wolf Creek Valley, p. 219, but this is incorrect. Godfrey ("Some Reminiscences") says, "November 25th we marched some distance up Wolf Creek and then turned in a southerly direction toward the Canadian," p. 488. Gibson, in Chandler, *Of Garryowen in Glory*, states, ". . . the Indian scouts . . . changed our course on the fourth day to nearly due south" (p. 16). Harvey ("Campaigning with Sheridan," pp. 84–85) gives the march mileage as twenty-five on November 23, eighteen on November 24, twenty-two on November 25, and thirty on November 26. His entry of the twenty-fifth states, ". . . we crossed over this morning at daybreak. We had a very hard march today, . . ." indicating they left

Wolf Creek early and crossed over the divide to the South Canadian River. The march records of the 7th give the daily mileage as November 23, fourteen; November 24, sixteen; November 25, eighteen, leaving Wolf Creek (Chandler, *Of Garryowen in Glory*, p. 27). The crossing of Wolf Creek and the first camp were evidently just west of Fargo, Oklahoma. Custer did his buffalo hunting south of Wolf Creek near the site of Gage, Oklahoma, and they camped the second night and turned south the next morning just east of Shattuck, Oklahoma.

Page 116
attacked a Comanche village . . . LeRoy R. Hafen and Carl Coke Rister, *Western America*, p. 300.

Page 117
"circle of snowy whiteness" . . . Custer, *My Life on the Plains*, p. 223.

Page 119
Lieutenant James M. Bell . . . Godfrey, "Some Reminiscences," p. 489.

Page 119
grandson of Alexander Hamilton . . . New York *Times*, December 6, 1868.

Page 120
"into battle by another" . . . "In Memoriam: Captain Louis McLane Hamilton," p. 366.

Page 122
"like a huge, black monster" . . . New York *Daily Tribune*, December 29, 1868.

Page 122
"Heaps Injuns" ahead . . . Custer, *My Life on the Plains*, p. 148.

Page 123
miles back on the trail . . . New York *Herald*, December 8, 1868.

Page 124
"river on the north side" . . . New York *Sun*, May 14, 1899, Fred S. Barde Collection, Oklahoma Historical Society.

Page 124
T. J. March and H. W. Smith . . . Chandler, *Of Garryowen in Glory*, p. 18. See Appendix A.

Page 125
and the other by West . . . Godfrey, "Some Reminiscences," p. 492; New York *Herald*, December 8, 1868, General Custer's official Report, November 28, 1868. Sam Robbins had been Chief of Cavalry in Colorado Territory at the time of Chivington's attack on Black Kettle's village there. But for some reason he was not at Sand Creek. A member of the anti-Chivington faction of the Colorado 1st Cavalry, he had accompanied a delegation to Washington in 1865 to testify before a Senate committee relative to Sand Creek. Following the Washita fight, Custer requested that "in consideration of the gallantry" displayed by Robbins and Second Lieutenant C. W. Smith, court-martial charges against the two be withdrawn. What these

charges were is not known. Records of U. S. Army Continental Commands, 1821–1920, Dept. of the Missouri, Letters Received, 1868. Custer to Crosby, Camp Supply, December 2, 1868.

Chapter IX   This Bloody Ground

Page 126
signal sent up by the Indians . . . Custer, *My Life on the Plains,* pp. 238–39. Clark said that Custer was so impressed that he called it the "Star of the Washita" and said that it presaged victory for him.
Page 128
warning to his village . . . Godfrey, "Some Reminiscences," *Cavalry Journal,* XXXVII, pp. 492–93.
Page 128
as it progressed . . . New York *Sun,* May 14, 1899, quoting Ben Clark.
Page 128
meandered on eastward . . . It is doubtful that any of Elliott's forces crossed the river prior to the attack, since the river looped conveniently well around the village and crossing it would have increased the danger of being discovered. Keim, who visited the battlefield with Sheridan and Custer, traces Elliott's route from the bluffs to the northeast of the battlefield (*Sheridan's Troopers,* pp. 142–43).
Page 129
to Lieutenant Johnson . . . Chandler, *Of Garryowen in Glory,* p. 18.
Page 129
village during the charge . . . Godfrey, "Some Reminiscences," *Cavalry Journal,* XXXVII, pp. 492–93.
Page 129
of the 7th Cavalry . . . Custer, *My Life on the Plains,* p. 241.
Page 130
after the soldiers had left . . . A Cheyenne woman later told of finding Black Kettle after the battle: "We all got on our ponies, and rode down to the river to find the spot where Black Kettle and his wife were killed. There was a sharp curve in the river where an old road-crossing used to be. Indian men used to go there to water their ponies. Here we saw the bodies of Black Kettle and his wife, lying under the water. The horse they had ridden lay dead beside them. We observed that they had tried to escape across the river when they were shot" (Ediger and Hoffman, "Some Reminiscences," p. 140). George Bent said that a Cheyenne told him that "the soldiers rode right over Black Kettle and his wife and their horse as they lay dead on the ground, and that their bodies were all splashed with mud by the charging soldiers" (Hyde, *Life of George Bent,* pp. 316–17). The charging soldiers would likely have been those in Elliott's detachment.

Page 131
"and left us alone" . . . Ediger and Hoffman, "Some Reminiscences,"
p. 139.

Page 131
"a vast slaughter pen" . . . New York *Tribune,* December 29, 1868. The
author of this account is unknown, but he was obviously a participant in the
fight. The story, dated in the field on November 29, was one of the first accounts of the battle written.

Page 132
"lacerated and disfigured" . . . New York *Herald,* December 24, 1868.
Only a week before, while at Camp Supply, Hamilton had written his parents that Custer "has given me the honor of arming my squadron with
Colt's revolvers, and making mine the light squadron" ("In Memoriam," p.
381).

Page 132
"Death was instantaneous" . . . File F, 421, Old Military Records, National
Archives, Official Report of Surgeon Henry Lippincott. See "Appendix B."

Page 132
"relatives and friends" . . . Godfrey, "Some Reminiscences," *Cavalry Journal,* XXXVII, p. 495.

Page 133
Barnitz whom he encountered . . . Brill, *Conquest of the Southern Plains,*
pp. 304–5.

Page 133
Black Kettle's nephew . . . Custer reported the boy as Black Kettle's son,
but George Bent said that the boy was a nephew of the Cheyenne chief and
his name was Blue Horse. Bent stated that Black Kettle had no children
(Hyde, *Life of George Bent,* p. 317).

Page 133
scalp, which he had taken . . . New York *Herald,* December 24, 1868;
Custer, *My Life on the Plains,* pp. 256–57. See "Appendix D," which lists
Private Daniel Morrison as having a flesh wound in the right temple.

Page 133
as he rode about . . . New York *Herald,* December 24, 1868; Custer, loc.
cit.

Page 134
"dropping upon the snow" . . . New York *Herald,* December 8, 1868.

Page 134
"a needless cruelty" . . . New York *Sun,* May 14, 1899; Kansas City *Star,*
December 3, 1904, Fred S. Barde Collection, Oklahoma Historical Society.
Clark tells, also, of an old, gray-haired woman who defiantly faced the
troops with an old cavalry saber until she was finally persuaded to put it
down.

Page 134
Black Kettle's sister . . . George Bent claimed that Black Kettle had no

sister. On September 27, 1869, he wrote Colonel Samuel Tappan from Fort Lyon: "Sir, I am sorry to say to you that Black Kettle and his wife were both killed at Battle of Washita. It is all mistake about Black Kettle's wife being taken prisoner. It was also mistake about his sister being taken prisoner. Black Kettle had no sister. I was at Camp Supply and saw all those that were taken prisoner at Washita" (Diary of Samuel Tappan, Colorado Historical Society).

Page 135
"*riding like devils incarnate*" . . . New York *Times*, February 14, 1869, Benteen letter.

Page 135
handfuls of ammunition . . . Colonel Charles Francis Bates, *Custer's Indian Battles*, p. 13.

Page 135
scattered about in groups . . . Godfrey, "Some Reminiscences," *Cavalry Journal*, XXXVII, pp. 493–94.

Page 137
"*would have reported it*" . . . Ibid., pp. 494–95.

Page 137
bridles, and other items . . . Senate Executive Document No. 18, part 1, 40th Cong., 3d sess., Report of Lt. Col. G. A. Custer, In the Field, on Washita River, November 28, 1868, pp. 27–29.

Page 137
"*powerful a chieftain*" . . . New York *Herald*, December 8, 1868, Keim's account.

Page 137
"*fires and destroyed*" . . . Godfrey tells of an Indian bridal gown, "adorned all over with bead work and elks' teeth on antelope skins as soft as the finest broad cloth. I started to show it to the General and ask to keep it, but as I passed a big fire, I thought, 'what's the use, "orders is orders,"' and threw it in the blaze. I have never ceased to regret the destruction" ("Some Reminiscences," *Cavalry Journal*, XXXVII, p. 496).

Page 138
"*behind hills and knolls*" . . . New York *Tribune*, December 29, 1868.

Page 139
officers and scouts . . . Clark claimed that some two hundred of the animals were thus distributed, with Custer taking four fine mules. New York *Sun*, May 14, 1899.

Page 139
"*about eight hundred ponies*" . . . Godfrey, "Some Reminiscences," *Cavalry Journal*, XXXVII, p. 496.

Page 139
"*death from a surer hand!*" . . . New York *Times*, February 14, 1869, Benteen letter.

Page 140
"three of their warriors" . . . Senate Executive Document No. 18, p. 28.
Page 140
"one hundred and three" . . . Godfrey, "Some Reminiscences," *Cavalry Journal*, XXXVII, p. 498. See also Chandler, *Of Garryowen in Glory*, p. 20, quoting Gibson.
Page 140
all by gunshot . . . New York *Herald*, December 24, 1868, Keim's account.
Page 140
who were in the camp . . . Ibid. These Indians were listed as Buffalo Tongue, Tall White Man, Tall Owl, Poor Black Elk, Big Horse, White Beaver, Bear Tail, Running Water, Wolf Ear, The Man That Hears the Wolf, and Medicine Walker—Cheyennes; Heap Timber and Tall Hat—Sioux; and Lame Man—Arapaho. George Bent lists eleven men killed: Black Kettle, Little Rock, Bear Tongue, Tall Bear, Blind Bear, White Bear, Cranky Man, Blue Horse, Red Teeth, Little Heart, and Red Bird. He said that two Arapahoes were killed (Hyde, *Life of Geoerge Bent*, p. 322).
Page 140
"the moment we attacked" . . . Senate Executive Document No. 18, p. 28.
Page 140
"though seriously wounded" . . . See "Appendix E."
Page 141
"savage alone can invent" . . . New York *Herald*, December 24, 1868.
Page 141
"brevet or a coffin" . . . Godfrey, "Some Reminiscences," *Cavalry Journal*, XXXVII, p. 493.
Page 142
only a few minutes . . . Custer, *My Life on the Plains*, p. 257.
Page 142
strategy of a feinting movement . . . According to Brill, Scout Ben Clark later claimed that Custer, encouraged by the ease of taking Black Kettle's camp, did intend to attack the other villages but that Clark talked him out of it. However, in a published account Clark made no such claim for himself: "As the hours of the afternoon wore away Custer abandoned his original plan of following the Indians and prepared to retreat under cover of night. The troops started at sundown, crossing the Washita where they had gone thundering over at daybreak" (New York *Sun*, May 14, 1899).
Page 143
clothing awaited them . . . Private Harvey, in his diary entry of November 27, wrote: "No rations tonight. The Indians captured them all from us by leaving it while charging. We will reach our train tomorrow by noon, then we will have plenty. I am very well so far. Plenty of snow" ("Campaigning with Sheridan," p. 86).

Page 143
watching his movements . . . On December 7, 1868, Captain Henry Alvord reported from Fort Cobb: "The last heard of the troops, they had crossed to the north side of the Canadian, followed only by two well-known braves of the Cheyennes whose relations were among the missing, and who announced their determination of rescuing their people or dying in the attempt" (*Senate Executive Document No. 18*, p. 37).

Page 143
"*gallant services rendered*" . . . Godfrey, "Some Reminiscences," *The Cavalry Journal*, October 1928, p. 499. Citing General Field Order No. 6, November 29, 1868.

Page 144
only four days off . . . Custer is wrong when he states in *My Life on the Plains*, p. 267, that the regiment returned to Camp Supply on December 2. Keim's report of December 1, 1868, and other evidence clearly indicate that the command was back at the post on December 1 (New York *Herald*, December 24, 1868).

Chapter X   For a Brevet or a Coffin

Page 145
chief of the Cheyennes . . . New York *Herald*, December 24, 1868, Keim's report, Fork of Beaver and Wolf Creek, I.T., December 1, 1868.

Page 146
"*adventurers and rugged men*" . . . Ibid.

Page 146
"*their proper officers*" . . . Ibid.

Page 147
around the fire . . . At the first camp on the return march, the Osages had hung the Cheyenne scalps outside their tents and fired several volleys over them to drive away the spirits of their recent owners (Ibid).

Page 147
camps, down the Washita . . . *Senate Executive Document No. 18*, Sheridan to Nichols, North Canadian, December 2 and December 3, 1868, pp. 34, 43.

Page 148
"*contented with their lot*" . . . New York *Herald*, December 26, 1868, Keim's report, Fork of Beaver and Wolf Creek, December 4, 1868.

Page 148
Camp Supply turning out . . . Ibid.

Page 148
"*than words can tell*" . . . Ibid.

Page 148
to Poughkeepsie for reburial . . . "In Memoriam," p. 374.
Page 148
in September 1861 . . . *War of the Rebellion Official Records of the Union and Confederate Armies,* Series I, Vol. XXXII, Part I, pp. 274–75; Series I, Vol. XXXIX, Part I, pp. 133–36; Series I, Vol. XLV, Part I, pp. 848–50 (Hadley, "The Nineteenth Kansas Cavalry," pp. 445–46).
Page 149
second in command of the unit . . . Godfrey, "Some Reminiscences," *Cavalry Journal,* XXXVII, p. 481.
Page 149
"troubles in my department" . . . New York *Tribune,* December 3, 1868, Sheridan report.
Page 150
"going to move soon" . . . Harvey, "Campaigning with Sheridan," p. 87.
Page 150
Indians without success . . . New York *Herald,* December 26, 1868.
Page 151
"in the distant plain" . . . Keim, *Sheridan's Troopers,* pp. 128–29.
Page 151
"left behind at Supply" . . . One of the dismounted 19th Kansas troopers was Private Joseph Phelps Rodgers, who tells of how he stole a horse from the 7th Cavalry picket line. Heating up an iron, he changed the brand from an "I" to an "F" so that he could join the march. His punishment would have been severe had he been caught. Rodgers, "A Few Years of Experiences," p. 8.
Page 151
"men all like him" . . . Spotts, "Campaigning with Custer," p. 72.
Page 151
"for a breech-clout" . . . Keim, *Sheridan's Troopers,* p. 129.
Page 152
slain chief Little Rock . . . Much is made by some historians of Custer's taking Mo-nah-se-tah along on the expedition, insisting on a romantic affair between Custer and the "Indian princess." But doubts are clearly put on this bit of historical gossip by the fact that Mo-nah-se-tah was then in the latter stages of pregnancy. In early January, less than two months after the battle on the Washita, while the 7th was bivouacked at the site of present Fort Sill, Mo-nah-se-tah gave birth to a child. E. B. Custer, *Following the Guidon,* citing a letter from Custer to Mrs. Custer, Medicine Bluff Creek, January 14, 1869.
Page 152
"forests of miniature oaks" . . . Keim, *Sheridan's Troopers,* p. 133.
Page 153
"stillness which prevailed" . . . Keim, *Sheridan's Troopers,* p. 136. The line of march was southwestward from Camp Supply to the approximate loca-

tion of present Fargo, Oklahoma; then due south to Hackberry Creek; on past the present site of Peek to the South Canadian, crossing at the southernmost bend of the river. Custer stated: "I aimed by a new route to strike the Washita below and near to the scene of the late battle . . ." (*Senate Executive Document No. 40,* 40th Cong., 3d sess., Custer report, In the Field, Indian Territory, December 22, 1868. Ben Clark wrote: "When we came on the second expedition from Camp Supply we struck below the Black Kettle camp" (Letter, Ben Clark to F. S. Barde, Fort Reno, O.T., May 1, 1903, Barde Collection, Oklahoma Historical Society).

Page 154
and his wife were gone . . . Brill quotes Magpie as saying he helped the women carry Black Kettle's body to higher ground and when he left they were debating where to bury it. Some said that he was "buried" in the forks of a tree. On July 13, 1934, a skeleton was unearthed on the west of the battlefield site, and it was believed that these were Black Kettle's bones (Brill, *Conquest of the Southern Plains,* pp. 25–26). In January 1891 the battle site was visited by Lieutenant H. L. Scott of the 7th Cavalry, who erected a monument and took a picture of a cottonwood tree at the foot of which Black Kettle was reportedly killed (Lewis N. Hornbeck, "The Battle of the Washita," *Sturm's Oklahoma Magazine,* V, No. 5 (January 1908), pp. 30–34).

Page 155
"to fight on foot" . . . Keim, *Sheridan's Troopers,* p. 145. Keim states: "All the missing bodies were found" (p. 146). But this was not so (see Appendix D). Custer's account of December 24, 1868, says: "At a short distance, here and there, from the spot where the bodies lay could be seen the carcasses of some of the horses of the party which had been probably killed early in the fight." He stated that a horse ridden by one of the men who was killed in the fight had been recognized in the hands of a Kiowa (*Senate Executive Document No. 40,* pp. 3–9).

Page 156
"party of eighteen men" . . . *Senate Executive Document No. 18,* p. 33, McCusker to Murphy, Fort Cobb, I.T., December 3, 1868.

Page 156
"if taken alive" . . . Keim, *Sheridan's Troopers,* p. 146. George Bent says that Clark told him that he had heard 7th Cavalry officers say that Custer ordered Major Elliott to take some of his men and drive those Indians out of the creek (Washita) that were firing at his men. Though perhaps of questionable significance, it is interesting to note that with the men of each company represented with Elliott was one non-commissioned officer.

Page 156
east of the village . . . Brill, *Conquest of the Southern Plains,* pp. 162–70.

Page 159
"and fought him again" . . . Hadley, "The Nineteenth Kansas Cavalry," p. 441, quoting letter, George Bent to Robert M. Peck. See also Hyde, *Life of George Bent,* pp. 318–20.

Page 160
"Major Elliott's horse yet" . . . William Nicholson, "A Tour of Indian Agencies in Kansas and the Indian Territory in 1870," *Kansas Historical Quarterly,* II, No. 4 (November 1934), p. 348.

Page 160
made another discovery . . . An unresolved mystery surrounds the death of Mrs. Blinn and her son, resulting from contradictory reports of where their bodies were found and charges that they were actually killed by Custer's troops as they attacked Black Kettle's village (see Appendix E).

Page 160
by one of the Kansans . . . Moore, "The Nineteenth Kansas Cavalry," p. 358.

Page 161
"and the mournful wintry wind" . . . Keim, *Sheridan's Troopers,* p. 151.

Page 161
Fort Arbuckle for interment . . . Keim, *Sheridan's Troopers,* p. 150; Custer, *My Life on the Plains,* p. 288.

Page 161
and the Indian Territory . . . *Rebellion Records,* Series I, Vol. XLI, Part IV, pp. 406, 441, 446, 461.

Page 161
received final approval . . . *Rebellion Records,* Series I, Vol. XLI, Part I, p. 477; Frederick H. Dyer, *Compendium of the War of the Rebellion,* III, pp. 1108, 1309–10.

Page 162
request that Clark refused . . . New York *Sun,* May 14, 1899.

Page 162
"rest their panting steeds" . . . New York *Times,* February 14, 1869, Benteen letter, Fort Cobb, I.T., December 22, 1869.

Page 162
riding quirt in the other . . . Colonel W. A. Graham, *The Custer Myth,* p. 213.

Chapter XI   Deliverance by Deception

Page 163
in their hurried exodus . . . One trooper was reported to have found a package of U.S. currency totaling nearly $400, while another a buckskin bag with $182 in gold coin in it (Hadley, "The Nineteenth Kansas," p. 445; Rodgers, "A Few Years of Experiences," p. 9).

Page 163
lost on the march . . . Moore stated that 148 animals were lost on the march from Camp Supply to Fort Cobb ("The Nineteenth Kansas Cavalry," p. 43).

Page 163
reportedly killing one . . . Harvey, "Campaigning with Sheridan," pp. 89–90.
Page 164
"also of our camp" . . . Senate Executive Document No. 40, p. 6.
Page 164
"permitted to feed them" . . . Senate Executive Document No. 18, p. 43.
Page 165
their armies behind them . . . Keim, Sheridan's Troopers, pp. 156–57. Charles Schreyvogel's beautiful painting of this meeting, entitled "Custer's Demand," contains several historical inaccuracies. Little Heart and Kicking Bird were not at the meeting, nor was Tom Custer. And the scout who has been identified as "Amos Grover (noted scout)" by some sources must be a mixture of Amos Chapman and Sharp Grover, the latter of whom was not with the expedition.
Page 165
"know him to be a friend" . . . Keim, loc. cit.
Page 166
under guard as hostages . . . Senate Executive Document No. 40, p. 6.
Page 166
before reaching the column . . . Leavenworth Evening Bulletin, December 31, 1868, Letter from Captain Thompson, Fort Cobb, December 22, 1868.
Page 166
and two Apache chiefs . . . Keim, Sheridan's Troopers, p. 157.
Page 166
"I get through with them" . . . Senate Executive Document No. 18, p. 40.
Page 167
"the approach of his people" . . . Moore, "The Nineteenth Kansas Cavalry," p. 43.
Page 167
"when I first met them" . . . House Executive Document, Vol. II, Pt. 1, 41st Cong., 2d sess., 1869–70, p. 49.
Page 167
people, who were starving . . . Senate Executive Document No. 18, Pt. 2, 40th Cong., 3d sess., p. 1.
Page 169
east of the Wichita Mountains . . . Grierson had discovered the location on a previous scout.
Page 169
visit the Indian camps . . . Custer, My Life on the Plains, pp. 316–17.
Page 170
month before her capture . . . Spotts, Campaigning with Custer, pp. 155–56.
Page 170
"corn and horse-flesh" . . . E. B. Custer, Following the Guidon, p. 50.
Page 170
for a similar offense . . . Spotts, Campaigning with Custer, pp. 134–35.

Page 170
"*looking at the sun*" . . . Ibid., p. 127.

Page 171
show in their faces . . . Ibid., pp. 131–32.

Page 171
released from their imprisonment . . . Keim, *Sheridan's Troopers*, p. 275.

Page 171
Indians as "wakaheaps" . . . Rodgers, "A Few Years of Experiences," p. 11.

Page 172
and a few provisions . . . Spotts, "Campaigning with Custer," p. 143; New York *Times*, April 7, 1869, Custer Report, In the Field on Washita, March 21, 1869.

Page 172
deliver the cattle . . . E. B. Custer, *Following the Guidon*, pp. 53–54.

Page 173
"*command moved out at once*" . . . Hadley, "The Nineteenth Kansas," pp. 448–49.

Page 175
"*impossible to estimate*" . . . Ibid., p. 450.

Page 175
"*their cheeks sunk in*" . . . Rodgers, "A Few Years of Experiences," pp. 12–13.

Page 176
in Medicine Arrow's village . . . Custer directly contradicts his official report in his book. In his report he states: "On my way to the village I learned that the two white women captured in Kansas last August . . . were then held captive in the Cheyenne village. It was then out of the question to assume a hostile attitude . . ." (New York *Times*, April 7, 1869). In *My Life on the Plains*, p. 359, he says that he did not learn this fact until Mo-nah-se-tah had come up with the command after he had left the Cheyenne village. The latter statement seems more logical, and the former an excuse for not attacking the village immediately.

Page 177
"*did not satisfy him*" . . . Custer, *My Life on the Plains*, pp. 362–63.

Page 177
as George Bent claims . . . Hyde, *Life of George Bent*, p. 326.

Page 178
toes barely touched the ground . . . Moore states: ". . . General Custer had the head chief taken down to the creek, a riata put around his neck and the other end thrown over a limb. A couple of soldiers took hold of the rope, and, by pulling gently, lifted him up onto his toes. He was let down, and Romero, the interpreter, explained to him that, when he was pulled up clear from the ground and left there, he would be hung" ("The Nineteenth Kansas Cavalry," p. 45).

Page 179
several months pregnant . . . *Kansas Daily Tribune*, April 2, 11, 1869.

Page 179
"before she was carried away" . . . Moore, "The Nineteenth Kansas Cavalry," p. 46. Many years later, Sarah White told her story of captivity to a reporter for the Kansas City *Star* (March 4, 1934). She said her feet had been badly frozen and had bothered her since. She described Mrs. Morgan as a "beautiful young woman with blue eyes and thick lustrous hair of yellow hue." . . . Mrs. Morgan bore a child with Indian features. Her husband left her, and she returned to her brother. She was eventually judged insane. Olive A. Clark, "Early Days Along the Solomon Valley," *Kansas Historical Collections, 1926–28,* Vol. XVII, pp. 728–29.

Page 180
"termination of the Indian war" . . . New York *Times,* April 7, 1869, Custer report.

Page 180
"they would not trust him" . . . Report of Hon. Vincent Colyer, 41st Cong., 2d sess., *House Executive Document No. 3,* pp. 524–25.

Page 181
"it was little wonder" . . . Hadley, "The Nineteenth Kansas," pp. 454–55.

Page 181
between the two regiments . . . Jenness, "History of the 19th Cavalry," p. 45. Jenness says concerning an inspection report made by Colonel J. W. Forsyth: "This report indicates plainly the hostile feeling entertained by regular officers for volunteers, and which have been very plainly indicated on several occasions during our associations with Custer and his officers."

Page 182
St. Louis but lost it there . . . *Kansas Daily Tribune,* May 15, 1869.

Page 182
train out of Hays . . . Brady was reported to be a 7th Cavalry deserter who had enlisted in the 19th Regiment under an assumed name.

Page 182
It proved to be Brady . . . Ibid., May 23, 1869.

Page 182
shot in the head and arm . . . Ibid., May 5, 8, 1869.

Page 182
Fat Bear was knocked unconscious . . . Letters Sent, Fort Hays, Report of Colonel Nelson Miles, May 9, 1869.

Page 183
"exposure and ill treatment" . . . Letters Sent, Fort Hays. There is a good chance that this was the same child who was with Black Kettle when he visited Hays City in August 1868, just a few months before the battle. This visit was described by the *Kansas Daily Tribune,* of Lawrence, in its August 14, 1868, issue, citing the Kansas City *Advance:* "A band of Cheyennes under command of Black Kettle, a noted chief, was in town on Thursday. They had a white child with them, which they claimed to be a half-breed, the offspring of an officer and a squaw of the tribe. Some think there is no Indian blood in the child, but that it was stolen from Texas by Kiowas or

Comanches and sold to the Cheyennes. Anyhow, if it belongs to any of our shoulder-strapped friends at Larned, they shouldn't be ashamed of it. Cheyenne stock is good." This visit is the subject of an article, "Black Kettle's Last Raid," by Hill P. Wilson, *Transactions of the Kansas State Historical Society*, VIII, pp. 110–17.

Chapter XII   A Quarrel of Conscience

Page 185
"*of the Indian reach them*" . . . New York *Times,* December 22, 1868, April 13, 1869.
Page 185
being organized by Sheridan . . . Ibid., October 11, 12, 13, 1868.
Page 186
"*Indians in his department*" . . . *Report of the Secretary of War, 1868, Executive Document No. 1*, pp. 20–21, Sheridan to Sherman, October 15, 1868.
Page 187
"*force them to war*" . . . New York *Tribune,* December 17, 1868, Tappan to Taylor, December 4, 1868.
Page 188
"*for their benefit*" . . . Brill, *Conquest of the Southern Plains,* p. 290, citing letter, Wynkoop to Taylor, October 7, 1868.
Page 189
"*fulfill the requirements of*" . . . New York *Times,* December 19, 1868, citing Leavenworth *Commercial,* December 9, 1868, Wynkoop to Taylor, November 29, 1868.
Page 189
"*reservation when attacked*" . . . Ibid.
Page 190
"*others to flight*" . . . New York *Times,* December 22, 1868.
Page 190
"*and forever settled*" . . . Ibid.
Page 190
"*people they have wronged*" . . . Ibid., December 24, 1868.
Page 190
"*and their oppressors*" . . . Ibid.
Page 191
"*citizens of the United States*" . . . Ibid., December 27, 1868, citing Kansas City (Missouri) *Journal,* December 6, 1868.
Page 191
"*these gallant officers*" . . . New York *Times,* February 9, 1869.

Page 191
"without any civil agent" . . . Ibid., February 21, 1869.
Page 191
"of the country at all" . . . Letters Received, Adjutant General's Office.
Page 192
"on the Washita River" . . . Ibid.
Page 192
"to massacre the settlers" . . . George W. Manypenny, *Our Indian Wards,*
p. 244.
Page 193
"women killed in wagons" . . . *Report of the Secretary of War, 1869–70,*
Sheridan to Sherman, Chicago, November 1, 1869; *House Executive Documents,* Vol. 2, Part 1, 41st Cong., 2d sess., SS-1412.
Page 193
"Black Kettle's band?" . . . Manypenny, *Our Indian Wards,* pp. 246–47.
Page 193
"expedition against the Utes?" . . . Ibid., pp. 249–50.

BIBLIOGRAPHY

Archival Materials

Fred S. Barde Collection, Oklahoma Historical Society.

Walter S. Campbell Papers, Division of Manuscripts, University of Oklahoma.

Cheyenne-Arapaho Agency, 1868–1935—Military Relations, Oklahoma Historical Society.

Fort Supply Letter Book, Division of Manuscripts, University of Oklahoma.

Jenness Manuscript on the March of the 19th Kansas, Kansas State Historical Society.

Memorandum of Trip from Topeka, Kansas, to the Indian Territory by Gus Johnson, Kansas State Historical Society.

Diary of A. Reed, Kansas State Historical Society.

"A Few Years of Experiences on the Western Frontier," by Joseph Phelps Rodgers, Kansas State Historical Society.

Papers of Generals W. T. Sherman and P. H. Sheridan, Rister Collection, Division of Manuscripts, University of Oklahoma.

Sheridan Papers, Division of Manuscripts, University of Oklahoma.

Diary of Samuel Tappan with various letters, Colorado Historical Society.

Dissertations

Carriker, Robert Charles. "Fort Supply, Indian Territory: Frontier Outpost on the Southern Plains, 1868–1894." University of Oklahoma, 1967.

Articles

"A. L. Runyon's Letters from the Nineteenth Kansas Regiment." *The Kansas Historical Quarterly,* Vol. IX (1940).

Anderson, Harry H., ed. "Stand at the Arikaree." *Colorado Magazine,* Vol. XLI, No. 4 (Fall 1964).

Bailey, Mahlon. "Medical Sketch of the Nineteenth Regiment of Kansas Cavalry Volunteers." *Kansas Historical Quarterly,* Vol. VI (1937).

"Battle of the Arickaree (or Beecher Island)." *Kansas Historical Quarterly,* Vol. XXXIV, No. 1 (Spring 1968).

"Beecher Island Monument." *Transactions of the Kansas State Historical Society, 1905–06,* Vol. IX (1906).

Brininstool, E. A. "The Rescue of Forsyth's Scouts." *Collections of the Kansas State Historical Society, 1926–1928,* Vol. XVII (1928).

Burgess, H. L. "The Eighteenth Kansas Volunteer Cavalry." *Collections of the Kansas State Historical Society, 1913–1914.* Vol. XIII (1915).

"Bypaths of Kansas History." *Kansas Historical Quarterly,* Vol. VI (1937).

"Bypaths of Kansas History." *Kansas Historical Quarterly,* Vol. XXXIV, No. 1 (Spring 1968).

"Bypaths of Kansas History." *Kansas Historical Quarterly,* Vol. XXXVI, No. 3 (Autumn 1970).

Carpenter, Brevet Colonel L. H. "Story of a Rescue." *Winners of the West,* Vol. II, No. 3 (February 1925).

Clark, Mrs. Olive A. "Early Days Along the Solomon Valley." *Collections of the Kansas State Historical Society, 1926–1928,* Vol. XVII (1928).

Cloud, Jim. "Evans' Christmas Day Battle." *The War Chief of the Indian Territory Posse of Oklahoma Westerners,* Vol. VI, No. 4 (March 1973).

Connelley, William E., ed. "The Life of George W. Brown." *Collections of the Kansas State Historical Society, 1926–1928,* Vol. XVII (1928).

Custer, Brevet Major General G. A. "In Memoriam: Louis McLane Hamilton, Captain 7th U. S. Cavalry." *Chronicles of Oklahoma,* Vol. XLVI, No. 4 (Winter 1968–69).

"General Custar's Battle." New York *Daily Tribune,* December 29, 1868.

"Custer's Oklahoma Fight." Kansas City *Star,* December 3, 1904.

"General Custer's Indian Battle, Another Version of." New York *Herald,* December 29, 1868.

"Custer's Washita Fight." New York *Sun,* May 14, 1899.

Davis, Theodore. "A Summer on the Plains." *Harper's New Monthly Magazine,* Vol. XXXVI, No. 213 (February 1868).

———. "Henry M. Stanley's Indian Campaign in 1867." *The Westerner's Brand Book, 1945–46.* Chicago: Chicago Westerners Posse, 1947.

Ediger, Theodore A., and Hoffman, Vinnie. "Some Reminiscences of the Battle of the Washita." *Chronicles of Oklahoma,* Vol. XXXIII, No. 2 (Summer 1955).

Fairfield, S. H. "The Eleventh Kansas Regiment at Platte Bridge." *Transactions of the Kansas State Historical Society, 1903–1904,* Vol. VIII (1904).

Freeman, Winfield. "The Battle of the Arickaree." *Transactions of the Kansas State Historical Society, 1897–1900,* Vol. VI (1900).

Godfrey, General E. S. "Medicine Lodge Treaty 60 Years Ago." *Winners of the West,* Vol. VI, No. 4 (March 30, 1929).

———. "Some Reminiscences, Including an Account of General Sully's Expedition Against the Southern Plains Indians, 1868." *The Cavalry Journal,* Vol. XXXVI, No. 148 (July 1927).

———. "Some Reminiscences, Including the Washita Battle, November 27, 1868." *The Cavalry Journal,* Vol. XXXVII, No. 153 (October 1928).

Hadley, James A. "The Nineteenth Kansas Cavalry and the Conquest of the Plains Indians." *Transactions of the Kansas State Historical Society, 1907–1908,* Vol. X (1908).

Harvey, Winfield Scott. "Campaigning with Sheridan: A Farrier's Diary." Edited by George Shirk. *Chronicles of Oklahoma,* Vol. XXXVII, No. 1 (Spring 1959).

Hazen, W. H. "Some Corrections of 'Life on the Plains.'" *Chronicles of Oklahoma,* Vol. III, No. 4 (December 1925).

Hornbeck, Lewis N. "The Battle of the Washita." *Sturm's Oklahoma Magazine,* Vol. V, No. 5 (January 1908).

Hurst, John. "The Beecher Island Fight." *Collections of the Kansas State Historical Society, 1919–1922,* Vol. XV (1923).

Jacob, Captain Richard T. "Military Reminiscences of Captain Richard T. Jacob." *Chronicles of Oklahoma,* Vol. II, No. 1 (1924).

Jenness, George B. "Lost in the Snow at Old Camp Supply." *Sturm's Oklahoma Magazine,* Vol. V, No. 4 (December 1907).

———. "Old Fort Sill and Stirring Events Preceding Its Establishment." *Sturm's Oklahoma Magazine,* Vol. V, No. 6 (February 1908).

Kroeker, Marvin. "Col. W. B. Hazen in the Indian Territory, 1868–69." *Chronicles of Oklahoma,* Vol. XLII, No. 1 (Spring 1964).

Lockard, F. M. "A Version of a Famous Battle." *Chronicles of Oklahoma,* Vol. V. No. 3 (September 1927).

McBee, John. "John McBee's Account of the Expedition of the Nineteenth Kansas," as told to William E. Connelley. *Collections of the Kansas State Historical Society, 1926–1928,* Vol. XVII (1928).

Millbrook, Minnie Dubbs. "Custer's First Scout in the West." *Kansas Historical Quarterly,* Vol. XXXIX, No. 1 (Spring 1973).

———. "The West Breaks In General Custer." *Kansas Historical Quarterly,* Vol. XXXVI, No. 2 (Summer 1970).

Montgomery, Mrs. Frank C. "Fort Wallace and Its Relation to the Frontier." *Collections of the Kansas State Historical Society, 1926–1928,* Vol. XVII (1928).

Moore, Colonel Horace L. "The Nineteenth Kansas Cavalry in the Washita Campaign." *Chronicles of Oklahoma,* Vol. II, No. 4 (December 1924).

Nesbit, Paul. "Battle of the Washita." *Chronicles of Oklahoma,* Vol. III, No. 1 (April 1925).

Nicholson, William. "A Tour of Indian Agencies in Kansas and the Indian Territory in 1870." *Kansas Historical Quarterly,* Vol. III, No. 4 (November 1934).

Robinson, W. Stitt, ed. "The Kiowa and Comanche Campaign of 1860 as Recorded in the Personal Diary of Lt. J. E. B. Stuart." *Kansas Historical Quarterly,* Vol. XXIII (1957).

Rucker, Alvin. "The Battle of the Washita." *The Daily Oklahoman,* August 2, 1925.

Runyon, A. L. "A. L. Runyon's Letters from the Nineteenth Kansas Regiment." *Kansas Historical Quarterly,* Vol. IX (1940).

"Scalped at the Washita." *Kansas Daily Tribune,* June 25, 1869.

Shirk, George. "The Journal of Private Johnson." *Chronicles of Oklahoma,* Vol. XLIX, No. 4 (Winter 1971–72).

Shlesinger, Sigmund. "The Beecher Island Battlefield Diary of Sigmund Shlesinger." *Colorado Magazine,* Vol. XXIX, No. 3 (July 1952).

————. "The Beecher Island Fight." *Collections of the Kansas State Historical Society, 1919–1922,* Vol. XV (1923).

Smith, Captain W. R. "Camp Starvation." *Winners of the West,* Vol. III, No. 7 (March 30, 1926).

Stanley, Henry M. "A British Journalist Reports the Medicine Lodge Peace Councils of 1867." *Kansas Historical Quarterly,* Vol. XXXIII, No. 3 (Autumn 1967).

Street, William D. "Cheyenne Indian Massacre on the Middle Fork of the Sappa." *Transactions of the Kansas State Historical Society, 1907–1908,* Vol. X (1908).

Tahan (Joseph K. Griffis). "The Battle of the Washita." *Chronicles of Oklahoma,* Vol. VIII, No. 3 (September 1930).

Taylor, Alfred A. "The Medicine Lodge Peace Council." *Chronicles of Oklahoma,* Vol. II, No. 2 (June 1924).

Watson, Elmo Scott. "Theodore R. Davis, Indian War Correspondent." *The Westerner's Brand Book.* Chicago: (privately printed), 1947.

————. "The Last Indian War, 1890–91—a Study of Newspaper Jingoism." *Journalism Quarterly,* Vol. XX, No. 3 (September 1943).

Whitney, Chauncey B. "Diary of Chauncey B. Whitney." *Collections of the Kansas State Historical Society, 1911–1912,* Vol. XII (1912).

Books

Abel, Annie Heloise. *The Slaveholding Indians.* 3 vols. Cleveland: The Arthur H. Clark Co., 1915, 1919, 1925.

Bates, Colonel Charles Francis. *Custer's Indian Battles*. Bronxville, N.Y.: (privately printed), 1936.

Berthrong, Donald J. *The Southern Cheyennes*. Norman: University of Oklahoma Press, 1963.

Boatner, Mark Mayo III. *The Civil War Dictionary*. New York: David McKay Co., Inc., 1959.

Brill, Charles J. *Conquest of the Southern Plains*. Oklahoma City: Golden Saga Publishers, 1938.

Chandler, Melbourne C. *Of Garryowen in Glory; The History of the Seventh United States Cavalry Regiment*. Annandale, Va.: The Turnpike Press, 1960.

Crawford, Samuel J. *Kansas in the Sixties*. Chicago: A. G. McClurg & Co., 1911.

Custer, Elizabeth B. *Following the Guidon*. Norman: University of Oklahoma Press, 1966.

————. *Tenting on the Plains*. Norman: University of Oklahoma Press, 1971.

Custer, George Armstrong. *My Life on the Plains or, Personal Experience with Indians*. Norman: University of Oklahoma Press, 1962. New edition copyright.

Dyer, Frederick H. *Compendium of the War of the Rebellion*. New York: Sagamore Press Inc., 1959.

Epple, Jess C. *Custer's Battle of the Washita and a History of the Plains Indian Tribes*. New York: Exposition Press, 1970.

Forsyth, General George A. *Thrilling Days in Army Life*. New York: Harper & Brothers, 1901.

Frost, Lawrence A. *The Court-Martial of General George Armstrong Custer*. Norman: University of Oklahoma Press, 1968.

Graham, Colonel W. A. *The Custer Myth*. Harrisburg, Pa.: The Stackpole Co., 1953.

Grinnell, George Bird. *The Fighting Cheyennes*. Norman: University of Oklahoma Press, 1956.

Hafen, LeRoy R.; and Rister, Carl Coke. *Western America*. New York: Prentice-Hall, Inc., 1941.

Hoig, Stan. *The Sand Creek Massacre*. Norman: University of Oklahoma Press, 1961.

Hunt, Frazier. *Custer, the Last of the Cavaliers*. New York: Cosmopolitan Book Corp., 1928.

Hyde, George E. *Life of George Bent, Written from His Letters*. Edited by Savoie Lottinville. Norman: University of Oklahoma Press, 1967.

Jones, Douglas C. *The Treaty of Medicine Lodge*. Norman: University of Oklahoma Press, 1966.

Keim, DeB. Randolph. *Sheridan's Troopers on the Borders: A Winter Campaign on the Plains*. Philadelphia: David McKay, 1885.

Manypenny, George W. *Our Indian Wards*. Cincinnati: Robert Clarke Co., 1880.

Miles, Nelson A. *Personal Recollections and Observations of General Nelson A. Miles.* Chicago: The Werner Co., 1897.

Monaghan, Jay. *Custer, the Life of General George Armstrong Custer.* Lincoln: University of Nebraska Press, 1971.

Nye, W. S. *Carbine and Lance.* Norman: University of Oklahoma Press, 1943.

O'Connor, Richard. *Sheridan, the Inevitable.* Indianapolis: Bobbs-Merrill, Co., Inc., 1953.

Rister, Carl Coke. *Border Command.* Norman: University of Oklahoma Press, 1944.

Sabin, Edwin L. *On the Plains with Custer.* Philadelphia: J. B. Lippincott Co., 1913.

Sheridan, P. H. *Personal Memoirs.* New York: Charles Webster & Co., 1888.

Spotts, David L. *Campaigning with Custer and the Nineteenth Kansas Volunteer Cavalry on the Washita Campaign, 1868–'69.* Edited and arranged by E. A. Brininstool. Los Angeles: Wetzer Publishing Co., 1928.

Stanley, Henry M. *My Early Travels and Adventures in America and Asia.* 2 vols. New York: Charles Scribner's Sons, 1905.

Stewart, Edgar I. *Custer's Luck.* Norman: University of Oklahoma Press, 1955.

Thoburn, Joseph B., and Wright, Muriel H. *Oklahoma, a History of the State and Its People.* 4 vols. New York: Lewis Historical Publishing Company, Inc., 1929.

Turner, Don. *Custer's First Massacre: The Battle of the Washita.* Amarillo, Texas: Humbug Gulch Press, 1968.

Van de Water, Frederic F. *Glory-Hunter.* New York: Bobbs Merrill Co., 1934.

Whittaker, Frederick. *A Complete Life of General George A. Custer.* New York: Sheldon & Co., 1876.

Newspapers

The Army and Navy Journal
The Chicago Times
The Chicago Tribune
The Cincinnati Commercial
The Cincinnati Gazette
The Daily Oklahoman (Oklahoma City)
The Emporia News
The Junction City Weekly Union

The Kansas City Journal
The Kansas City Star
The Kansas Daily Tribune (Lawrence)
The Kansas State Journal (Lawrence)
The Kansas Weekly Tribune (Lawrence)
The Leavenworth Commercial
The Leavenworth Conservative
The Leavenworth Evening Bulletin
The Leavenworth Times
The Missouri Democrat (St. Louis)
The Missouri Republican (St. Louis)
The New York Herald
The New York Sun
The New York Times
The New York Tribune
The Times and Conservative (Leavenworth)

Government Documents—Published

Report of the Commissioner of Indian Affairs, 1858–1869.
Report of the Secretary of War, 1867, 1868–69, 1869–70.
Report of an Interview between Colonel E. W. Wynkoop, United States Indian agent, and Little Rock, a Cheyenne chief, held at Fort Larned, Kansas, August 19, 1868, in *Report of the Commissioner of Indian Affairs, 1868.*
Special Report on Washita Battlefield, Oklahoma, by William E. Brown, The National Survey of Historic Sites and Buildings, U. S. Department of Interior, National Park Service, July 1967.
The War of the Rebellion, A Compilation of the Official Records of the Union and Confederate Armies. Washington: GPO, 1880–91.
Senate Executive Document No. 40, 40th Cong., 3d sess.
Senate Executive Document No. 18, 40th Cong., 3d sess. Letters and reports from Indian Territory prior to and following the Washita battle.
House Executive Document No. 40, 41st Cong., 2d sess. "Difficulties with the Indian Tribes."
Record of Engagements with Hostile Indians.
House Executive Document, 41st Cong., 2d sess. "Report of Hon. Vincent Colyer on Visit to Indian Territory."

Government Documents—Unpublished

Records of the Adjutant General's Office—Medical Records, Report on Diseases and Individual Cases. File F, 421, National Archives.

Office of the Adjutant General—Letters Received.
Records of the Adjutant General—Miscellaneous File.
Office of Indian Affairs, 1824–69, Letters Sent.
Office of Indian Affairs, Central Superintendency, Letters Received.
Records of U. S. Army Commands, North America, 1868–72.

Department of the Missouri: District of Indian Territory, Letters Sent
District of Nebraska, Selected Letters
District of Upper Arkansas, Letters
    Sent in Field
Fort Dodge, Selected Letters Sent
Fort Hays, Letters Sent
    Letters Received
    Orders
Fort Lyon, Letters Sent
Fort Supply, Letters Sent
    Medical History
Fort Wallace, Letters Sent

Regimental Returns of the 7th U. S. Cavalry.

INDEX